A POCKETEXPERT  W9-CUO-829

MARINE
FISHES

The POCKETEXPERT™ Guide Series
for Aquarists and Underwater Naturalists

This book has been published with the intent to provide accurate and authoritative information in regard to the subject matter within. While every precaution has been taken in preparation of this book, the publisher and author assume no responsibility for errors or omissions. Neither is any liability assumed for damages resulting from the use of the information herein.

Front Cover: Emperor Angelfish (*Pomacanthus imperator*)
Front and back cover photographs by Scott W. Michael

T.F.H. Publications, Inc.
One TFH Plaza
Third and Union Avenues
Neptune City, NJ 07753
www.tfh.com

A PocketExpert™ Guide

MARINE FISHES

500+ ESSENTIAL-TO-KNOW AQUARIUM SPECIES

TEXT AND PRINCIPAL PHOTOGRAPHY BY

SCOTT W. MICHAEL

MICROCOSM

t.f.h.

PROFESSIONAL
SERIES™

T.F.H. Publications
One T.F.H. Plaza
Third and Union Avenues
Neptune City, NJ 07753
www.tfh.com

Copyright © 2001 by T.F.H. Publications, Inc.
All rights reserved. No part of this publication may be reproduced, stored, or transmitted in any form, or by any means electronic, mechanical, or otherwise, without written permission from the publisher, except where permitted by law. Requests for permission or further information should be directed to the above address.

ISBN 1-890087-38-6

If you purchased this book without a cover, you should be aware that this book is stolen. It was reported as unsold and destroyed to the publisher, and neither the author nor the publisher has received any payment for this "stripped book."

Library of Congress Cataloging-in-Publication Data
Michael, Scott W.
Marine fishes: 500+ essential-to-know aquarium species / text and photographs by Scott W. Michael.
    p. cm.—(The PocketExpert guide series for aquarists and underwater naturalists; 1)
Includes bibliographical references.
ISBN 1-890087-38-6
1. Marine aquarium fishes. 2. Marine aquariums. I. Title.
II. Series.
SF457.1.M52 1999   99-35858
639.34'2—dc21

Designed by Eugenie Seidenberg Delaney and Alice Z. Lawrence

Co-published by
Microcosm Ltd.
P.O. Box 550
Charlotte, VT 05445
www.microcosm-books.com

CONTENTS

ACKNOWLEDGMENTS

THIS BOOK WOULD HAVE BEEN IMPOSSIBLE TO assemble without years of input and help from many different people with many different connections to the world of coral reef fishes and marine aquariums.

Many aquarists, both professional and amateur, have shared their observations with me, while many others have helped me acquire fishes for observation and photography. These include Bill Addison (C-Quest), J. Charles Delbeek (Waikiki Aquarium), Dr. Bruce Carlson (Waikiki Aquarium), Millie Chua (All Seas Marine), Thomas Frakes (Aquarium Systems), Steven Freed (Seashell Pet Shop), Kyle and Mark Haeffner (Fish Store Inc.), Richard Harker, Roy Herndon (Sea Critters), John Hoover, Kelly ("Puffer Queen") Jedlicki, Scott Larson (Bellevue Pet Center), Morgan Lidster (Inland Aquatics), Ron Mascarin, Bronson Nagareda, Alf Jacob Nilsen, Michael Paletta, Richard Pyle, Mike Schied (Reef Tectonics), Matt Schuler, Phil Shane (Quality Marine), David and Kathy Smith (Reef Encrustaceans), Julian Sprung, Wayne Sugiyama (Wayne's Ocean World), Dr. Hiroyuki Tanaka, Robert Tomasetti, Jeff Turner (Oceans, Reefs & Aquariums/Exotic Aquaria), Jeff Voet (Tropical Fish World), Matt Walker (Animal Talk Pet Center), Randy Walker (Marine Center), Jim Walters (Old Town Aquarium), Kathleen Wood (*Aquarium Fish Magazine*), Forrest Young and Angus Barnhart (Dynasty Marine), and Bill Zarnick (Animal Graphics).

Special recognition should be given to my friend—and expert fish finder—Dennis Reynolds of Aqua Marines in Hermosa Beach, California, for all the unusual specimens and reliable information he has generously provided over the years. At the same time, I would like to acknowledge the work of ecologically responsible fish collectors, especially Tony Nahacky and Chip Boyle, who provide healthy fishes to aquarists, as well as being good stewards of the coral reef environment. I also wish to thank Dr. Gerald Allen, Foster Bam, Fred Bavendam, Stephen Frink, John P. Hoover, Paul Humann, and Aaron Norman for providing supplemental photographs. Aquarist Larry Jackson deserves special thanks for reviewing the manuscript and making a number of valuable suggestions.

Finally, I am thankful for the patience and assistance of my wife, Janine Cairns-Michael, and extremely appreciative of the publishing crew at Microcosm (Alesia Depot, Eugenie Seidenberg Delaney, Alice Lawrence, and James Lawrence) for the time, energy, and care they have invested in this book.

*To my parents, Donna and Duane Michael,
for all their love and support—and for
encouraging a Nebraska youth's early fascination
with sea life and marine aquariums.*

As bedazzling as any environment on Earth, the coral reef is home to some 7,000 species of fishes and countless invertebrate life forms. Although they are but relative specks in the world's oceans, coral reefs are oases of shelter, phenomenally productive calcareous labyrinths that support a disproportionate number of saltwater fish species.

Of the approximately 48,000 recognized species of living vertebrates on Earth, more than half—or about 24,600—are fishes. Of these, more than 60% live exclusively in marine environments. Although coral reefs account for much less than 1% of the total area of the world's oceans, about half of all known species of marine fishes are found concentrated in these shallow tropical waters. (True coral reefs are limited in their distribution to areas where the minimal surface temperature is 18°C [64.4°F] or higher.)

Almost every niche on the reef, as well as nearby ecosystems—lagoons, mangrove swamps, seagrass beds, and the like—is occupied by one or more fish species. To the eye of an aquarist, these fishes hold tremendous appeal, not just for their brilliant colors, but for their fascinating behaviors and marvelous survival adaptations (including bizarre anatomical features, astonishing camouflage systems, highly varied swimming patterns, and feeding modes that range from blinding predatory speed to elaborately deceptive "fishing" skills).

In general terms, reef fishes are smaller, more colorful, and

Reef scene in Kimbe Bay, Papua New Guinea, with Pyramid Butterflyfish (*Hemitaurichthys polylepis*), Purple Queen Anthias (*Pseudanthias tuka*), and others.

more diverse than the pelagic, or oceanic, fishes. They are also relatively sedentary, often spending their entire adult lives on the same reef; many are content to occupy a particular limited territory or zone that best suits their anatomical, behavioral, and feeding profile.

Aquarium Specimens

Given their visual appeal and life habits, many coral reef fishes make outstanding candidates for keeping in the home marine aquarium. Hundreds of species have proved relatively easy to acclimate to captive conditions and foods and are long-lived when given proper care and attention.

With recent advances in filtration, nutrition, and disease prevention and control, as well as the opening of collecting stations in far-flung locations and vastly improved shipping and handling possibilities, there is no better time to be a marine fishkeeper. It is now feasible for landlocked reef lovers to enjoy marine fishes from reefs around the world, rather than only being able to observe them in public aquariums or on those infrequent dive trips.

For the saltwater aquarist, however, this brings with it the ethical responsibility of being a caretaker to some of nature's most beautiful subjects. An aquarist's obligation should not be taken lightly. Among the reef fish species commonly kept by aquarists, none is considered endangered at this writing—a consequence of their widespread distributions, the localized activities of most ornamental fish collectors, and the prolific reproduction capabilities of most reef species. Nevertheless, this is a resource that must be harvested and used with care and respect.

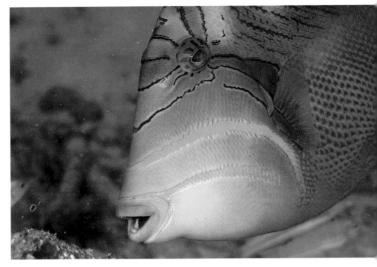

Queen Triggerfish (*Balistes vetula*): a hardy, aggressive Caribbean species.

Reef Impact

Most assessments of reef fish collection for the aquarium trade have shown minimal environmental impact when traditional hand-fishing methods, primarily nets, are used. The use of sodium or potassium cyanide to stun reef fishes, for sales both to gourmet markets in the Orient and to the pet-fish trade, has had tragic consequences on reefs in the Philippines and Indonesia. Cyanide application can kill or weaken coral heads, and areas heavily fished with these chemicals typically lose their natural habitat and their population of fishes and invertebrates. In addition to the environmental damage, fishes harvested with cyanide may never recover fully, and informed aquarists are actively involved in trying to put a stop to this and other nonsustainable collection practices.

Golden Butterflyfish pair (*Chaetodon semilarvatus*): Red Sea icons.

Aquarists can help improve the situation by purchasing "net-caught" and, if available, "certified" livestock that has been harvested sustainably and without chemicals or other destructive methods. The aquarist who ensures that his or her specimens have been properly collected and that they survive well in captivity is helping to prevent needless pressure on natural stocks. (Many marine fishes can live from 5 to 25 years in the aquarium with proper care.)

Captive-bred marine fishes are also becoming more commonly available, an exciting development that is providing the aquarist with specimens that are beautiful, well-adapted to aquarium conditions, and also have a propensity to reproduce in captive conditions. These fishes are highly recommended, especially for new aquarists and would-be breeders.

Challenging Species

Some species, on the other hand, should be avoided by most aquarists, in many cases because they present special feeding challenges. For example, unless you are willing to provide the natural diet of those butterflyfishes that eat only stony coral polyps, they should be left on the reef to thrive and procreate.

The clearest message that can be sent to the collectors, who have no way of knowing the relative aquarium survivability of the species they catch, is for aquarists to refuse to buy those fishes that are nearly impossible to keep. Without a demand for them, collectors will stop removing them from the wild in large numbers.

Some of the species offered in the trade also get far too large for the vast majority of home aquariums. The juvenile Giant Grouper (*Epinephelus lanceolatus*) is attractively marked, "personable," and occasionally shows up in the aquarium trade. But what is the ill-informed hobbyist going to do when junior grows into a ravenous behemoth? This fish can reach a maximum length of 9.8 ft. (300 cm) and weigh over 882 lbs. (400 kg)!

There are many other species that reach considerable proportions and need more room than the hobbyist can readily provide. If these fishes are forced to live in crowded confines, they usually perish prematurely.

In this book, I have attempted to give the aquarist, diver, biologist, and reef naturalist a snapshot of some 500 species that are most commonly encountered in the aquarium trade.

I especially hope that these insights will aid aquarists in selecting the species most appropriate to their own aquariums, interests, and husbandry skills. To a certain extent, it is meant

Hawaiian Longfin Anthias (*Pseudanthias hawaiiensis*): delicate endemic species.

to steer the beginning hobbyist away from those fishes that are hard to keep, that grow too large, or that are destined to threaten their tankmates.

Despite the unsuitability of certain families and species, we have a huge selection of reef fishes that make excellent aquarium specimens, able to lead long, healthy lives in captivity, giving us great satisfaction and providing countless others with an educational, face-to-face look at some of the living creatures of the coral reef.

U SING PHOTOGRAPHS TO PROVIDE QUICK VISUAL identification, this guide is designed primarily for marine aquarists, divers, and coral reef naturalists with a special focus on behaviors as they apply to captive husbandry. Species appearing here have been selected for their availability in the aquarium trade and are organized in classic taxonomic order, starting with the elasmobranchs (sharks and rays), followed by the bony fishes, from the moray eels to the porcupinefishes and burrfishes. (Fishes are arranged alphabetically by genus and species within their family groupings.)

Those seeking information on additional species or more in-depth coverage of identifying features, ranges, behaviors, and captive care advice may wish to consult the author's **Reef Fishes** series (see page 446).

Subheadings within each species account contain concise reference material, advice, and comments organized as follows:

Scientific Name

This is the most current Latin name applied to the fish by the scientific community. The name is in the form of a binomial. The first name indicates the genus to which the fish belongs, while the second name is the species name. Following the scientific name is the name of the "author." This is the ichthyologist or naturalist who formally described the species. If the name is in parentheses, it indicates that the species was originally placed in a different genus. For example, the Hispid Frogfish (*Antennarius hispidus*) (Bloch & Schneider, 1801) was originally placed in the genus *Lophius* by its describers, but has since been moved to the genus *Antennarius*.

Common Name

One or more common names are listed for each species. The first name provided is the name most frequently used in the authoritative checklists and field guides written by ichthyologists. It is the preferred name in this series. In many cases, a name frequently used in the aquarium trade is not given as the name of choice. This is often because the trade name is confusing and lends little insight into the systematics or relatedness of various species. For example, in aquarium shops, the name "scooter blenny" is often applied to members of the Family Pinguipedidae as well as the Family Callionymidae. Members of these two families are referred to respectively as sand perches and dragonets by ichthyologists, while blennies belong to the Family Blenniidae. In assigning the preferred common name to each species, I have attempted to steer away from such misnomers and toward names that will minimize confusion and bring science and hobby closer together.

The names used in ichthyological circles often incorporate the scientific name into the common name. For instance, *Dendrochirus biocellatus* is called the Twinspot Lionfish—*biocellatus* means "two ocelli" or "two spots." Some in the aquarium trade call this the Fu Manchu Lionfish, but I believe that by using a common name that is derived from the scientific name, amateur aquarists, divers, and marine scientists can all better communicate with one another. However, to make the book more user-friendly, I have tried to include most of the common names used in the aquarium hobby. These other common names are listed after the preferred name. In the Common Name Index (page 438), all the choices are included.

Maximum Length

This indicates the greatest length that an individual of that particular species can attain—or the longest ever reported—measuring from the end of the snout to the tip of the tail. In most cases, the length of a specimen will fall short of this measure, but the aquarist should always plan for the prospect of his or her fish reaching a maximum length close to that presented.

Range

This entry notes the broad geographical area where each species occurs. The distribution of a fish is of great value to those aquarists wishing to set up a tank that represents a natural community from a certain geographical region.

Minimum Aquarium Size

This is the minimum suitable aquarium volume for an adult individual of the species. Of course, juveniles and adolescents can be housed in smaller tanks. Activity levels and behavior patterns of a particular species have been accounted for whenever possible. As this is the minimum suitable size, please note that providing as much room as possible will allow any fish to acclimate better and display less aggression toward its tankmates.

Foods & Feeding

Marine fishes vary dramatically in their feeding preferences and requirements. Advice in this section includes the type of foods generally preferred by the species and whether or not it may be difficult to initiate a feeding response. Suggestions are given for enticing those species that may be finicky eaters, and a daily feeding frequency is recommended.

Meaty foods for carnivorous fishes include: fresh or frozen seafoods (e.g., shrimp, scallop, squid, mussels, clams, marine fish flesh); dried and frozen aquarium foods, including mysid and brine shrimp, krill, marine plankton, worms of various types, anchovy-like silversides, and others. High-quality prepared rations may also contain sea urchins, sea worms, and other high-protein marine ingredients that are relished by many fishes. A number of prepared frozen foods are specially formulated for angelfishes (sponge-feeders), sharks and rays, triggerfishes, and others.

Live foods include feeder fish, adult or newly hatched brine shrimp, mysid (or *Mysis*) shrimp, grass shrimp, black worms, and many other items from pet and bait shops.

Herbivore foods range from dried and frozen preparations that contain unicellular algae (especially *Spirulina*) and various types of red, green, and brown marine algae to table vegetables, such as spinach, zucchini, broccoli, or even carrots. (These are usually microwaved, blanched, or frozen and thawed before feeding.)

An increasing number of marine rations—both dried and frozen—contain added vitamins and pigments, such as carotenoids, to help maintain the fish's natural bright colors.

Live rock and live sand are indicated as important sources of food for some carnivores and herbivores. There are many protozoans, small crustaceans, and worms, as well as micro- and macroalgae growth, that thrive on and within such natural substrates, and these will supplement the diet of many fishes.

Aquarium Suitability Index

This rating, ranging from a low of 1 to a top mark of 5, gives an indication of the durability, hardiness, and/or adaptability of each species to captive conditions and foods.

Factors such as readiness to feed, dietary breadth, competitiveness, tolerance of sudden changes, and ability to withstand less-than-ideal water conditions have been taken into account when applying a rating. For example, a species typically loses one rating point on this scale if live food is usually required. The following is a breakdown of the rating system:

1 = These species are almost impossible to keep and should be left on the reef.

These fishes may rarely feed, may be prone to disease, may be incurably shy, and, for one or more of these reasons, will almost always waste away and die in the home aquarium.

2 = Most individuals of these species do not acclimate to the home aquarium, often refusing to feed and wasting away in captivity.

The occasional individual may adapt if kept in optimal water conditions and housed on its own or with noncompetitive tankmates. These species are best left in the wild or ordered only by the experienced aquarist with the aptitude and willingness to devote the time and energy to maintaining them.

3 = These species are moderately hardy, with most individuals acclimating to the home aquarium if special care is provided.

This may include offering live food to induce a feeding response, keeping them with less-competitive (and less-aggressive) tankmates, and providing aquarium conditions that resemble those of their natural habitats. For some of these species, a lush growth of filamentous algae may provide a natural source of food and increase the chances of their successful maintenance.

4 = These species are generally durable and hardy, with most individuals acclimating to the home aquarium.

Fishes in this category should thrive, provided they are not exposed to dramatic changes in environment or poor water conditions. They will accept a wide range of commercially available foods. Live food may either be required to induce feeding or may be the only type of food accepted. These fishes are recommended for aquarists who have gained some husbandry experience (at least 6 months with a marine aquarium).

5 = These species are very hardy with almost all individuals readily acclimating to aquarium confines.

They are undemanding by marine fish standards and are more likely to withstand some neglect and deteriorating conditions. They will accept a wide range of commercially available fish foods and will not require live food to survive. These species are great for the beginning hobbyist.

V Venomous = These species have spines or barbs that bear toxins with varying degrees of toxicity. The effects range from mild stings to severe pain and even death. They

should be handled with caution and not displayed in systems within reach of children or uninformed viewers.

Note: While the aquarium suitability rankings are arbitrary, they are based on the collected experiences of hundreds of amateur and professional aquarists, marine biologists, aquarium trade importers, distributors, retailers, and others. (Readers with additional information are invited to contact the publisher at the address listed on page 446.)

Reef Aquarium Compatibility

The information in this section predicts whether the species will fit into a captive system containing corals, tridacnid clams, ornamental crustaceans, and/or other invertebrates. Fishes that are likely to feed on such invertebrates or otherwise impact the health of such a system are noted.

Captive Care

This section includes general comments on the relative desirability of the species as a marine aquarium subject, as well as its specific husbandry requirements, color fastness, aggressiveness toward conspecifics (members of its own species), congeners (other members of its genus) and heterospecifics (nonrelated fishes), unusual habits, and captive-breeding information, if available.

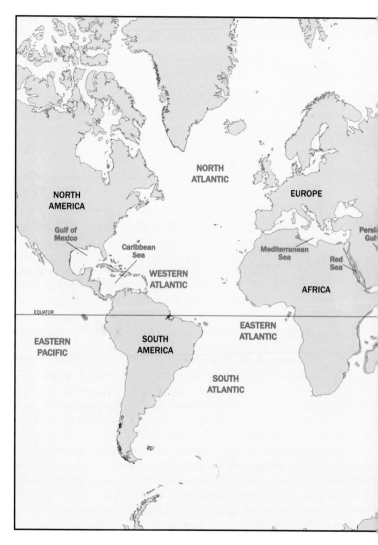

NORTH
ATLANTIC

EUROPE

NORTH
AMERICA

Gulf of
Mexico

Persi
Gul

Caribbean
Sea

Mediterranean
Sea

Red
Sea

WESTERN
ATLANTIC

AFRICA

EQUATOR

EASTERN
ATLANTIC

EASTERN
PACIFIC

SOUTH
AMERICA

SOUTH
ATLANTIC

Mercator Projection, Compiled by Microcosm Ltd.
References: Defense Mapping Agency, World Resources Institute,
International Union for Conservation of Nature and Natural Resources

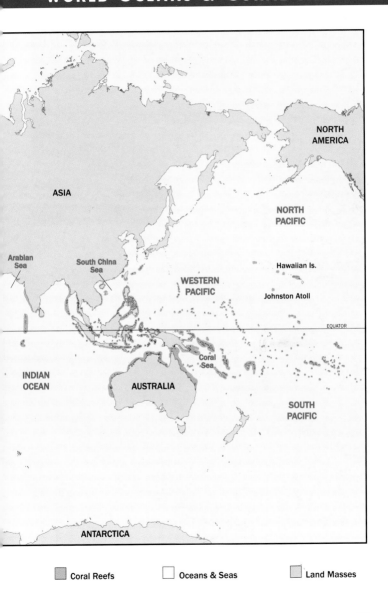

NORTH
AMERICA

ASIA

NORTH
PACIFIC

Arabian
Sea

South China
Sea

WESTERN
PACIFIC

Hawaiian Is.

Johnston Atoll

EQUATOR

Coral
Sea

INDIAN
OCEAN

AUSTRALIA

SOUTH
PACIFIC

ANTARCTICA

Coral Reefs   Oceans & Seas   Land Masses

Orectolobus maculatus (Bonnaterre, 1788)
Spotted Wobbegong (Common Wobbegong)

Maximum Length: 10.4 ft. (3.2 m).
Range: Western Pacific.
Minimum Aquarium Size: 3,150 gal. (11,970 L).
Foods & Feeding: Meaty foods, including pieces of fresh shrimp, scallop, or marine fish flesh impaled on a feeding stick. Feed to satiation, 2 times a week. Do not feed large prey items—the fish may become bloated and float to the surface of the aquarium like a cork.
Aquarium Suitability Index: 1. ▮▮
Reef Aquarium Compatibility: Not recommended. Will eat ornamental crustaceans and any fish tankmate that will fit into its large mouth. May topple corals not securely attached to rockwork.
Captive Care: An ambush predator that will put on an explosive feeding display, the wobbegong makes an unusual and durable aquarium specimen, but one that will outgrow the vast majority of home tanks. Unfortunately, it is inactive during the day and is extremely voracious, ingesting any fish or crustacean that can be swallowed whole. More than one can be kept, although they will consume other sharks (including members of their own species). Provide with a stable cave or sheltering ledge where it can hide.

Ginglymostoma cirratum (Bonnaterre, 1788)
Nurse Shark

Maximum Length: 14.1 ft. (4.3 m).
Range: Tropical Atlantic and Eastern Pacific.
Minimum Aquarium Size: 4,800 gal. (18,240 L)
Foods & Feeding: Meaty foods, including pieces of fresh shrimp, scallop, or marine fish flesh impaled on a feeding stick or dropped to the aquarium bottom. Feed to satiation, 2 times a week.
Aquarium Suitability Index: 1.
Reef Aquarium Compatibility: Will eat ornamental crustaceans and small fishes; may topple corals not securely attached to rockwork.
Captive Care: This behemoth is very common in the aquarium trade, despite the fact that it is certain to outgrow virtually all home aquariums. Grows approximately 7.5 inches (19 cm) a year in captivity. When acquiring small juveniles, aquarists often assume that a public aquarium will eventually take their overgrown pet shark, but most will not. It is a hardy animal in captivity, but highly predaceous, consuming fish and crustacean tankmates. Its aggressiveness as a feeder can hamper attempts to get food items to more-reclusive sharks or rays housed with it. It often spends its days resting on the bottom, although it can spring into action if a stimulus appears.

Chiloscyllium plagiosum (Bennett, 1830)
Whitespotted Bamboo Shark

Maximum Length: 37.4 in. (95 cm).
Range: Indo-west-Pacific.
Minimum Aquarium Size: 160 gal. (608 L).
Foods & Feeding: Meaty foods, including pieces of fresh shrimp, scallop, or marine fish flesh impaled on a feeding stick. Juveniles should be fed finely chopped food. Feed to satiation, 3 times a week.
Aquarium Suitability Index: 5.
Reef Aquarium Compatibility: Will eat ornamental crustaceans and small fishes. May topple corals not securely attached to rockwork.
Captive Care: An appealing fish that haunts reef crevices in the wild and is one of the sharks better suited to keeping in the home aquarium. A juvenile can easily be kept in smaller quarters, even in a tank as small as a 20-gallon long (76 L), but the aquarist must be prepared to provide a larger system as the shark grows (It will grow fast if well fed.). Provide stable ledges and caves; it is a proficient digger and an unstable reef structure can topple and crush it. More than one can be kept, although mature males may fight or harass females. May be picked on by angelfishes, triggers, and puffers. Will reproduce in larger aquariums.

__Chiloscyllium punctatum__ Müller & Henle, 1838
Brownbanded Bamboo Shark

Maximum Length: 40.9 in. (104 cm).
Range: Western Pacific.
Minimum Aquarium Size: 170 gal. (646 L).
Foods & Feeding: Meaty foods, including pieces of fresh shrimp, scallop, or marine fish flesh impaled on a feeding stick. Also will eat frozen foods made especially for sharks. Feed to satiation, 3 times a week.
Aquarium Suitability Index: 5.
Reef Aquarium Compatibility: Will eat crustaceans and small fishes. May topple corals not securely attached to rockwork.
Captive Care: This handsome fish readily acclimates to the home aquarium, although juveniles can be reclusive and may take some time before starting to feed. Will grow as much as 11.8 in. (30 cm) in a year; an appropriately sized tank should be available. Provide stable ledges and caves; it is a proficient digger and an unstable reef structure can topple and crush it. Will breed in larger aquariums, laying adhesive egg cases on the bottom or sides of the aquarium. Egg cases are frequently available and usually take from 138-160 days to hatch, but this is highly temperature-dependent.

Hemiscyllium ocellatum (Bonnaterre, 1788)
Epaulette Shark

Maximum Length: 42.1 in. (107 cm).
Range: Western Pacific.
Minimum Aquarium Size: 260 gal. (988 L).
Foods & Feeding: Meaty foods, including pieces of fresh shrimp, scallop, or marine fish flesh impaled on a feeding stick. May fast for weeks before it begins eating. Feed to satiation, 3 times a week.
Aquarium Suitability Index: 5. ▇
Reef Aquarium Compatibility: Will eat ornamental crustaceans and small fishes. Normally lives among staghorn corals, but may topple loose rockwork or coral colonies that are not firmly anchored.
Captive Care: A denizen of tidepools and smaller niches within the coral reef, this is one the best sharks for the home aquarium. Will readily acclimate to aquarium confines. Adult males may behave aggressively toward consexuals, as well as toward male sharks of other species. They will also harass female Epaulette Sharks. Provide with a stable cave or ledge; it is a very effective digger so cable ties should be used to create a secure hiding place. It will reproduce in large aquariums and will lay adhesive, golden brown egg cases. May bite if provoked.

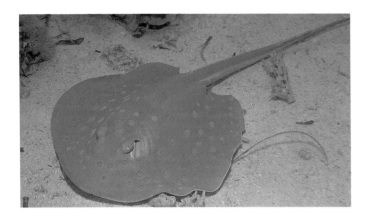

Taeniura lymma (Forsskål, 1775)
Bluespotted Ribbontail Ray (Bluespotted Stingray)

Maximum Length: 28.0 in. (71 cm); attains a maximum disc width of 11.8 in. (30 cm).
Range: Western Pacific.
Minimum Aquarium Size: 260 gal. (988 L).
Foods & Feeding: Can be difficult to feed. Offer live grass shrimp or marine worms to initiate a feeding response. Some individuals will accept pieces of fresh shrimp, scallop, or marine fish flesh impaled on a feeding stick or dropped onto the substrate. Feed once a day.
Aquarium Suitability Index: 2.
Reef Aquarium Compatibility: Will eat ornamental crustaceans and small fishes. Needs a broad expanse of uncluttered sand bottom.
Captive Care: With its electric-blue spots and graceful swimming habits, this attractive ray has great appeal to aquarists, but it rarely does well in home aquariums. Many individuals never accept food; others do, but then suddenly die or cease feeding for no apparent reason. May be sensitive to low levels of copper and contaminants in tap water; use only reverse osmosis or deionized water. Provide ample swimming room, a large open area of sand, and little or no decor (with the exception of a secure ledge under which it can hide).

Enchelycore carychoa Böhlke & Böhlke, 1976
Chestnut Moray (Viper Moray)

Maximum Length: 13.4 in. (34 cm).
Range: Tropical Atlantic.
Minimum Aquarium Size: 20 gal. (76 L).
Foods & Feeding: Meaty foods, including fresh and frozen fish and crustacean flesh. Feed to satiation, 2 times a week. Live feeder fish or grass shrimp may be necessary to initiate feeding.
Aquarium Suitability Index: 4.
Reef Aquarium Compatibility: Will eat ornamental crustaceans and small fishes; may topple loose corals or rockwork.
Captive Care: This is a vicious-looking moray that is actually rather shy and able to be kept in a small aquarium. Should be provided with good hiding places, where it will spend much of its time with its head protruding. Will eat any fish tankmates small enough to swallow, but because of its small size a wide range of fish can be kept with it. Does not tend to be aggressive toward heterospecifics. Solitary in the wild; keep only one per aquarium. Can be kept with other small moray species. Vulnerable to being preyed upon by larger eels. Prone to escaping from open tanks or small openings in the aquarium cover.

Enchelycore pardalis (Temminck & Schlegel, 1843)
Dragon Moray (Hawaiian Dragon Moray)

Maximum Length: 31.5 in. (80 cm).
Range: Indo-Pacific.
Minimum Aquarium Size: 55 gal. (208 L).
Foods & Feeding: Meaty foods, including fresh and frozen fish and crustacean flesh. Sometimes difficult to feed. Live feeder fish may be necessary to initiate feeding. It may take months for larger specimens to commence feeding. Over time, it should be switched to long strips of fish flesh (e.g., smelt, orange roughy, haddock) and squid presented on a feeding stick. Feed to satiation, 2 times a week.
Aquarium Suitability Index: 4.
Reef Aquarium Compatibility: Will eat ornamental crustaceans and fish tankmates; may topple loose corals or rockwork.
Captive Care: A menacing appearance and colorful attire make this a great display animal for a larger aquarium. It is a fish eater and will ingest anything that can fit into its expandable jaws. Must be provided with suitable shelter sites to facilitate acclimation. With time, it will spend more of the daylight hours with at least its head protruding. Some will even begin to lie out in full view. Keep singly except in mated pairs. Prone to escaping from open tanks.

Echidna catenata (Bloch, 1795)
Chainlink Moray (Chain Moray)

Maximum Length: 28.0 in. (71 cm).
Range: Tropical Atlantic.
Minimum Aquarium Size: 30 gal. (114 L).
Foods & Feeding: May be difficult to feed at first, requiring live foods. Once acclimated, offer fresh or frozen fish, crustacean flesh, and krill using a feeding stick. Feed to satiation, two times a week.
Aquarium Suitability Index: 4. ◥
Reef Aquarium Compatibility: Will eat ornamental crustaceans and small fishes; may topple corals that are not securely attached to the rockwork.
Captive Care: This is a handsome and modestly sized moray that readily adjusts to captivity, but may require live crustacean foods to initiate a feeding response. Occasional individuals will accept pieces of fresh shrimp impaled on a feeding stick, but grass shrimp or small fiddler crabs may be needed at first. Once settled in, it will often eat meaty foods greedily, and some individuals will snap at other fishes in the tank when food is present. Provide plenty of hiding places, as this is a secretive moray that will often spend most of the day hiding under or between the aquarium decorations.

Echidna nebulosa (Ahl, 1789)
Snowflake Moray (Clouded Moray, Starry Moray)

Maximum Length: 29.5 in. (75 cm).
Range: Indo-Pacific.
Minimum Aquarium Size: 30 gal. (114 L).
Foods & Feeding: Meaty foods, including fresh and frozen fish, crustacean flesh, and krill using a feeding stick. Feed to satiation, 2 times a week.
Aquarium Suitability Index: 5. ■
Reef Aquarium Compatibility: Will eat ornamental crustaceans and small fishes; may topple corals not securely attached to rockwork.
Captive Care: This is a great aquarium fish that adapts quickly to life in captivity, readily accepts most foods, stays relatively small, and is less of a threat to its fish tankmates than members of the genus *Gymnothorax*. Normally mild-mannered, it can become pugnacious when food is present, and a larger specimen may occasionally latch onto a fellow tankmate. Use of a feeding stick can train the eel to feed predictably. Can be kept with other eels, but a resident specimen may attack a newly introduced conspecific, and cannibalism is occasionally reported. Does not tend to be as shy as *E. polyzona* and *Gymnomuraena zebra*.

Echidna polyzona (Richardson, 1844)
Banded Moray (Ringed Moray, Barred Moray)

Maximum Length: 23.6 in. (60 cm).
Range: Indo-Pacific.
Minimum Aquarium Size: 30 gal. (114 L).
Foods & Feeding: Can be difficult to feed. May require live fiddler crabs for food. Feed to satiation, 2 times a week.
Aquarium Suitability Index: 2-3.
Reef Aquarium Compatibility: Will eat ornamental crustaceans and small fishes; may topple corals that are not securely attached to the rockwork.
Captive Care: Especially attractive in its bold juvenile coloration, this smaller moray is readily available to marine hobbyists and suitable for the home aquarium if provided with live crustaceans, especially small fiddler crabs. With time and persistence, it is possible to switch some individuals over to fresh crustacean and fish flesh. Needs numerous holes and crevices in which to refuge—these will help it to acclimate and discourage it from seeking an escape from the aquarium. This is a nonaggressive species that can be kept with other morays and fishes too large to swallow whole.

Gymnomuraena zebra (Shaw, 1797)
Zebra Moray

Maximum Length: 4.9 ft. (1.5 m); specimens over 3.3 ft. (1 m) are rare.
Range: Indo-Pacific.
Minimum Aquarium Size: 55 gal. (208 L).
Foods & Feeding: Can be difficult to feed, and may require live feeder crabs at first. Meaty foods. Feed to satiation, twice a week.
Aquarium Suitability Index: 3.
Reef Aquarium Compatibility: Will eat ornamental crustaceans; may topple corals that are not securely attached to the rockwork.
Captive Care: This is an eyecatching and extremely docile species that is an ideal moray for the community fish tank. It may appear menacing, but poses no threat to its fish tankmates—even smaller specimens—or to the aquarist. Naturally reclusive, it must be provided with crevices that are large enough to conceal its entire body. In time it can become bold enough to move about the tank searching for food when the lights are still on. Juveniles accept food more readily and will usually take a wider variety of prey, including fish flesh, clam meat, scallop, and squid, all from a feeding stick. When using a feeding stick, gently nudge the eel's snout with the food.

Gymnothorax chilospilus Bleeker, 1865
Whitelip Moray (Lipspot Moray)

Maximum Length: 19.7 in. (50 cm).
Range: Indo-west-Pacific.
Minimum Aquarium Size: 30 gal. (114 L).
Foods & Feeding: Meaty foods, including fresh and frozen fish and crustacean flesh. Feed to satiation, 2 times a week.
Aquarium Suitability Index: 5.
Reef Aquarium Compatibility: Will eat ornamental crustaceans and small fishes; may topple corals that are not securely attached to the rockwork.
Captive Care: Many members of the genus *Gymnothorax* grow too large for the average home aquarium, but this eel's modest maximum size makes it an ideal choice, even for a smaller tank. Must be provided with numerous hiding places, and does best in a reef-type setting aquascaped with live rock. Do not house with larger morays —especially those species known to consume smaller eels (e.g., *Gymnothorax favagineus*). A white spot or spots on the lower jaw help distinguish many individuals of this species.

Gymnothorax meleagris (Shaw & Nodder, 1795)
Whitemouth Moray (Comet Moray, Guineafowl Moray)

Maximum Length: 3.9 ft. (1.2 m).
Range: Indo-Pacific.
Minimum Aquarium Size: 35 gal. (132 L).
Foods & Feeding: Meaty foods. Feed to satiation with fresh and frozen fish and crustacean flesh, 2 times a week.
Aquarium Suitability Index: 5. ■
Reef Aquarium Compatibility: Will eat ornamental crustaceans and small fishes; may topple corals that are not securely attached to the rockwork.
Captive Care: This is an attractive aquarium animal that can be kept with other morays and with fishes that are too large for it to ingest. It is not unusual for this species to fast when first introduced to the aquarium and for occasional repeat episodes after it has been kept in the aquarium for some time. This behavior is to be expected when keeping moray eels, and is typically not a cause for alarm, provided that water conditions are good. The eel will usually resume eating within several weeks. Normally accepts both living and nonliving foods.

Gymnothorax miliaris (Kaup, 1856)
Goldentail Moray (Golden Moray)

Maximum Length: 23.6 in. (60 cm).
Range: Tropical Atlantic.
Minimum Aquarium Size: 30 gal. (114 L).
Foods & Feeding: Meaty foods, including fresh or frozen fish and crustacean flesh. Feed to satiation, 2 times a week.
Aquarium Suitability Index: 5. ▆
Reef Aquarium Compatibility: Will eat ornamental crustaceans and small fishes; may topple corals that are not securely attached to the rockwork.
Captive Care: This is a hardy and desirable aquarium inhabitant that tends not to be especially aggressive. It is readily available from dealers or collectors specializing in fishes from the tropical Atlantic and Caribbean. Although it does not grow particularly large, it can be a threat to smaller fishes and to crustacean tankmates. Cleaner shrimp may be safe if they are established in the aquarium prior to the arrival of the eel. An all-gold or -yellow phase of this moray is sometimes available from Brazil, but it is considered a rare find for aquarists and always commands a premium price.

Gymnothorax richardsonii (Bleeker, 1852)
Richardson's Moray

Maximum Length: 12.6 in. (32 cm).
Range: Indo-Pacific.
Minimum Aquarium Size: 20 gal. (76 L).
Foods & Feeding: Meaty foods, including fresh or frozen fish and crustacean flesh. Feed to satiation, 2 times a week.
Aquarium Suitability Index: 5. ■
Reef Aquarium Compatibility: Will eat ornamental crustaceans and small fishes; may topple corals that are not securely attached to the rockwork.
Captive Care: This is a small species that is commonly sold in the aquarium trade as an "assorted moray." It tends to be secretive and more active once the lights are dimmed. It does well in the home aquarium and has a voracious appetite—which can be a mixed blessing with some individuals. Most will eat not only live foods, but also fresh and frozen fish, crustacean, and scallop flesh. A word of warning: I have seen several of these morays simultaneously attack and tear chunks of flesh from fishes that were too large for them to swallow whole.

Gymnothorax favagineus
Honeycomb or Tessellated Moray
Max. Length: 5.9 ft. (1.8 m).
Aquarium Suitability: 5.

Gymnothorax flavimarginatus
Yellowmargin Moray
Max. Length: 3.9 ft. (1.2 m).
Aquarium Suitability: 5.

Gymnothorax funebris
Green Moray
Max. Length: 7.5 ft. (2.3 m).
Aquarium Suitability: 5.

Gymnothorax moringa
Spotted Moray
Max. Length: 4.0 ft. (1.2 m).
Aquarium Suitability: 5.

Gymnothorax thyrsoidea
White-eye Moray
Max. Length: 25.6 in. (65 cm).
Aquarium Suitability: 5.

Gymnothorax vicinus
Purplemouth Moray
Max. Length: 4 ft. (1.2 m).
Aquarium Suitability: 5.

__Rhinomuraena quaesita__ Garmann, 1888
Ribbon Eel (Black Ribbon Eel, Blue Ribbon Eel)

Maximum Length: 3.9 ft. (1.2 m).
Range: Indo-west-Pacific.
Minimum Aquarium Size: 30 gal. (114 L).
Foods & Feeding: Difficult to nourish in captivity. Live feeder fish are necessary to elicit feeding behavior. Start with mollies or guppies and gradually switch to marine fish and crustacean flesh. Feed to satiation 2 times per week.
Aquarium Suitability Index: 2.
Reef Aquarium Compatibility: May eat crustaceans and small fishes.
Captive Care: Ribbon eels make striking display animals for the marine aquarium, but will refuse to feed in some captive venues. To acclimate a specimen to captivity, provide a good concentration of potential prey in its vicinity by adding a dozen small mollies or feeder guppies to its aquarium. It will help to house it in a smaller tank (e.g., 30 gal. [114 L]), at least at first, or to partition off the eel's preferred hiding place in a larger aquarium. Some specimens can be trained to take small pieces of fish from a feeding stick or to take food off the aquarium bottom. Provide sand and coral rubble for burrowing, or an aquascape of live rock for hiding. They are especially profi-

Pseudechidna brummeri
White Ribbon Eel
Max. Length: 40.6 in. (103 cm).
Aquarium Suitability: 2.

Rhinomuraena quaesita (black form)
Ribbon Eel
Max. Length: 3.9 ft. (1.2 m).
Aquarium Suitability: 2.

Rhinomuraena quaesita (yellow form)
Ribbon Eel
Max. Length: 3.9 ft. (1.2 m).
Aquarium Suitability: 3.

Strophidon sathete
Longtail Moray
Max. Length: 12.2 ft. (3.75 m)
Aquarium Suitability: 3.

cient at finding and escaping through small cracks and holes in the aquarium back stripping, and will swim up siphon tubes that lack strainer caps. Ribbon eels are protandric hermaphrodites (all females are derived from males that have changed sex). As sexual transformation occurs, this eel undergoes a chromatic metamorphosis. The juvenile is jet black with a yellow dorsal fin. At a size between about 25-32 in. (65-80 cm), it begins to transform into a male and its coloration begins to change from black to blue. The snout and lower jaw turn bright yellow. At about 33 in. (85 cm), it begins to develop female sex organs and changes colors until it is either yellowish blue or entirely yellow.

Myrichthys breviceps (Richardson, 1844)
Sharptail Snake Eel

Maximum Length: 3.4 ft. (102 cm).
Range: Tropical Western Atlantic.
Minimum Aquarium Size: 180 gal. (681 L).
Foods & Feeding: Difficult to feed. Live foods, such as grass shrimp and fiddler crabs, are most effective for catalyzing a feeding response. May accept shrimp, squid, or marine fish flesh from a feeding stick after it is has fully acclimated to captive life. Feed to satiation, 2-3 times a week.
Aquarium Suitability Index: 2. ◣
Reef Aquarium Compatibility: May eat ornamental crustaceans and small fishes. Requires an expanse of open, sandy bottom.
Captive Care: A common sight for snorkelers and divers in south Florida and the Caribbean, this species is often seen probing reef rubble for crabs, shrimps, and urchins. It can be a challenge to feed in captivity and will often require live foods. It may ingest fish tankmates small enough to swallow whole, but it can be kept with larger fishes and other eels, including members of its own species, as long as the snake eel is the first fish in the tank and tankmates are introduced only after the snake eel is feeding.

Myrichthys colubrinus (Boddaert, 1781)
Banded Snake Eel (Harlequin Snake Eel)

Maximum Length: 34.6 in. (88 cm).
Range: Indo-Pacific.
Minimum Aquarium Size: 180 gal. (681 L).
Foods & Feeding: Difficult to feed. Offer live grass shrimp or small benthic fishes to initiate a feeding response. May accept pieces of fresh shrimp, scallop, or marine fish flesh impaled on a feeding stick. Feed to satiation, 2 times a week.
Aquarium Suitability Index: 1. ▮
Reef Aquarium Compatibility: May eat ornamental crustaceans and small fishes; may topple corals not securely attached to rockwork.
Captive Care: This boldly striped fish bears some resemblance to the venomous Banded Sea Snake (*Laticauda colubrina*), but is a very finicky eater and difficult to keep in captivity. Its tank should have at least 2 in. (5 cm) of fine coral sand, as it often buries. Right out of the shipping bag, it is not uncommon for it to lie on the bottom with parts of its body rigid and curled up off the substrate. Use care when choosing tankmates, as many fishes are inclined to nip at it. The author has observed juvenile tobies (*Canthigaster* spp.) biting this eel's tail, irritating it and forcing it to try to escape.

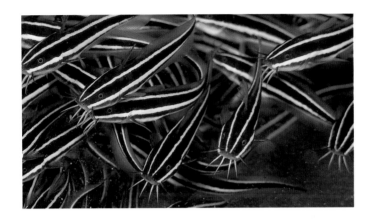

Plotosus lineatus (Thünberg, 1787)
Striped Eel Catfish (Coral Catfish)

Maximum Length: 12.6 in. (32 cm).
Range: Indo-Pacific.
Minimum Aquarium Size: 75 gal. (284 L).
Foods & Feeding: Varied diet, including fresh and frozen seafoods, frozen preparations, and flake foods. Feed 2 times a day.
Aquarium Suitability Index: 5. ■ **V**
Reef Aquarium Compatibility: Juveniles are innocuous; as they grow, they will eat ornamental shrimps and fishes.
Captive Care: These effective scavengers grub in the sand and around the decor to get at any food. Juveniles form an egalitarian school—all individuals are the same in "rank" and display little or no aggression. They do best when kept in groups and may hide constantly and stop eating if kept on their own. Occasionally succumb to parasitic infections; exercise caution when treating with copper-based medications or organophosphates. Can be treated with freshwater dips. One drawback: cute juveniles gradually transform into less attractive, secretive big fish with big appetites that threaten smaller tankmates, take up a ponderous amount of room, and place a significant burden on the biological filter.

Dinematichthys riukiuensis Aoyagi, 1952
Yellow Brotula (Lycopod Goby, Yellow Eel Goby)

Maximum Length: 3.9 in. (10 cm).
Range: Western Pacific.
Minimum Aquarium Size: 10 gal. (38 L).
Foods & Feeding: Difficult to feed. Live foods (brine shrimp, grass shrimp, frozen mysid shrimp) or frozen meaty foods. Feed after dark (use a red light to see that they are eating) or be sure the food gets behind the rockwork where the fish lives.
Aquarium Suitability Index: 1. ▪▪▪
Reef Aquarium Compatibility: Has been known to bite clam mantles; an unlikely threat to most sessile invertebrates.
Captive Care: This is one of the most secretive fishes available to marine aquarists and is thus not a very desirable display animal. It will rarely be seen in a tank full of live rock. Best housed in a small tank (10-30 gal. [38-114 L]) with limited decor but with one or two desirable hiding places. To increase viewing opportunities, use dim lighting. Can be observed at night by placing a red bulb (incandescent or fluorescent) over the tank. Capable of ingesting ornamental shrimp and small fishes. Sometimes picked on by other crevice dwellers, such as larger dottybacks and pygmy angelfishes.

Opsanus beta (Goode & Bean, 1879)
Gulf Toadfish (Orange Toadfish)

Maximum Length: 11.8 in. (30 cm).
Range: Western Atlantic.
Minimum Aquarium Size: 30 gal. (114 L).
Foods & Feeding: Meaty foods, including marine fish and crustacean flesh. Live fish may be needed to initiate feeding. Feed 2-4 times a week.
Aquarium Suitability Index: 5.
Reef Aquarium Compatibility: Voracious predator on ornamental shrimps and small fishes. Burrowing activities may topple live rock and corals.
Captive Care: This is a durable fish that fares well in the home aquarium. It is the only member of its genus regularly encountered by the aquarist; most individuals are collected by live rock farmers along the Gulf coast of Florida. Often found in polluted water in the wild, it can tolerate suboptimal conditions in captivity. Rarely succumbs to disease, even when other fishes in the aquarium are infected. Will burrow under aquarium decor and hide much of the time. When food is added, it will dash from its hiding place to capture it, then quickly return to the safety of its shelter.

Antennarius commerson (Latreille, 1804)
Giant Frogfish (Commerson's Frogfish)

Maximum Length: 11.8 in. (30 cm).
Range: Indo-Pacific.
Minimum Aquarium Size: 30 gal. (114 L).
Foods & Feeding: Meaty foods, including marine fish and crustacean flesh. Live fish may be needed to initiate feeding. Feed 2 times a week.
Aquarium Suitability Index: 4.
Reef Aquarium Compatibility: Will eat ornamental shrimps and fish tankmates. May perch on and irritate corals.
Captive Care: Equipped with an angling lure (a modified spine known as the illicium and esca) that dangles temptingly near its mouth, the frogfishes make fascinating aquarium specimens. This is a large species with a rainbow of changeable colors. Can be kept in smaller tanks, but as it grows it will become a greater threat to a wider range of tankmates. Like other frogfishes, it is susceptible to *Cryptocaryon* and *Amyloodinium.* Will spawn in captivity. Although notorious for luring and eating other fishes—and even conspecifics—it is well suited for a species aquarium or reef system with large tankmates because it often spends most of the daylight hours in full view.

Antennarius maculatus (Desjardins, 1840)
Wartskin Frogfish (Warty Frogfish, Clown Frogfish)

Maximum Length: 3.9 in. (10 cm).
Range: Indo-west-Pacific.
Minimum Aquarium Size: 20 gal. (76 L).
Foods & Feeding: Meaty foods, including marine fish and crustacean flesh. Live fish may be needed to initiate feeding. Feed 2 times a week.
Aquarium Suitability Index: 4.
Reef Aquarium Compatibility: Will eat ornamental shrimps and fish tankmates. May perch on and irritate corals.
Captive Care: A camouflage artist that can change colors to adapt to its environment, this is one of the best of the frogfish species for a reef aquarium because of its propensity to spend more time in full view. May behave aggressively toward other frogfishes, especially members of its own species or closely related forms. These agonistic encounters usually consist only of lateral displays, pushing with the pectoral fins, and tail slapping. Like most frogfishes, this species will ingest slender fishes that are much longer than itself, as well as crustacean tankmates. Its lure, or esca, sometimes mimics a small fish, complete with an eyespot and vertical bands.

Antennarius striatus Shaw & Nodder, 1794
Striated Frogfish (Striped Frogfish)

Maximum Length: 8.6 in. (22 cm).
Range: Western Atlantic, Eastern Atlantic, and Indo-Pacific.
Minimum Aquarium Size: 30 gal. (144 L).
Foods & Feeding: Meaty foods, including marine fish and crustacean flesh. Live fish may be needed to initiate feeding. Do not feed oversized prey items. Feed 2 times a week.
Aquarium Suitability Index: 4.
Reef Aquarium Compatibility: Will eat ornamental shrimps and small fishes. May perch on and irritate corals.
Captive Care: One of the most fascinating of the frogfishes and a master angler. It makes an interesting addition to the species tank or reef aquarium and, unlike some members of the genus, will spend most of its time in full view. Can and will eat tankmates as long as itself. Also likely to be picked on by more-pugnacious species or fishes that feed on sessile invertebrates. Can be kept with other frogfishes, although it has been known to eat members of its own species and its relatives. Do not lift this fish out of the water as it may ingest air, which it could have difficulty expelling. A number of reports document captive spawning in this species.

Antennarius coccineus
Scarlet or Freckled Frogfish
Max. Length: 5.1 in. (13 cm).
Aquarium Suitability: 4.

Antennarius hispidus
Hispid or Shaggy Frogfish
Max. Length: 7.9 in. (20 cm).
Aquarium Suitability: 4.

Antennarius maculatus (variant)
Wartskin, Warty, or Clown Frogfish
Max. Length: 3.9 in. (10 cm).
Aquarium Suitability: 4.

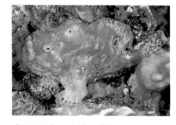

Antennarius multiocellatus
Longlure Frogfish
Max. Length: 7.9 in. (20 cm).
Aquarium Suitability: 4.

Antennarius nummifer
Coinbearing or Whitefingered Frogfish
Max. Length: 5.1 in. (13 cm).
Aquarium Suitability: 4.

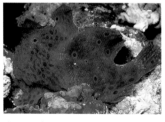

Antennarius pictus (variant)
Painted Frogfish
Max. Length: 3.9 in. (10 cm).
Aquarium Suitability: 4.

Cleidopus gloriamaris De Vis, 1882
Pineapple Fish

Maximum Length: 8.7 in. (22 cm).
Range: Western and Eastern Australia.
Minimum Aquarium Size: 55 gal. (208 L).
Foods & Feeding: Requires live foods, including small grass, mysid, and brine shrimp, baby livebearers, and live black worms. Feed 2 times a day.
Aquarium Suitability Index: 4.
Reef Aquarium Compatibility: Will eat ornamental shrimps. Prefers dim lighting.
Captive Care: Appealing and unusual, these cave dwellers can be successfully kept in a quiet species aquarium or with other peaceful fish species. Does best in small groups. Bioluminescent bacteria colonize a patch of skin near the edge of each side of the mouth and glow green in the dark. Feeding can be a challenge. To switch this fish from living to nonliving foods, mix the latter with the live items to gradually wean it off the live food. It may feed best at night and will be rather inactive during the day, spending most of its time hanging in the corner of the tank. If provided with a large enough cave, it will hang inside. Has been kept as long as 10 years in captivity.

Sargocentron diadema (Lacépède, 1801)
Crown Squirrelfish

Maximum Length: 6.7 in. (17 cm).
Range: Indo-Pacific.
Minimum Aquarium Size: 75 gal. (284 L).
Foods & Feeding: Chopped seafoods, live or frozen brine shrimp, mysid shrimp, and frozen preparations. Feed two times a day.
Aquarium Suitability Index: 4.
Reef Aquarium Compatibility: Will eat a variety of motile invertebrates, such as worms, crustaceans, snails, and serpent stars. Tends to hide from intense lighting.
Captive Care: This is an attractive and relatively common species that does well in an aquarium provided with good hiding caves and crevices. It is often shy initially, but with time it will become bolder, spending more time in the open when the lights are on. It will be a more conspicuous part of the fish community in a tank with less lighting. Usually not aggressive toward heterospecifics, but may bicker with members of its own species. Will also eat bristleworms, including the notorious Fire Worm (*Hermodice carunculata*).

Sargocentron rubrum (Forsskål, 1775)
Redcoat Squirrelfish

Maximum Length: 10.6 in. (27 cm).

Range: Indo-west-Pacific.

Minimum Aquarium Size: 75 gal. (284 L).

Foods & Feeding: Chopped seafoods, live or frozen brine shrimp, mysid shrimp, and frozen preparations. Feed two times a day.

Aquarium Suitability Index: 4.

Reef Aquarium Compatibility: Not safe with smaller fishes and will eat a variety of motile invertebrates, such as worms, crustaceans, snails, and serpent stars.

Captive Care: Often sold as an "assorted" squirrelfish or even as a "Hawaiian" squirrelfish, even though it is not found around these islands, this is a hardy aquarium species. It can be kept singly or in small groups if the tank is of substantial size (100 gal. [379 L] or larger). The red color of this and other squirrelfishes and soldierfishes is relatively unusual among coral reef fishes. While bold and conspicuous under aquarium lights, these fishes actually appear gray in deeper water in their natural environment, because red light is effectively absorbed by the dense saltwater medium.

Sargocentron xantherythrum (Jordan & Evermann, 1903)
Hawaiian Squirrelfish

Maximum Length: 6.7 in. (17 cm).
Range: Johnston and Hawaiian Islands.
Minimum Aquarium Size: 75 gal. (284 L).
Foods & Feeding: Chopped seafoods, live or frozen brine shrimp, mysid shrimp, and frozen preparations. Feed two times a day.
Aquarium Suitability Index: 4. ◤
Reef Aquarium Compatibility: Will eat a variety of motile invertebrates, such as worms, crustaceans, and serpent stars.
Captive Care: These nocturnal fish need plenty of good shelter sites in which to refuge when the lights are on. They can be greedy eaters, but nonliving food introduced to the tank must be moving in the water column in order for a squirrelfish to ingest it; food items that come to rest on the bottom will usually go uneaten. Most of the squirrelfishes are not aggressive toward heterospecifics, although they may defend a hiding place and may spar among themselves if placed in a smaller tank or in an aquarium with limited shelter sites. They are likely to stay hidden in the shadows if kept in a brightly lit reef aquarium.

Myripristis violacea Bleeker, 1851
Violet Soldierfish (Orangefin Soldierfish)

Maximum Length: 7.9 in. (20 cm).
Range: Indo-Pacific.
Minimum Aquarium Size: 55 gal. (208 L).
Foods & Feeding: Chopped seafoods, live or frozen brine shrimp, mysid shrimp, and frozen preparations. Feed two times a day.
Aquarium Suitability Index: 4.
Reef Aquarium Compatibility: May eat smaller ornamental shrimps and some sand-dwelling worms. Prefers dim lighting.
Captive Care: Large, bulbous eyes and a downturned mouth that appears to be frowning distinguish the soldierfishes from the similar squirrelfishes. This is a durable aquarium species that can be kept singly, although it may adapt better in small groups in a larger aquarium. Provide with rocky overhangs, caves, or large crevices to observe its natural behaviors. It is rarely aggressive toward other fishes, although an occasional dominant individual will pester subordinates and may have to be removed. It should be captured in a specimen container, not a net, as the large eyes are reported to be easily damaged by abrasive net material. May be bullied by larger, more-aggressive species that occupy the same hideouts.

Myripristis adusta
Bronze Soldierfish
Max. Length: 12.6 in. (32 cm).
Aquarium Suitability: 4.

Myripristis berndti
Bigscale Soldierfish
Max. Length: 11.8 in. (30 cm).
Aquarium Suitability: 4.

Myripristis hexagona
Doubletooth Soldierfish
Max. Length: 7.9 in. (20 cm).
Aquarium Suitability: 4.

Myripristis jacobus
Blackbar Soldierfish
Max. Length: 7.9 in. (20 cm).
Aquarium Suitability: 4.

Myripristis kuntee
Pearly Soldierfish
Max. Length: 7.5 in. (19 cm).
Aquarium Suitability: 4.

Myripristis vittata
Whitetip or Big-eye Soldierfish
Max. Length: 7.9 in. (20 cm).
Aquarium Suitability: 4.

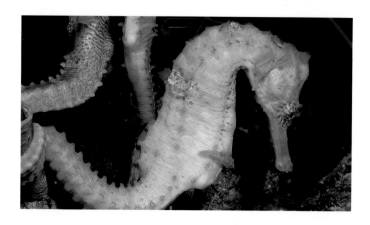

Hippocampus erectus Perry, 1810
Lined Seahorse

Maximum Length: 5.9 in. (15 cm).
Range: Atlantic Ocean.
Minimum Aquarium Size: 20 gal. (76 L).
Foods & Feeding: Feed live or vitamin-enriched frozen mysid shrimp. Seahorses must have frequent feeding sessions—with prey items available for at least 20-30 minutes 3 times a day.
Aquarium Suitability Index: 2.
Reef Aquarium Compatibility: Will not harm invertebrates. Do not keep with corals or anemones that possess potent stinging tentacles.
Captive Care: This species is common and will thrive and reproduce in captivity if fed often and properly. They are easier to feed in smaller tanks because food densities will be higher. Frequent feedings demand attention to water quality, with regular water changes and, ideally, the use of a protein skimmer to reduce the level of dissolved organics. Best kept in a quiet species tank without competitive tankmates or excessive water flow. They require stationary perches around which they can wrap their prehensile tails. Note that seahorses are becoming threatened worldwide by shoreline development and overharvesting, mostly for Asian folk-medicine markets.

Hippocampus histrix Kaup, 1856
Thorny Seahorse (Spiny Seahorse)

Maximum Length: 6.7 in. (17 cm).
Range: Indo-Pacific.
Minimum Aquarium Size: 20 gal. (76 L).
Foods & Feeding: Feed live or vitamin-enriched frozen mysid shrimp. Seahorses must have frequent feeding sessions—with prey items available for at least 20-30 minutes 3 times a day.
Aquarium Suitability Index: 2.
Reef Aquarium Compatibility: Will not harm invertebrates but may itself become the victim of anemones or the stinging tentacles of various corals. Very difficult to feed properly in a typical reef aquarium.
Captive Care: This medium-sized species is recognized by its elongated snout. Colors range from brown to yellow, red, and white. It is not especially common in the aquarium trade, but its husbandry is similar to that of the other larger seahorse species—*Hippocampus erectus* and *Hippocampus kuda*. Mysid shrimp have proved to be the best food for captive seahorses, although they will accept brine shrimp, which should be vitamin-enriched. Baby seahorses require almost constant exposure to live brine shrimp nauplii.

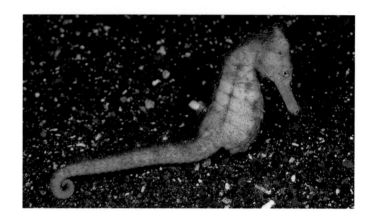

Hippocampus kuda Bleeker, 1852
Common Seahorse (Spotted Seahorse, Yellow Seahorse, Black Seahorse)

Maximum Length: 11.8 in. (30 cm).
Range: Indo-Pacific.
Minimum Aquarium Size: 20 gal. (76 L).
Foods & Feeding: Feed live or vitamin-enriched frozen mysid shrimp. Seahorses must have frequent feeding sessions—with prey items available for at least 20-30 minutes 3 times a day.
Aquarium Suitability Index: 2.
Reef Aquarium Compatibility: Will not harm invertebrates. Do not keep with anemones or corals with large, stinging tentacles.
Captive Care: This is probably the most frequently encountered seahorse in the aquarium trade, with most individuals originating from Indonesia and the Philippines. Often less hardy than its Atlantic counterparts, because the latter are usually treated with greater care and experience less shipping stress. If possible, purchase only specimens that are active and already feeding. Good specimens can do well in captivity, and as many as 5 generations of *H. kuda* have been kept and raised in one public aquarium. Its care requirements are similar to those of other seahorses.

Corythoichthys intestinalis (Ramsay, 1881)
Messmate Pipefish (Dragon Pipefish)

Maximum Length: 6.7 in. (17 cm).
Range: Western and South Pacific.
Minimum Aquarium Size: 20 gal. (76 L).
Foods & Feeding: Difficult to feed properly. Usually requires live foods initially, with frequent feedings. Offer live adult brine shrimp, daphnia, mosquito larvae, baby guppies and mollies, and live grass shrimp. Frozen mysid shrimp and brine shrimp may be accepted if the prey items are moving in the water column.
Aquarium Suitability Index: 2.
Reef Aquarium Compatibility: Can be kept in a reef aquarium; may benefit from the small crustaceans living on the rocks and sand.
Captive Care: Slinking along or hovering close to the bottom in the manner of "horizontal seahorses," pipefishes make interesting aquarium specimens for experienced aquarists. They are easier to feed in a smaller tank without fleet food competitors or aggressive species likely to pick at them—including blennies, wrasses, tobies, triggerfishes, and porcupinefishes. It is often said that pipefishes and seahorses make suitable tankmates, but pipefishes tend to be more efficient predators and may not leave the seahorses enough to eat.

Doryrhamphus dactyliophorus (Bleeker, 1853)
Banded Pipefish (Ringed Pipefish)

Maximum Length: 7.9 in. (20 cm).
Range: Indo-Pacific.
Minimum Aquarium Size: 20 gal. (76 L).
Foods & Feeding: Vitamin-enriched live brine shrimp and/or live or frozen mysid shrimp. Feed several times daily.
Aquarium Suitability Index: 2. ◣
Reef Aquarium Compatibility: Will not harm invertebrates. Do not keep with corals or anemones that possess potent stinging tentacles.
Captive Care: Very handsome and bolder than many other pipefishes, this species is relatively common in the aquarium trade but requires the care of a dedicated aquarist. Provide with suitable shelter sites, such as an overhang or a cave, and place with nonaggressive tankmates only. Will typically consume live food only, such as adult brine shrimp. Should be switched to frozen mysid shrimp, which are more nutritionally complete, but pipefishes will only ingest non-living food if it is moving in the water column. If it will not accept frozen mysid shrimp, feed live brine shrimp that have been vitamin enriched. In nature, it is found singly, in pairs, and in small groups.

Paracentropogon longispinus (Cuvier & Valenciennes, 1829)
Longspine Waspfish

Maximum Length: 4.7 in. (12 cm).
Range: Indo-west-Pacific.
Minimum Aquarium Size: 20 gal. (76 L).
Foods & Feeding: Feed marine fish and crustacean flesh. May require live foods to initiate a feeding response. Feed several times a week.
Aquarium Suitability Index: 3. **V**
Reef Aquarium Compatibility: Harmless to sessile invertebrates, but a threat to ornamental crustaceans and small, bottom-dwelling fishes.
Captive Care: With a potent sting and the habit of mimicking dead leaves or other reef flotsam, the waspfishes make curious specimens for small specialty tanks—well out of the reach of children. They are relatively easy to keep if provided with live black worms, grass shrimp, small feeder fish, and live adult brine shrimp. They are nocturnal feeders and should not be kept with aggressive species that will compete with them for food, or with fishes that rasp on sessile invertebrates. Provide suitable places where the fish can refuge during the day. Warning: waspfishes have highly venomous spines that can deliver a very painful or even lethal sting.

Inimicus didactylus (Pallas, 1769)
Spiny Devilfish (Sea Goblin)

Maximum Length: 7.1 in. (18 cm).
Range: Indo-west-Pacific.
Minimum Aquarium Size: 30 gal. (114 L).
Foods & Feeding: Feed marine fish and crustacean flesh. Live grass shrimp or feeder fish may be needed to initiate feeding. Feed 2-4 times a week.
Aquarium Suitability Index: 3. **V**
Reef Aquarium Compatibility: Will eat ornamental shrimps and smaller fishes. Requires plenty of open bottom space and sand substrate.
Captive Care: Cryptic bottom-dwellers that can inflict excruciating pain on divers and fishermen who come in contact with their venomous spines, members of this genus are sometimes called bearded ghouls or demon stingers. A devilfish makes an unusual captive specimen, flaring its colorfully patterned pectoral fins as a warning when threatened. Requires a tank with at least 1 in. (2.5 cm) of fine coral sand substrate. An occasional specimen will refuse even live food, while others can be enticed into taking strips of fresh marine fish flesh from a feeding stick. Keep only one per aquarium. Warning: devilfishes possess highly venomous spines.

Scorpaena brasiliensis Cuvier & Valenciennes, 1829
Barbfish (Orange Scorpionfish)

Maximum Length: 9.1 in. (23 cm).
Range: Tropical Western Atlantic.
Minimum Aquarium Size: 20 gal. (76 L).
Foods & Feeding: Meaty foods, including marine fish and crustacean flesh. Live grass shrimp or feeder fish may be needed to initiate feeding. Feed 2-4 times a week.
Aquarium Suitability Index: 4. ◣ **V**
Reef Aquarium Compatibility: Will eat ornamental shrimps and fishes.
Captive Care: This commonly seen scorpionfish ranges from Virginia to Brazil and occurs in a wide variety of color variants, some drab and others very colorful. It is a durable aquarium species, but should not be housed with fishes that feed on encrusting invertebrates or algae. For example, pygmy angelfishes may persistently pick at the skin of smaller individuals, despite the venomous spines. Provide with plenty of hiding places, including caves and crevices in the rockwork. Warning: all scorpionfishes and lionfishes are equipped with venomous spines. Handle with care, use caution in cleaning or working in the aquarium, and do not place within reach of children.

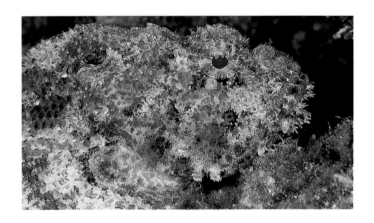

Scorpaena plumieri Bloch, 1789
Spotted Scorpionfish

Maximum Length: 14.2 in. (36 cm).
Range: Tropical Western Atlantic and Eastern Pacific.
Minimum Aquarium Size: 30 gal. (144 L).
Foods & Feeding: Meaty foods, including marine fish and crustacean flesh. Live grass shrimp or feeder fish may be needed to initiate feeding. Feed 3-4 times a week.
Aquarium Suitability Index: 4. **V**
Reef Aquarium Compatibility: Will eat ornamental shrimps and fishes.
Captive Care: A sometimes flamboyantly pigmented species, this larger scorpionfish is found on both eastern and western coasts of North and South America. It is a good aquarium species, but it should not be kept with fishes that are less than three-quarters of its total body length. In the wild, it has been reported to eat deep-bodied species like surgeonfishes, as well as long, slender forms, like conger eels. A good scorpionfish for the reef aquarium because of its less cryptic nature and its tendency to spend more time on the sand bottom than perching on soft or hard corals, making it less likely to cause stress or mechanical damage. Warning: venomous spines.

Scorpaenopsis macrochir Ogilby, 1910
Flasher Scorpionfish

Maximum Length: 5.1 in. (13 cm).
Range: Western Pacific.
Minimum Aquarium Size: 20 gal. (76 L).
Foods & Feeding: Meaty foods, including marine fish and crustacean flesh. Live grass shrimp or feeder fish may be needed to initiate feeding. Feed 3-4 times a week.
Aquarium Suitability Index: 4. ◣ **V**
Reef Aquarium Compatibility: Will eat ornamental shrimps and fishes.
Captive Care: This is a fantastic camouflage artist and an ambush predator whose sometimes beautiful pectoral fins are flashed to warn away other predators. It is one of the most common members of the scorpionfish family in the aquarium trade and easy to keep, although it may be reluctant to accept anything other than live foods. It is a fish-eater with a large mouth, and extreme care is advised when selecting tankmates. Can be housed with other scorpionfishes, but it will eat smaller specimens. Spends most of its time in the open; rarely roosts on hard and soft corals. Warning: venomous spines.

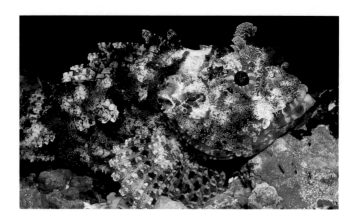

Sebastapistes strongia (Cuvier, 1829)
Barchin Scorpionfish

Maximum Length: 4.0 in. (10 cm).
Range: Indo-Pacific.
Minimum Aquarium Size: 20 gal. (76 L).
Foods & Feeding: Meaty live foods, including grass shrimp and feeder fish. Can occasionally be coaxed into accepting pieces of food from a feeding stick. Feed 3-4 times a week.
Aquarium Suitability Index: 4.
Reef Aquarium Compatibility: Will eat ornamental shrimps and small fishes.
Captive Care: This attractive little scorpionfish has dark bars on its lower jaw and orange-red spokes radiating from the pupils of its eyes. It makes a hardy aquarium inhabitant, putting on a display of unexpected predatory speed when food items come within its striking range. Provide it with plenty of hiding places, including scattered pieces of coral rubble. It will often lie up against the rubble in full view. Sessile-invertebrate-feeding fishes may pick at its fins and skin. Warning: venomous spines.

Taenianotus triacanthus Lacépède, 1802
Leaf Scorpionfish (Leaf Fish, Paper Fish)

Maximum Length: 3.9 in. (10 cm).
Range: Indo-Pacific.
Minimum Aquarium Size: 20 gal. (76 L).
Foods & Feeding: Meaty foods, including marine fish and crustacean flesh. Live grass shrimp or feeder fish may be needed to initiate feeding. Feed 3-4 times a week.
Aquarium Suitability Index: 4. ◥ **V**
Reef Aquarium Compatibility: Will not harm sessile invertebrates, but will eat small ornamental shrimps and smaller fishes.
Captive Care: A great aquarium fish that can be kept in groups of two or three for an unusual display in a small tank with several pieces of live rock; it spends much of its time on exposed perches. Will rarely accept anything but live food, such as small feeder fish or grass shrimp. Has a small mouth for a scorpionfish, so choose potential prey items accordingly. Should not be placed in a tank with more-aggressive feeders or any fish that might nip at its leaflike body. The best way to feed it in a reef tank is to place its food in a net and slowly move it toward the fish. Can be taught to jump into the net to capture live food. Warning: venomous spines.

Dendrochirus biocellatus (Fowler, 1934)
Twinspot Lionfish (Ocellated Lionfish, Fu Manchu Lionfish)

Maximum Length: 3.9 in. (10 cm).
Range: Indo-Pacific.
Minimum Aquarium Size: 20 gal. (76 L).
Foods & Feeding: Meaty foods, including marine fish and crustacean flesh. May be difficult to feed. Live grass shrimp or feeder fish may be needed to initiate feeding. Feed 3-4 times a week.
Aquarium Suitability Index: 3. ▨ **V**
Reef Aquarium Compatibility: Will eat ornamental shrimps and smaller fishes.
Captive Care: This appealing dwarf species, with twin eyespots on its soft dorsal fin, may be the most difficult lionfish to maintain, with some specimens refusing to eat. Best kept with less-aggressive tank-mates, and it must have caves, crevices, and overhangs in order to acclimate. Larger specimens (presumably males) will behave aggressively toward conspecifics and cannibalism can occur. Not a threat to most active fish species. Smaller specimens tend to be more secretive than adults; some larger individuals will come out into the open as they become accustomed to aquarium life. Warning: venomous spines.

Dendrochirus brachypterus (Cuvier, 1829)
Shortfin Lionfish (Dwarf Lionfish, Fuzzy Dwarf Lionfish)

Maximum Length: 6.7 in. (17 cm).
Range: Indo-Pacific.
Minimum Aquarium Size: 30 gal. (114 L).
Foods & Feeding: Meaty foods, including marine fish and crustacean flesh. Live grass shrimp or feeder fish may be needed to initiate feeding. Feed 3-4 times a week.
Aquarium Suitability Index: 4. ◥ **V**
Reef Aquarium Compatibility: Will eat ornamental shrimps and smaller fishes.
Captive Care: Naturally reclusive during daylight hours, this small species should be kept in an aquarium with plenty of hiding places. May be kept in groups in larger aquariums (75 gal. [284 L] or larger); it is best to purchase one larger individual and one or more smaller specimens. If serious antagonism occurs between specimens, they will have to be separated. Often reluctant to eat anything but live food; if more-boisterous eaters are present, it may be difficult to feed. It is more likely to spend time in the open in a reef aquarium than its close relative _D. zebra_. Warning: venomous spines.

Dendrochirus zebra (Quoy & Gaimard, 1825)
Zebra Lionfish (Dwarf Lionfish)

Maximum Length: 7.1 in. (18 cm).
Range: Indo-Pacific.
Minimum Aquarium Size: 30 gal. (114 L).
Foods & Feeding: Meaty foods, including marine fish and crustacean flesh. Live grass shrimp or feeder fish may be needed to initiate feeding. Feed 3-4 times a week.
Aquarium Suitability Index: 4. ◥ **V**
Reef Aquarium Compatibility: Will eat ornamental shrimps and smaller fishes.
Captive Care: Although somewhat secretive, this is one of the most common lionfish species in the marine aquarium trade. The most important husbandry prerequisites are plenty of good hiding places, especially rocky caves, and a varied diet. May behave aggressively toward conspecifics or other lionfishes in the genus *Dendrochirus*. Can be kept in a reef aquarium but will often spend much of its time in hiding. It is more likely to venture into the open in a deep-water reef tank because of the reduced light levels. Warning: venomous spines.

Pterois antennata (Bloch, 1787)
Spotfin Lionfish (Antennata Lionfish, Ragged-finned Firefish)

Maximum Length: 7.9 in. (20 cm).
Range: Indo-Pacific.
Minimum Aquarium Size: 30 gal. (114 L).
Foods & Feeding: Meaty foods, including marine fish and crustacean flesh. Live grass shrimp or feeder fish may be needed to initiate feeding. Feed 3-4 times a week.
Aquarium Suitability Index: 5. ■ **V**
Reef Aquarium Compatibility: Will eat ornamental shrimps and smaller fishes.
Captive Care: This is an attractive and durable aquarium fish that readily adapts to captive life if provided with adequate hiding places. It is easily distinguished by blue, brown, or black spots on its flared pectoral fins. (Compare to *Pterois radiata,* page 75). When keeping more than one specimen, provide various shelter sites so that each individual can find its own refuge. Although it feeds on crustaceans in the wild, it will eat any tankmate small enough to fit into its mouth. Can be kept in a shallow- or deep-water reef aquarium. Warning: venomous spines.

Pterois mombasae (Smith, 1957)
Deepwater Lionfish (Mombasa Turkeyfish, Mile's Lionfish)

Maximum Length: 6.3 in. (16 cm).
Range: Indo-west-Pacific.
Minimum Aquarium Size: 30 gal. (114 L).
Foods & Feeding: Meaty foods, including marine fish and crustacean flesh. Live grass shrimp or feeder fish may be needed to initiate feeding. Feed 3-4 times a week.
Aquarium Suitability Index: 5. ⬛ **V**
Reef Aquarium Compatibility: Will eat ornamental shrimps and smaller fishes.
Captive Care: This durable aquarium fish readily adapts to captive life if provided with adequate hiding places. Often misidentified as the "Antennata Lionfish" in the aquarium trade. Recognized by its lack of a series of dark spots on the pectoral fins (as in *P. antennata,* page 73), short pectoral fin filaments, a complex barring pattern on the caudal peduncle, and larger eyes. To keep more than one, provide each with its own shelter site. Although it feeds on crustaceans in the wild, it will eat any fish in the aquarium small enough to fit into its mouth. Can be kept in a shallow- or deep-water reef aquarium. Best kept in a dimly lit tank. Warning: venomous spines.

Pterois radiata Cuvier, 1829
Clearfin Lionfish (Radiata Lionfish)

Maximum Length: 9.4 in. (24 cm).
Range: Indo-Pacific.
Minimum Aquarium Size: 30 gal. (114 L).
Foods & Feeding: Meaty foods, including marine fish and crustacean flesh. Can be difficult to feed initially and usually requires live food to initiate the process; offer grass shrimp, small freshwater crayfish, or fiddler crabs. Feed 3-4 times a week.
Aquarium Suitability Index: 4. ◥ **V**
Reef Aquarium Compatibility: Will eat ornamental shrimps and smaller fishes.
Captive Care: Very common in the Red Sea, but less frequently seen—and more highly prized—in the aquarium trade than its close relative, *P. antennata*. Should be provided with a place to hide, either a cave or an overhang, and should not be kept with overly aggressive tankmates that might interfere with its feeding. Feeds almost entirely on crustaceans in the wild, but will eat small fishes in the aquarium. Can be kept in pairs or small groups in a larger aquarium. Warning: venomous spines.

Pterois russelli Bennett, 1828
Russell's Lionfish (Spotless Lionfish, Red Volitans Lionfish, Soldier Lionfish, Plaintail Firefish, Largetail Turkeyfish, Military Turkeyfish)

Maximum Length: 11.8 in. (30 cm).
Range: Indo-west-Pacific.
Minimum Aquarium Size: 55 gal. (208 L).
Foods & Feeding: Meaty foods, including marine fish and crustacean flesh. Live grass shrimp or feeder fish may be needed to initiate feeding. Feed 3-4 times a week.
Aquarium Suitability Index: 5. ▨ **V**
Reef Aquarium Compatibility: Will eat ornamental shrimps and smaller fishes.
Captive Care: This durable aquarium species will spend much of its time in full view. It is distinguished by the absence of spots on its dorsal, anal, and tail fins and no bands on the dorsal spines. Can be trained to eat pieces of fresh seafood, but live prey may be necessary to feed a finicky newcomer. Like its relatives, Russell's Lionfish is typically not aggressive toward other fishes, with the possible exception of other lionfishes. Does well in both shallow- and deep-water reef tanks. Warning: venomous spines

Pterois volitans (Linnaeus, 1758)
Volitans Lionfish (Common Lionfish, Turkeyfish, Red Firefish, Butterfly Cod, Devilfish)

Maximum Length: 15.0 in. (38 cm).
Range: Indo-Pacific.
Minimum Aquarium Size: 55 gal. (208 L).
Foods & Feeding: Meaty foods, including marine fish and crustacean flesh. Live grass shrimp or feeder fish may be needed to initiate feeding. Feed 3-4 times a week.
Aquarium Suitability Index: 5. ▬ **V**
Reef Aquarium Compatibility: Will eat ornamental shrimps and smaller fishes.
Captive Care: A great, long-lived aquarium species that spends most of its time in the open. Can grow large and should be provided with plenty of open space so it can hover in the water column or sit in repose on the substrate. Will eat fish and crustacean tankmates, which must be chosen accordingly. May be kept in groups in large tanks, but on rare occasions, it may behave aggressively toward a conspecific or another member of the genus *Pterois*. Because of its boldness, it is one of the best species of this subfamily for both the shallow- and deep-water reef aquarium. Warning: venomous spines.

Dactyloptena orientalis (Cuvier, 1829)
Oriental Helmet Gurnard

Maximum Length: 15.0 in. (38 cm).
Range: Indo-Pacific.
Minimum Aquarium Size: 180 gal. (681 L).
Foods & Feeding: May be difficult to feed. Offer meaty foods, including small pieces of shrimp or fish flesh offered from a feeding stick. Feed at least 3-4 times a week.
Aquarium Suitability Index: 3.
Reef Aquarium Compatibility: May feed on small ornamental shrimps. Need open, unrestricted swimming spaces without much rockwork.
Captive Care: With fanlike pectoral fins that resemble wings when they swim over the substrate, these are graceful fishes to encounter on the reef but somewhat challenging to keep in a home aquarium. Even a smaller specimen needs a large tank with plenty of open, sandy bottom. Feed marine worms, black worms, brine and mysid shrimp (they will pick these off the substrate), amphipods, and grass shrimp. Do not house with aggressive tankmates, such as angelfishes, large damselfishes, puffers, porcupinefishes, and triggerfishes. Oriental Helmet Gurnards have relatively large mouths and will eat small bottom-dwelling fishes, such as gobies.

Serranus baldwini (Evermann & Marsh, 1900)
Lantern Bass

Maximum Length: 2.8 in. (7 cm).
Range: Tropical Western Atlantic.
Minimum Aquarium Size: 20 gal. (76 L).
Foods & Feeding: Meaty foods, including marine fish and crustacean flesh, mysid shrimp, and frozen foods. Feed at least once a day.
Aquarium Suitability Index: 5. ■
Reef Aquarium Compatibility: May eat ornamental crustaceans and smaller fishes.
Captive Care: This is a hardy little dwarf seabass that is disease-resistant and will accept most foods. Should be placed in a tank with numerous hiding places and housed with moderately aggressive tankmates (e.g., hamlets, grunts, pygmy angelfishes, larger hawkfishes, hogfishes, other large wrasses, damselfishes, surgeonfishes). Should not be kept with passive fishes, especially in smaller aquariums. Keeping two in a larger tank is possible. Select smaller specimens, add simultaneously, and observe carefully for the first week or more. If they begin to fight, be prepared to remove one. Suitable for a shallow- or deep-water reef aquarium.

Serranus tabacarius (Cuvier & Valenciennes, 1829)
Tobacco Fish (Tobacco Bass)

Maximum Length: 7.1 in. (18 cm).
Range: Tropical Western Atlantic.
Minimum Aquarium Size: 55 gal. (208 L).
Foods & Feeding: Meaty foods, including marine fish and crustacean flesh, mysid shrimp, and frozen foods. Feed at least once a day.
Aquarium Suitability Index: 5. ▮
Reef Aquarium Compatibility: May eat ornamental crustaceans and smaller fishes.
Captive Care: This dwarf seabass is a very hardy aquarium species whose interesting behavior and relatively peaceful disposition make it a great choice for a fish community as well as a reef tank. It will, however, eat any ornamental shrimps or fishes that can fit into its mouth. Because it attains a larger maximum size than many other dwarf seabasses, it will become a greater threat to more-diminutive species, such as damselfishes, gobies, and blennies, as it grows. More than one can be kept in a larger aquarium (100 gal. [379 L] or more), but individuals should all be small when acquired and ought to be introduced to the tank at the same time. Larger specimens are socially dominant and may bully smaller members of the same species.

Serranus tigrinus (Bloch, 1790)
Harlequin Bass

Maximum Length: 3.9 in. (10 cm).
Range: Tropical Western Atlantic.
Minimum Aquarium Size: 20 gal. (76 L).
Foods & Feeding: Meaty foods, including marine fish and crustacean flesh, mysid shrimp, and frozen foods. Feed at least once a day.
Aquarium Suitability Index: 5. ■
Reef Aquarium Compatibility: May eat ornamental crustaceans and smaller fishes.
Captive Care: This is a handsome and hardy dwarf seabass well suited for aquariums of all sizes. It will eat fishes, including cleaner species like the neon gobies (genus _Gobiosoma_) or crustaceans small enough to ingest. To avoid serious aggression, do not keep more than one Harlequin Bass unless a mated pair can be acquired. In a larger tank, two specimens can be added simultaneously, but they should be watched carefully. If they start chasing and biting each other, remove one immediately. If they ignore each other or swim close together, there is good chance that they have already formed a pair or will pair-up. Can be kept in shallow- or deep-water reef aquariums.

Serranus tortugarum Longley, 1935
Chalk Bass

Maximum Length: 3.1 in. (8 cm).
Range: Tropical Western Atlantic.
Minimum Aquarium Size: 20 gal. (76 L).
Foods & Feeding: Meaty foods for zooplankton feeders, including mysid shrimp, vitamin-enriched brine shrimp, and frozen preparations. Feed at least once a day.
Aquarium Suitability Index: 5. ■
Reef Aquarium Compatibility: Excellent species for reef tanks. Larger individuals may prey on small shrimps.
Captive Care: With electric-blue vertical bands, this is a beautiful little seabass that thrives even in smaller tanks and is a great choice for beginning aquarists. Does best with plenty of hiding places and nonaggressive tankmates, but is not especially shy. It will spend most of its time hanging a few inches above the bottom or swimming high in the water column, often in the open. Usually not aggressive, and fares best in small groups that are introduced simultaneously. Individuals will form dominance hierarchies, their pecking order being determined by size. It will not bother crabs or most shrimps, with the possible exception of the delicate *Periclimenes* species.

Hypoplectrus unicolor (Walbaum, 1792)
Butter Hamlet

Maximum Length: 5.1 in. (13 cm).
Range: Tropical Western Atlantic.
Minimum Aquarium Size: 30 gal. (114 L).
Foods & Feeding: Meaty foods, including marine fish and crustacean flesh, mysid shrimp, and frozen foods. Feed at least once a day.
Aquarium Suitability Index: 4.
Reef Aquarium Compatibility: May eat ornamental crustaceans and smaller fishes.
Captive Care: Hamlets are attractive and hardy members of the Subfamily Serraninae, which includes the dwarf seabasses. Young specimens tend to adjust more readily to captivity, but larger individuals are prone to acclimation difficulties. A specimen that does not acclimate will hide constantly and refuse to feed. Only one specimen should be kept per tank, unless the tank is at least 55 gal. (208 L) or larger. In a larger tank, it is possible to keep several species of *Hypoplectrus* together; but all specimens are best added to the tank simultaneously. Although Butter Hamlets are rarely aggressive toward unrelated species, more belligerent fishes occasionally attack them.

Hypoplectrus abberans
Yellowbelly Hamlet
Max. Length: 4.8 in. (12 cm).
Aquarium Suitability: 4.

Hypoplectrus chlorurus
Yellowtail Hamlet
Max. Length: 5.1 in. (13 cm).
Aquarium Suitability: 4.

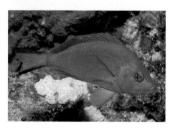

Hypoplectrus gemma
Blue Hamlet
Max. Length: 5.1 in. (13 cm).
Aquarium Suitability: 4.

Hypoplectrus guttavarius
Shy Hamlet
Max. Length: 5.1 in. (13 cm).
Aquarium Suitability: 4.

Hypoplectrus indigo
Indigo Hamlet
Max. Length: 5.5 in. (14 cm).
Aquarium Suitability: 4.

Hypoplectrus puella
Barred Hamlet
Max. Length: 5.1 in. (13 cm).
Aquarium Suitability: 4.

MALE

Nemanthias carberryi Smith, 1954
Threadfin Anthias

Maximum Length: 3.9 in. (10 cm).
Range: Indian Ocean.
Minimum Aquarium Size: 55 gal. (208 L).
Foods & Feeding: Meaty foods for zooplankton feeders, including mysid shrimp, vitamin-enriched brine shrimp, and frozen preparations. Feed at least 4 times a day.
Aquarium Suitability Index: 3.
Reef Aquarium Compatibility: Excellent. Can be kept in a shallow- or deep-water reef tank.
Captive Care: This is a gorgeous fish, and a great addition to the reef aquarium. Will do best if housed in a medium- to large-sized system with nonaggressive tankmates and plenty of hiding places. Best kept in a group consisting of one male and eight or more females. Strong water movement and good water quality are prerequisites. Live foods, such as adult brine shrimp, may be necessary to induce feeding. Introducing this fish into a tank that already contains a well-established school of less-aggressive anthias may stimulate feeding responses and facilitate acclimation.

MALE

Pseudanthias bartlettorum (Randall & Lubbock, 1981)
Bartlett's Anthias

Maximum Length: 3.5 in. (9 cm).
Range: Western Pacific.
Minimum Aquarium Size: 55 gal. (208 L).
Foods & Feeding: Meaty foods for zooplankton feeders, including mysid shrimp, vitamin-enriched brine shrimp, and frozen preparations. Feed at least 4 times a day.
Aquarium Suitability Index: 4.
Reef Aquarium Compatibility: Excellent.
Captive Care: An excellent species for both shallow- and deep-water reef aquariums and one of the easiest anthias to maintain. Although not a large species, it needs ample swimming room in the upper part of the aquarium. Will quickly acclimate to captivity as long as hiding places are plentiful and there are no aggressive or highly competitive fishes. Can be pugnacious, especially toward other anthias and similarly shaped zooplankton feeders. Males should not be kept with members of their own kind, or even other male _Pseudanthias_ spp., except in larger aquariums.

MALE

Pseudanthias bicolor (Randall, 1979)
Bicolor Anthias

Maximum Length: 5.1 in. (13 cm).
Range: Indo-Pacific.
Minimum Aquarium Size: 55 gal. (208 L).
Foods & Feeding: Meaty foods for zooplankton feeders, including mysid shrimp, vitamin-enriched brine shrimp, and frozen preparations. Feed at least 4 times a day.
Aquarium Suitability Index: 3-4.
Reef Aquarium Compatibility: Excellent. Will not harm invertebrates, but will acclimate more readily to a dimly lit aquarium.
Captive Care: This is a great species for the reef aquarium, and easier to keep than many of the other anthias. Young specimens acclimate much more readily than large adults. To keep a group of these fish, which should consist of a single male and eight or more females, a tank of at least 135 gal. (511 L) is required. Adults can be kept with moderately aggressive tankmates, such as pygmy angelfishes, small- to medium-sized dottybacks, and surgeonfishes, as long as the anthias are introduced and established first. Can be kept in a shallow-water reef tank, but expose it to higher light levels gradually. Prone to color loss unless fed an enriched diet high in carotenoids.

MALE

Pseudanthias pascalus (Jordan & Tanaka, 1927)
Purple Queen Anthias (Amethyst Anthias, Sailfin Anthias)

Maximum Length: 6.7 in. (17 cm).
Range: Western and South Pacific.
Minimum Aquarium Size: 55 gal. (208 L).
Foods & Feeding: Meaty foods for zooplankton feeders, including mysid shrimp, vitamin-enriched brine shrimp, and frozen preparations. Feed at least 4 times a day.
Aquarium Suitability Index: 2.
Reef Aquarium Compatibility: Will not harm invertebrates. Best kept in a deep-water reef aquarium.
Captive Care: Sadly, this lovely species is difficult to maintain in the aquarium, often refusing food and wasting away or succumbing to parasitic infections. It is best kept in groups of one male and five or more females in a medium to large aquarium with plenty of swimming room in the upper levels of the tank. It must have ready access to shelter sites and cannot be housed with aggressive species. A plankton-laden refugium attached to the tank is ideal for providing a constant infusion of live foods. Adding individuals to a tank with docile anthias that are already established and feeding may facilitate acclimation. May lose its intense coloration unless fed enriched foods.

MAIN PHOTO, MALE; INSET, FEMALE

Pseudanthias pleurotaenia (Bleeker, 1857)
Squarespot Anthias (Squareblock Anthias, Squareback Anthias)

Maximum Length: 7.9 in. (20 cm).
Range: Western and South Pacific.
Minimum Aquarium Size: 70 gal. (265 L).
Foods & Feeding: Meaty foods for zooplankton feeders, including mysid shrimp, vitamin-enriched brine shrimp, and frozen preparations. Feed at least 4 times a day.
Aquarium Suitability Index: 3.
Reef Aquarium Compatibility: Excellent, but does not adapt well to intense reef lighting.
Captive Care: Nearly fluorescent in color intensity, this flashy species can do well in a larger aquarium with several hiding places into which it can dive when threatened. Acclimation is often slow; a new specimen may hide for a week or more. In time it will become less shy and accept live and prepared foods. Juveniles and smaller females (under 3.9 in. [10 cm]) adjust more readily. Keep singly, unless the tank is large (135 gal. [511 L] or more). Even then, keep only one male and six or more females to avoid terminal battles. May wrangle with other zooplankton feeders.

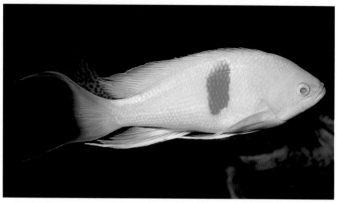

MALE

Pseudanthias rubrizonatus (Randall, 1983)
Redbelted Anthias (Redgirdled Anthias, Redbar Anthias, Redband Anthias, Tricolor Anthias)

Maximum Length: 3.9 in. (10 cm).
Range: Indo-west-Pacific.
Minimum Aquarium Size: 55 gal. (208 L).
Foods & Feeding: Meaty foods for zooplankton feeders, including mysid shrimp, vitamin-enriched brine shrimp, and frozen preparations. Feed at least 4 times a day.
Aquarium Suitability Index: 4.
Reef Aquarium Compatibility: Good for the reef aquarium. Likely to retain brilliant colors in a dimly lit setting.
Captive Care: This is a hardy but aggressive anthias species. Best to keep solitary individuals, except in extra-large aquariums, where a group should consist of one male and eight or more females. Its pugnacious disposition makes it risky to keep with most other anthias species and more-peaceful zooplankton feeders, such as fairy or flasher wrasses. Prone to color and weight loss if not given a varied diet and an ample quantity of food. Does well in both shallow-water and deep-water reef aquariums. Less likely to fade in deep-water tanks.

MAIN PHOTO, MALE; INSET, FEMALE

Pseudanthias squamipinnis (Peters, 1855)
Lyretail Anthias (Scalefin Anthias, Jewel Anthias)

Maximum Length: 4.7 in. (12 cm).
Range: Indo-Pacific.
Minimum Aquarium Size: 55 gal. (208 L).
Foods & Feeding: Meaty foods for zooplankton feeders, including mysid shrimp, vitamin-enriched brine shrimp, and frozen preparations. Feed at least 4 times a day.
Aquarium Suitability Index: 4.
Reef Aquarium Compatibility: Excellent.
Captive Care: Often photographed in huge swarms over Indo-Pacific reefs, this is a common, hardy anthias that is surprisingly territorial. Solitary individuals do best. To keep a group, choose one male and eight or more females and house them in an extra-large tank (180 gal. [681 L] or larger). Battling individuals will chase and nip at each other or may even lock jaws; weaker specimens may be killed or will eventually starve. Its aggressive disposition makes it risky to keep males with most other members of the genus or with peaceful zooplankton feeders. A varied diet is necessary for good health and color. The color of males is highly variable from one geographic location to another.

Pseudanthias cooperi (male)
Cooper's or Redbar Anthias
Max. Length: 5.5 in. (14 cm).
Aquarium Suitability: 3.

Pseudanthias dispar (male)
Dispar, Redfin, or Peach Anthias
Max. Length: 3.7 in. (9.5 cm).
Aquarium Suitability: 2-3.

Pseudanthias huchtii (male)
Redcheek, Green, or Threadfin Anthias
Max. Length: 4.7 in. (12 cm).
Aquarium Suitability: 4.

Pseudanthias lori (female)
Lori's or Tiger Queen Anthias
Max. Length: 4.7 in. (12 cm).
Aquarium Suitability: 3.

Pseudanthias smithvanizi (female)
Princess Anthias
Max. Length: 3.7 in. (9.5 cm).
Aquarium Suitability: 3.

Pseudanthias tuka (female)
Yellowstripe or Purple Anthias
Max. Length: 4.7 in. (12 cm).
Aquarium Suitability: 2.

MALE

Pseudanthias ventralis (Randall, 1979)
Longfin Anthias

Maximum Length: 2.1 in. (5.5 cm).
Range: Western and South Pacific.
Minimum Aquarium Size: 30 gal. (114 L).
Foods & Feeding: Meaty foods for zooplankton feeders, including mysid shrimp, vitamin-enriched brine shrimp, and frozen preparations. Will also ingest small motile invertebrates off the sides or bottom of the aquarium. A productive refugium will aid in its care. Feed at least 4 times a day.
Aquarium Suitability Index: 2.
Reef Aquarium Compatibility: Excellent, but difficult to acclimate to the intense lighting and high water temperatures associated with a shallow-water reef aquarium. Can be kept in the more dimly lit deep-water reef aquarium.
Captive Care: A stunning deep-water species with great appeal to rare-fish enthusiasts. It is shy, often reluctant to eat, and a regular victim of bright lights, tankmate aggression, and disease. Tends to ship better than its Hawaiian counterpart, _P. hawaiiensis_ (Hawaiian Longfin Anthias), but may be less hardy in captivity. Males may fight if placed together and may pick on females, especially in smaller tanks.

MALE

Serranocirrhitus latus Watanabe, 1949
Fathead Anthias (Hawkfish Anthias)

Maximum Length: 5.1 in. (13 cm).
Range: Western and South Pacific.
Minimum Aquarium Size: 30 gal. (114 L).
Foods & Feeding: Meaty foods for zooplankton feeders, including mysid shrimp, vitamin-enriched brine shrimp, and frozen preparations. Feed at least 2-4 times a day.
Aquarium Suitability Index: 3.
Reef Aquarium Compatibility: Excellent, but better suited to dimly lit deep-water reef tanks than to shallow-water tanks.
Captive Care: This is a beautiful fish that must be provided with subdued lighting, rocky caves and archways, and passive tankmates, such as gobies, comets, reef basslets, assessors, and dragonets. Keep singly in a small- to medium-sized aquarium; will fight with members of its own species. In the wild, pairs and trios are usually seen with one larger individual (probably the male). For larger aquariums, acquire an obvious pair, or choose individuals that differ greatly in size. Can be sensitive to inadequate decompression during collection. These individuals will constantly perch between rocks and have difficulty maintaining their position in the water column.

Cephalopholis argus (Schneider, 1801)
Peacock Hind (Bluespotted Grouper)

Maximum Length: 16.5 in. (42 cm).
Range: Indo-Pacific.
Minimum Aquarium Size: 180 gal. (681 L).
Foods & Feeding: Meaty foods, including marine fish and crustacean flesh. Feed 2-4 times a week.
Aquarium Suitability Index: 5. ▬
Reef Aquarium Compatibility: Will eat ornamental crustaceans and fish tankmates.
Captive Care: As with many groupers, this is an ambush predator that is secretive and will spend much of its time hiding, especially when first introduced to the aquarium. Over time, many specimens become bolder, even to the point of taking food from the aquarist's hand. Can be kept with other groupers, but only one Peacock Hind should be kept per tank. Needs plenty of swimming space and one or two good shelter sites. All larger groupers are greedy eaters and waste producers that place extra demands on aquarium filtration systems. Can be housed in a shallow- or deep-water reef aquarium, but will eat small fishes and crustaceans.

Cephalopholis miniata (Forsskål, 1775)
Coral Hind (Miniata Grouper, Coral Grouper)

Maximum Length: 16.1 in. (41 cm).
Range: Indo-west-Pacific.
Minimum Aquarium Size: 100 gal. (379 L).
Foods & Feeding: Meaty foods, such as marine fish and crustacean flesh. Feed 2-4 times a week.
Aquarium Suitability Index: 5.
Reef Aquarium Compatibility: Will eat ornamental crustaceans and fish tankmates.
Captive Care: A gaudy species that will thrive in the marine aquarium. Can be quite shy when initially introduced; over time it will spend more time in the open. Like all other members of its genus, it greedily accepts chopped fresh or frozen seafoods, other frozen preparations, and freeze-dried krill. Keep one per aquarium, as they are prone to fight with each other. May be kept in a shallow- or deep-water reef aquarium, but will eat crustaceans and smaller fishes. It will eat any fish it can swallow whole (including cleaner wrasses) and will behave aggressively toward tankmates that intrude on its preferred hiding places. Can outgrow smaller tanks and place a strain on aquarium filtration and water quality.

Cephalopholis cruentatus
Graysby
Max. Length: 13.8 in. (35 cm).
Aquarium Suitability: 5. █

Cephalopholis formosa
Bluelined Hind or Bluelined Grouper
Max. Length: 13.4 in. (34 cm).
Aquarium Suitability: 5. █

Cephalopholis fulva
Coney
Max. Length: 16.1 in. (41 cm).
Aquarium Suitability: 5. █

Cephalopholis fulva (variant)
Coney
Max. Length: 16.1 in. (41 cm).
Aquarium Suitability: 5. █

Cephalopholis leoparda
Leopard Hind
Max. Length: 9.4 in. (24 cm).
Aquarium Suitability: 5. █

Cephalopholis urodeta
Darkfin Hind, V-tail or Flagtail Grouper
Max. Length: 10.6 in. (27 cm).
Aquarium Suitability: 5. █

Cromileptes altivelis (Valenciennes, 1828)
Panther Grouper (Panther Fish, Polkadot Grouper, Barramundi Cod, Humpback Grouper)

Maximum Length: 27.6 in. (70 cm).
Range: Indo-Pacific.
Minimum Aquarium Size: 180 gal. (681 L).
Foods & Feeding: Meaty foods, including marine fish and crustacean flesh. Feed 2-4 times a week.
Aquarium Suitability Index: 5. ■
Reef Aquarium Compatibility: Will eat ornamental crustaceans and fish tankmates.
Captive Care: With its striking color pattern, unusual appearance, amusing swimming behavior, and charming personality, this is a favorite aquarium fish. It is a bold, long-lived species suitable for aquarists at all levels. Although juveniles are a tempting acquisition for smaller tanks, it is essential to know that they grow rapidly and very large if fed frequently. Requires hiding places and a tank of at least 180 gal. (681 L) to house the fish for its entire life. Rarely aggressive, it will ignore its fish tankmates unless they are small enough to swallow whole. Several adults can be housed together in a very large system.

Epinephelus cyanopodus (Richardson, 1790)
Speckled Grouper

Maximum Length: 39 in. (99 cm).
Range: Indo-west-Pacific.
Minimum Aquarium Size: 240 gal. (908 L).
Foods & Feeding: Meaty foods, including marine fish and crustacean flesh. Feed 2-4 times a week.
Aquarium Suitability Index: 4.
Reef Aquarium Compatibility: Will eat ornamental crustaceans and fish tankmates.
Captive Care: A very hardy species that can be housed in larger aquariums. It is fast-growing and will quickly outgrow smaller tanks (juveniles may grow 12 in. [30 cm] in as little as a year). Tends to spend more time in the open than many of its family mates, and often hovers in the water column. Because of this tendency, and the fact that it is more active than many other groupers, it needs plenty of uncluttered swimming room. A voracious predator, it will make short work of smaller fishes and crustaceans. It is possible to keep more than one in an extra-large aquarium, but individuals may fight if space is limited.

Epinephelus ongus (Bloch, 1790)
Specklefin Grouper (Whitespotted Grouper)

Maximum Length: 11.8 in. (30 cm).
Range: Indo-west-Pacific.
Minimum Aquarium Size: 75 gal. (284 L).
Foods & Feeding: Meaty foods, such as marine fish and crustacean flesh. Feed 2-4 times a week.
Aquarium Suitability Index: 5.
Reef Aquarium Compatibility: Will eat ornamental crustaceans and fish tankmates.
Captive Care: This is one of the better grouper choices for the home aquarium because of its smaller maximum size. Interestingly, this fish can even be acclimated to a brackish-water aquarium, but should be kept at a specific gravity of 1.014 or more. Can be kept in a shallow- or deep-water reef aquarium, but it will eat ornamental crustaceans and small fishes.

Liopropoma rubre Poey, 1861
Swissguard Basslet (Peppermint Basslet)

Maximum Length: 3.1 in. (8 cm).
Range: Tropical Western Atlantic.
Minimum Aquarium Size: 20 gal. (76 L).
Foods & Feeding: Meaty foods, including marine fish and crustacean flesh. Feed 2-4 times a week.
Aquarium Suitability Index: 5. ▮▮
Reef Aquarium Compatibility: Great reef tank resident. May eat smaller ornamental crustaceans.
Captive Care: Difficult to approach and capture in the wild, this handsome species is not commonly available; when it is, it commands a high price. It is however, the most common member of a genus prized by reef aquarists. Should be housed with nonaggressive species. More than one can be kept in the same aquarium, if the tank is large enough, but the dominant fish may intimidate and behave aggressively toward the subordinate. Overt aggression may not be witnessed, but if one specimen starts to hide all the time, it is probably being picked on. Be prepared to remove one if this occurs. Has been bred in captivity. Larger individuals may behave aggressively toward other crevice-dwellers.

Paranthias furcifer (Cuvier, 1828)
Creolefish

Maximum Length: 13.7 in. (35 cm), usually less than 7.8 in. (20 cm).
Range: Tropical Atlantic.
Minimum Aquarium Size: 75 gal. (284 L).
Foods & Feeding: Meaty foods, including mysid shrimp, vitamin-enriched brine shrimp, and frozen preparations. Feed 3 times a day.
Aquarium Suitability Index: 5. ▄
Reef Aquarium Compatibility: May eat small, ornamental crustaceans. Otherwise, not a threat to ornamental invertebrates.
Captive Care: This is a durable aquarium species appropriate for the Caribbean biotope aquarium. Although a shoaling species in nature, they are best kept singly in the home aquarium where they often behave aggressively toward each other. Will also pester smaller, passive fishes. Best kept with moderately aggressive tankmates, such as squirrelfishes, angelfishes, larger wrasses, damselfishes, and surgeonfishes. It will eat most aquarium foods, from flakes to live feeder fish. Provide plenty of open swimming space. May jump from an uncovered tank. (The individual in the photo above has a large gnathiid isopod attached to its "cheek.")

Plectropomus maculatus (Bloch, 1790)
Spotted Coral Grouper

Maximum Length: 27.5 in. (70 cm).
Range: Indo-west-Pacific.
Minimum Aquarium Size: 300 gal. (1,136 L).
Foods & Feeding: Meaty foods, such as marine fish and crustacean flesh. Feed 2-4 times a week.
Aquarium Suitability Index: 5. ■
Reef Aquarium Compatibility: Too large for most reef tanks. Will eat ornamental crustaceans and cleaner wrasses on occasion.
Captive Care: This is one of the largest members of the grouper family regularly available to aquarists. It is very active and must be housed in a large, uncluttered aquarium with suitable refuge sites. If startled, it will often dash about the tank recklessly and harm itself. Members of the same species, or similarly marked species, should not be housed together, but it can be kept with other groupers of similar size with distinctly different color patterns. It is best to introduce all groupers simultaneously or add the smaller specimens first. *Plectropomus* spp. will eat any fishes they can swallow whole. Don't underestimate the size of its mouth—it is immense.

MAIN PHOTO, ADULT; INSET, JUVENILE

Variola albimarginata Baissac, 1952
Whitemargin Lyretail Grouper

Maximum Length: 21.7 in. (55 cm).
Range: Indo-Pacific.
Minimum Aquarium Size: 240 gal. (908 L).
Foods & Feeding: Meaty foods, such as marine fish and crustacean flesh. Feed 2-4 times a week.
Aquarium Suitability Index: 5. ▆
Reef Aquarium Compatibility: Too large for most reef aquariums. Will eat ornamental crustaceans and fish tankmates.
Captive Care: Juveniles of this species commonly appear in the aquarium trade, but they grow quite large and inevitably have to be moved to a huge aquarium. Should be provided with plenty of swimming room, as well as several holes or crevices in which to shelter. Tends to be less shy than many of the other large groupers (e.g., *Plectropomus* spp.), making it a better display animal. It will eat any fish tankmate it can ingest. Small individuals can be kept in a very large shallow- or deep-water reef aquarium, although adolescents and adults need more swimming room than that provided by a tank packed with live rock, and it will eat many desirable specimens.

MAIN PHOTO, JUVENILE; INSET, ADULT

Variola louti (Forsskål, 1775)
Lyretail Grouper (Coronation Grouper)

Maximum Length: 35.4 in. (90 cm).
Range: Indo-Pacific.
Minimum Aquarium Size: 300 gal. (1,136 L).
Foods & Feeding: Meaty foods, including marine fish and crustacean flesh. Feed 2-4 times a week.
Aquarium Suitability Index: 5. ▆
Reef Aquarium Compatibility: Will eat ornamental crustaceans and fish tankmates.
Captive Care: This is a spectacular fish that will do well in the aquarium as a juvenile. However, it grows huge and will inevitably have to be moved to a very large aquarium. Should be provided with plenty of swimming room, as well as several holes or crevices in which to shelter. Tends to be less shy than many of the other large groupers (e.g., *Plectropomus* spp.), making it a better display animal. Small individuals can be kept in a shallow- or deep-water reef aquarium, although adolescents and adults need more swimming room than that provided by a tank packed with live rock. It will also eat desirable crustaceans and any fish tankmate it can ingest.

Diploprion bifasciatum (Cuvier, 1828)
Twobanded Soapfish (Barred Soapfish, Yellow Emperor)

Maximum Length: 9.8 in. (25 cm).
Range: Indo-west-Pacific.
Minimum Aquarium Size: 75 gal. (284 L).
Foods & Feeding: Varied diet, including finely chopped fresh seafood, frozen brine shrimp, mysid shrimp, carnivore preparations, and even flake food. Occasionally live guppies are necessary to induce a feeding response. Feed 2-4 times a week.
Aquarium Suitability Index: 4.
Reef Aquarium Compatibility: Harmless to sessile invertebrates, but will eat crustaceans and small fishes.
Captive Care: This species makes an unusual display animal that is well suited to captivity. As with other soapfishes, it may release grammistin, a toxic substance exuded from the skin, when stressed or frightened. This can kill it and its tankmates. Discard shipping water and do not harass this fish during tank maintenance. May hide when initially introduced, but usually within hours it will start swimming about the tank. Not aggressive toward other fishes, but will eat any tankmate it can swallow whole. May be kept in pairs or groups; they are rarely aggressive toward each other.

Grammistes sexlineatus (Thünberg, 1792)
Sixline Soapfish (Sixstripe Soapfish, Goldstriped Soapfish, Skunk Fish)

Maximum Length: 11.8 in. (30 cm).
Range: Indo-Pacific.
Minimum Aquarium Size: 55 gal. (208 L).
Foods & Feeding: Meaty foods, including marine fish and crustacean flesh. Feed 2-4 times a week.
Aquarium Suitability Index: 4.
Reef Aquarium Compatibility: Will eat ornamental crustaceans and any fishes that will fit into its mouth.
Captive Care: Here is a hardy species with some fascinating behaviors that make it a candidate for special aquarium situations only. Like all soapfishes, when stressed it exudes a toxic slime that can poison its fish tankmates. (Always discard the shipping water of this and other fishes.) It also has an incredible appetite, and will eat any tankmate—fish or crustacean—that will fit into its capacious mouth, including other groupers, members of its own species, and other prey items almost as large as itself. Will eagerly suck up live feeder fish and live grass shrimp and can usually be coaxed into accepting chunks of fresh seafood, krill, or cubes of frozen preparations.

Pogonoperca punctata (Valenciennes, 1830)
Leaflip Soapfish (Spotted Soapfish, Snowflake Soapfish, Leaflip Grouper)

Maximum Length: 13.8 in. (35 cm).
Range: Indo-Pacific.
Minimum Aquarium Size: 75 gal. (284 L).
Foods & Feeding: Meaty foods, including marine fish and crustacean flesh. Feed 2-4 times a week.
Aquarium Suitability Index: 4.
Reef Aquarium Compatibility: Will eat ornamental crustaceans and any fishes that will fit into its mouth.
Captive Care: Equipped with a poisonous mucus coat that deters predators, this is a hardy species that makes an interesting display animal. Although young specimens can be quite secretive, with time they become bolder and spend more time in the open. This is a ravenous predator that will eat any fishes or crustaceans it can swallow whole, and will even eat poisonous fishes (e.g., tobies [*Canthigaster* spp.]). While only one Leaflip Soapfish should be kept per aquarium, it can be housed with other groupers and even other soapfish species. Under unusual stress, it can release a slime that will kill tankmates. (Always discard shipping water after transporting a soapfish.)

Congrogadus subducens (Richardson, 1843)
Carpet Eel Blenny (Wolf Eel)

Maximum Length: 17.7 in. (45 cm).
Range: Western Indian Ocean and Western Pacific.
Minimum Aquarium Size: 55 gal. (208 L).
Foods & Feeding: Meaty foods, including fresh or frozen marine fish flesh, shrimp, and squid. Reluctant feeders can be given live feeder fish and grass shrimp. Feed once a day.
Aquarium Suitability Index: 5. ▮
Reef Aquarium Compatibility: Not a threat to sessile invertebrates, but will make short work of crustaceans and small fishes.
Captive Care: Despite its name, this is neither an eel nor a blenny, but rather an unusual pseudochromid (dottyback) that makes an interesting addition to the aggressive community tank. Keep only one per tank, provide with plenty of suitable hiding places, and keep the tank covered—it is a proficient jumper. If a male and female are acquired, it is best to add the female first and let her adjust before adding the male. This predator will eat smaller fishes, but may itself fall prey to piscivorous morays.

Cypho purpurascens (De Vis, 1884)
Oblique-lined Dottyback

Maximum Length: 2.9 in. (7.5 cm).
Range: Western Pacific.
Minimum Aquarium Size: 20 gal. (76 L).
Foods & Feeding: Meaty foods, including marine fish, crustacean flesh, mysid shrimp, and frozen preparations. Feed daily.
Aquarium Suitability Index: 5. ■
Reef Aquarium Compatibility: Safe with corals, but will eat small tubeworms and small ornamental shrimps.
Captive Care: A colorful dottyback with an aggressive temperament, attacking smaller, more-docile fishes. Can be kept with demoiselles, larger wrasses, and shrimp gobies in a capacious reef aquarium with a profusion of hiding places in the live rock, but it can be lethal to small fishes in a confined or barren environment. Avoid keeping it with any other red, similarly shaped fishes (e.g., *Cirrhilabrus rubripinnis*, page 289) and other dottybacks. Can be kept in pairs or small groups (e.g., one male, two females), but only in a spacious tank (100 gal. [379 L] or larger) with numerous hiding places. If a pair can be obtained, there is a good chance they will spawn in typical dottyback fashion, depositing a cluster of eggs in the male's lair.

Labracinus cyclophthalmus (Müller & Troschel, 1849)
Red Dottyback (Dampiera, Red Grouper)

Maximum Length: 7.9 in. (20 cm).
Range: Western Pacific.
Minimum Aquarium Size: 30 gal. (114 L).
Foods & Feeding: Meaty foods, including marine fish and crustacean flesh. Feed 2-4 times a week.
Aquarium Suitability Index: 5. ▪
Reef Aquarium Compatibility: Will eat ornamental crustaceans and small fishes.
Captive Care: Although undeniably attractive, this is a dottyback that can terrorize an entire aquarium. Its aggressiveness and size make it a potentially destructive member of many typical aquarium fish communities. It should not be kept with smaller, passive species, but with eels, large squirrelfishes, groupers, snappers, larger angelfishes, large hawkfishes, and triggerfishes. This species is a voracious predator that will eat almost anything, including frozen prepared foods, chopped seafoods, and even "pinky" (newborn) mice normally fed to reptiles. (Not recommended.) If smaller fishes are too large to swallow whole, this dottyback will break them into pieces by bashing them against a rock or piece of coral.

Labracinus melanotaenia (Bleeker, 1852)
Spotfin Dottyback

Maximum Length: 7.8 in. (20 cm).
Range: Western Pacific.
Minimum Aquarium Size: 30 gal. (114 L).
Foods & Feeding: Feed marine fish, crustacean flesh, mysid shrimp, and frozen preparations. Feed daily, unless housed with live rock.
Aquarium Suitability Index: 5. ▮
Reef Aquarium Compatibility: Will eat or attack smaller, docile fishes and crustaceans. Will eat pestilent species in reef aquariums, including bristleworms and small mantis shrimps.
Captive Care: Pugnacious behavior, coupled with its larger size, makes this a potentially destructive aquarium inhabitant. Never attempt to house it with smaller, passive fishes or other dottybacks. Appropriate tankmates include eels, large squirrelfishes, groupers, snappers, larger angelfishes, large hawkfishes, and triggerfishes. Keep singly, except in pairs in an extra-large aquarium. Eats smaller fishes; if they are too large to swallow whole it will break them into pieces by bashing them against a rock or piece of coral.

Ogilbyina novaehollandiae (Steindachner, 1880)
Australian Dottyback (Multicolored Dottyback)

Maximum Length: 3.9 in. (10 cm).
Range: Southern Great Barrier Reef.
Minimum Aquarium Size: 30 gal. (114 L).
Foods & Feeding: Meaty foods, including marine fish, crustacean flesh, mysid shrimp, and frozen preparations. Feed daily.
Aquarium Suitability Index: 5. ■
Reef Aquarium Compatibility: Will eat or attack smaller, docile fishes and crustaceans. Will eat pestilent species in reef aquariums, including bristleworms and small mantis shrimps.
Captive Care: Here is one of the more-aggressive members of a naturally tough family. It will attack almost anything that enters its domain, even if the intruding species is larger. Should not be housed with placid species or other dottyback species. Best kept with squirrelfishes, soldierfishes, larger angelfishes, hawkfishes, surgeonfishes, and triggerfishes. Even a male-female pair is risky, as they tend to tear each other up. Spends most of its time moving through tunnels and crevices and will occasionally dart from one nook to another or come out to feed. Rarely collected for the aquarium trade, but captive-bred specimens are occasionally available.

Pseudochromis aldabraensis Bouchot & Boutin, 1958
Arabian Bluelined Dottyback (Neon Dottyback)

Maximum Length: 3.3 in. (8.5 cm).
Range: Arabian Gulf to Sri Lanka.
Minimum Aquarium Size: 20 gal. (76 L).
Foods & Feeding: Meaty foods, including marine fishes, crustacean flesh, mysid shrimp, and frozen preparations. Feed daily.
Aquarium Suitability Index: 5. ■
Reef Aquarium Compatibility: Will eat small tubeworms and ornamental shrimps.
Captive Care: Exotically pigmented, this is an eyecatching fish well suited to the moderately aggressive community tank. However, it has a well-documented belligerent streak and is a real threat to many aquarium cohabitants. It may attack and even disembowel tankmates of smaller or equal size. Best kept with larger and more-aggressive species, such as large angelfishes, surgeonfishes, large damselfishes, and hawkfishes. Retains its colors well if fed a varied diet. In reef aquariums it feeds heavily on fireworms, even those too large to swallow whole. It is being reproduced in captivity and lays demersal eggs in large shells, but the sexes are not readily separable, and establishing a breeding pair is a challenge.

Pseudochromis cyanotaenia Bleeker, 1857
Bluelined Dottyback (Bluebarred Dottyback, Surge Dottyback)

Maximum Length: 2.4 in. (6 cm).
Range: Western Pacific.
Minimum Aquarium Size: 20 gal. (76 L).
Foods & Feeding: Meaty foods, including marine fish, crustacean flesh, mysid shrimp, enriched brine shrimp. Feed daily.
Aquarium Suitability Index: 5. ▮
Reef Aquarium Compatibility: Will eat small tubeworms and may attack ornamental shrimps, especially those introduced after the dotty-back. May grasp the operculum of upended *Astraea* snails and attempt to rip them from their shells.
Captive Care: An interesting little dottyback that should be an excellent candidate for captive breeding, owing to its hardiness, size and sexual dichromatism—males have yellow heads. Tends to be shy, especially if kept with larger fishes; may starve if kept with aggressive tankmates. It is not as territorial as many of its congeners and can be successfully housed with more-peaceful species if it is one of the last additions to the tank. Conspecifics of the same sex should not be kept together, but a male and female may tolerate each other. Provide with ample hiding places.

Pseudochromis diadema Lubbock & Randall, 1978
Diadem Dottyback

Maximum Length: 2.4 in. (6 cm).
Range: Western Pacific.
Minimum Aquarium Size: 20 gal. (76 L).
Foods & Feeding: Meaty foods, such as marine fish, crustacean flesh, mysid shrimp, and frozen preparations. Feed daily.
Aquarium Suitability Index: 5. ▇
Reef Aquarium Compatibility: Will eat smaller ornamental shrimps.
Captive Care: Feisty for its size, this fish is made popular by its colors, but it can be very aggressive toward other fish species, bullying tankmates of smaller or similar size. Will attack damselfishes, fire gobies, gobies, grammas, anthias, and juveniles of larger species; will even harass cleaner shrimps. When kept with larger fishes (e.g., tangs, angelfishes, butterflyfishes), it tends to be much less belligerent. A moderately hardy dottyback, this species is prone to radical color loss (the magenta stripe often fades). Feeding high-quality, vitamin-enriched and color-enhancing marine foods is advised. Small groups of these dottybacks can be kept in larger reef aquariums that offer profuse cover among the corals and live rock aquascaping.

Pseudochromis flavivertex Rüppell, 1835
Sunrise Dottyback

Maximum Length: 3.1 in. (8 cm).
Range: Red Sea and the Gulf of Aden.
Minimum Aquarium Size: 20 gal. (76 L).
Foods & Feeding: Meaty foods, including marine fish, crustacean flesh, mysid shrimp, and frozen preparations. Feed daily.
Aquarium Suitability Index: 5. ▨
Reef Aquarium Compatibility: May eat smaller ornamental crustaceans.
Captive Care: This is one of the less boisterous of the dottybacks, and is a worthy addition to any reef tank, especially when certain invertebrate pests need to be controlled. Larger specimens have been observed to capture and feed on small mantis shrimps. It will eat small fireworms with relish. This less-aggressive dottyback is suitable for some community situations, and it will often tolerate closely related species in the same tank. However, it can be intimidated by larger tankmates, and it may hide constantly and starve to death. Feed a high-quality, varied diet to retain colors. Captive-bred specimens are often available.

Pseudochromis fridmani Klausewitz, 1968
Orchid Dottyback (Fridman's Dottyback)

Maximum Length: 2.8 in. (7 cm).
Range: Red Sea.
Minimum Aquarium Size: 20 gal. (76 L).
Foods & Feeding: Meaty foods, including marine fish, crustacean flesh, mysid shrimp, and frozen preparations. Feed daily.
Aquarium Suitability Index: 5. ▇
Reef Aquarium Compatibility: Excellent. May eat bristleworms.
Captive Care: This dazzling Red Sea native once fetched a king's ransom from aquarists, but is now commonly available from commercial breeders at reasonable prices. It is a great aquarium fish that can be housed singly, in mated pairs, or in small aggregations as long as the tank is large enough and has plenty of live rock and hiding places. Usually shy initially, it will become bolder and remain mostly in the open, unless housed with larger, more-aggressive species. Although the most sociable member of the genus, this species will occasionally pester smaller, more-passive fishes (e.g., fire gobies, gobies, small wrasses), other dottybacks, and grammas, and will defend its shelter sites from intrusion. It is extremely hardy and easy to feed.

Pseudochromis fuscus Müller & Troschel, 1849
Dusky Dottyback (Yellow Dottyback)

Maximum Length: 3.9 in. (10 cm).
Range: Western Pacific.
Minimum Aquarium Size: 30 gal. (114 L).
Foods & Feeding: Meaty foods, including marine fishes, crustacean flesh, mysid shrimp, and frozen preparations. Feed daily.
Aquarium Suitability Index: 5. ▉
Reef Aquarium Compatibility: Will eat ornamental shrimps.
Captive Care: Sporting several color forms, including one that is yellow and one that is dusky or purplish brown, this is one of the bolder members of the genus, spending a considerable amount of time in the open. In the aquarium it may hide initially, but will soon begin to spend more time in view. It tends to be territorial, but its disposition varies greatly between individuals; in most cases it should not be kept with small or inoffensive fishes or with members of its own kind, unless a male-female pair can be acquired. If you do get a boisterous individual, this species' larger size makes it an even greater threat than one of its smaller cousins. As with all dottybacks, it may jump out of uncovered aquariums.

Pseudochromis paccagnellae Axelrod, 1973
Royal Dottyback (Bicolor Dottyback)

Maximum Length: 3.1 in. (8 cm).
Range: Western Pacific.
Minimum Aquarium Size: 20 gal. (76 L).
Foods & Feeding: Meaty foods, including marine fishes, crustacean flesh, mysid shrimp, and frozen preparations. Feed daily.
Aquarium Suitability Index: 5. ▉
Reef Aquarium Compatibility: Will eat smaller ornamental shrimps.
Captive Care: Inch for inch, one of the most aggressive dottybacks available. This species may viciously attack aggressive fish three times its size, and aquarium shop owners frequently see Royal Dottybacks returned because of this agonistic nature. It is highly inadvisable to keep this fish with placid species (e.g., gobies, dart gobies, fire gobies, small wrasses, cleaner fishes) except in a large aquarium with ample hiding places. It is reported to maintain a territory of several square yards in the wild, so keeping more than one in anything but a very large home aquarium may be foolhardy. Despite its belligerence, it is a durable aquarium fish. It has a tendency to lose some of its chromatic brilliance, and should be offered foods enriched with vitamins and color enhancers, including carotenoids.

Pseudochromis sp.
Allen's Dottyback

Maximum Length: 4.7 in. (12 cm).

Range: Western Pacific.

Minimum Aquarium Size: 30 gal. (114 L).

Foods & Feeding: Meaty foods, including marine fish, crustacean flesh, mysid shrimp, and frozen preparations. Feed daily.

Aquarium Suitability Index: 5. ■

Reef Aquarium Compatibility: Will eat small tubeworms and small ornamental shrimps.

Captive Care: A relative newcomer to the aquarium trade, this fish has long pelvic fins, each with a patch of red or yellow coloration at the base. It is not overly quarrelsome, although, like most dottybacks, care should be taken when housing it with smaller, peaceful fish species. Offer a rocky aquascape with plenty of hiding spots and refrain from keeping it with other dottybacks, especially species that may be more aggressive—for example, *Ogilbyina novaehollandiae*. Keep only one Allen's Dottyback per tank unless a mated pair is acquired.

Pseudochromis porphyreus Lubbock & Goldman, 1974
Magenta Dottyback (Purple Dottyback, Strawberry Dottyback)

Maximum Length: 2.4 in. (6 cm).
Range: Western and South Pacific.
Minimum Aquarium Size: 20 gal. (76 L).
Foods & Feeding: Meaty foods, including marine fish, crustacean flesh, mysid shrimp, and frozen preparations. Feed daily.
Aquarium Suitability Index: 5. ▪
Reef Aquarium Compatibility: Will eat smaller ornamental shrimps.
Captive Care: This species is sometimes mistaken for *P. fridmani*, page 118, but the latter is easily distinguished by a black slash through its eye and purple, rather than clear, fins. Although it can be a behavioral problem in the "passive" community tank, it is less aggressive than many members of the genus. Like most of its relatives, it will harass fire gobies, dart gobies, grammas, and other small, mild-mannered reef fishes. More than one can be kept in a moderate-sized (e.g., 90 gal. [341 L]) aquarium if they are introduced simultaneously and the tank is heavily decorated. It is moderately hardy and will accept most fresh or prepared foods. In captivity it tends to lose its chromatic brilliance; offering a varied, enriched diet will help to prevent this tendency.

Pseudochromis sankeyi Lubbock, 1975
Sankey's Dottyback

Maximum Length: 3.1 in. (8 cm).
Range: Southern Red Sea to the Gulf of Aden.
Minimum Aquarium Size: 20 gal. (76 L).
Foods & Feeding: Meaty foods, including marine fish, crustacean flesh, mysid shrimp, and frozen preparations. Feed daily.
Aquarium Suitability Index: 5. ▇
Reef Aquarium Compatibility: Excellent.
Captive Care: This striking black-and-white fish was once rare in the aquarium trade but is much more commonly available as a result of captive breeding. It is not a terribly aggressive species and can even be kept in small groups in larger aquariums with many hiding holes; all specimens should be introduced simultaneously. Will quarrel if housed in a smaller aquarium, and if one individual becomes overly aggressive either it or the subordinates may have to be evacuated. May eat smaller bristleworms in systems with live rock. May jump from open aquariums.

Pseudochromis springeri Lubbock, 1975
Springer's Dottyback

Maximum Length: 1.6 in. (4 cm).
Range: Red Sea.
Minimum Aquarium Size: 20 gal. (76 L).
Foods & Feeding: Meaty foods, including marine fish, crustacean flesh, mysid shrimp, and frozen preparations. Feed daily.
Aquarium Suitability Index: 5. ■
Reef Aquarium Compatibility: Excellent, but will eat smaller ornamental shrimps.
Captive Care: With flashes of electric blue on a jet black body, this is a hardy, relatively colorfast dottyback that is a favorite of many aquarists. This species is very active, flitting from one hiding place to another, and is moderately aggressive. Best kept singly, except in large, well-aquascaped systems, or unless a mated pair is obtained. Will pester anthias, dart gobies, fire gobies, and fairy wrasses, especially in more limited confines. It accepts a wide variety of prepared foods and is relatively resistant to disease. One advantage to keeping it in the reef aquarium is that it will eat small bristleworms. This Red Sea species is especially attracted to the shelter of branching stony coral colonies. Captive-bred specimens are available.

Gramma brasiliensis Sazima, Gasparini & Mourra, 1998
Brazilian Gramma

Maximum Length: 3.1 in. (8 cm).
Range: Brazil.
Minimum Aquarium Size: 20 gal. (76 L).
Foods & Feeding: Feed finely chopped fresh or frozen marine fish flesh, shrimp and/or squid, mysid shrimp, vitamin-enriched brine shrimp, and frozen preparations for carnivores. Feed at least 2 times a day.
Aquarium Suitability Index: 5. ■
Reef Aquarium Compatibility: Excellent.
Captive Care: This flashy species is as durable as its much more commonly seen northern cousin, *Gramma loreto*, page 126. It differs from *G. loreto* in that it has a larger mouth and lacks yellow streaks on the head. The Brazilian Gramma is more aggressive, and it is riskier to keep more than one, except in a reasonably spacious aquarium (75 gal. [284 L] or larger) or as a confirmed male-female pair. This species is more likely to harass smaller, docile species and should not be kept with *G. loreto*. May eat small, delicate shrimps.

Gramma loreto Poey, 1868
Royal Gramma (Fairy Basslet)

Maximum Length: 3.0 in. (8 cm).
Range: Tropical Western Atlantic.
Minimum Aquarium Size: 20 gal. (76 L).
Foods & Feeding: Meaty foods, including marine fish, crustacean flesh, mysid shrimp, and frozen preparations. Feed daily.
Aquarium Suitability Index: 5. ▓
Reef Aquarium Compatibility: Excellent.
Captive Care: A hardy, intensely colorful aquarium fish that tends to do well even for beginning aquarists. It is generally nonaggressive, but will viciously defend a preferred hiding place from intrusion. An irregular vertical reef wall or an overhang of live rock will replicate its natural habitat. Can be kept in groups, but should not be overcrowded. Several juveniles can be kept in tanks as small as 30 gal. (114 L), but an aggregation of adults should be housed in a tank no smaller than 55 gal. (208 L). Ideally a group will be composed of one medium-sized or large individual and two or more smaller specimens. On average, males are larger than females; choosing one larger adult and several small ones will increase the chances of creating a reproductive unit. Will build nests and spawn in captivity.

Gramma melacara Böhlke & Randall, 1963
Blackcap Basslet (Blackcap Gramma)

Maximum Length: 3.9 in. (10 cm).
Range: Tropical Western Atlantic.
Minimum Aquarium Size: 30 gal. (114 L).
Foods & Feeding: Meaty foods, including marine fish, crustacean flesh, mysid shrimp, and frozen preparations. Feed daily.
Aquarium Suitability Index: 5. ▆
Reef Aquarium Compatibility: Excellent, but may eat small, delicate shrimps.
Captive Care: Found on deeper walls and reef faces, this species was once considered rare and very expensive. Now more widely available, it is a durable fish similar in overall disposition to *G. loreto*. However, a large male *G. melacara* can become quite aggressive once established in the aquarium community and may be especially fervent about defending its cave or hiding hole. May be slightly shyer than *G. loreto* initially, and must be kept with less-belligerent tankmates if it is to acclimate. Because they tend to inhabit deeper reef areas, Blackcap Basslets will adjust better in less-intense lighting. May be kept in groups in a tank of at least 100 gal. (379 L), with plenty of hiding places.

Assessor flavissimus Allen & Kuiter, 1976
Yellow Assessor

Maximum Length: 2.3 in. (5.5 cm).
Range: Western Pacific.
Minimum Aquarium Size: 20 gal. (76 L).
Foods & Feeding: Meaty foods, such as finely chopped fresh or frozen marine fish flesh, shrimp and/or squid, mysid shrimp, vitamin-enriched brine shrimp, and frozen preparations for carnivores. Feed at least 2 times a day—less often in a healthy, established reef tank.
Aquarium Suitability Index: 5. ■
Reef Aquarium Compatibility: Excellent.
Captive Care: This is a lovely fish, ideal for the new marine aquarist and a great species for the reef tank—disease-resistant and completely uninterested in ornamental invertebrates. Its natural habitat is rocky caves or ledges, and it should be given appropriate places to hide. It commonly swims upside down if given appropriate overhanging decor. This is a peaceful fish that is a likely target of aggression if kept with overly boisterous species. Its smaller size makes it vulnerable to many piscivorous fishes. Can be kept in aggregations (see *A. macneilli* Captive Care notes, page 129). May jump out of an uncovered tank if disturbed.

Assessor macneilli Whitley, 1935
Blue Assessor

Maximum Length: 2.4 in. (6 cm).
Range: Western Pacific.
Minimum Aquarium Size: 20 gal. (76 L).
Foods & Feeding: Meaty foods, such as finely chopped fresh or frozen marine fish flesh, shrimp and/or squid, mysid shrimp, vitamin-enriched brine shrimp, and frozen preparations for carnivores. Feed at least 2 times a day—less often in a healthy, established reef tank.
Aquarium Suitability Index: 5. ■
Reef Aquarium Compatibility: Excellent.
Captive Care: Deep blue coloration and a good disposition make this an ideal aquarium fish for reef aquariums and quiet community tanks. Can be kept on its own or in small aggregations. To establish a group, the tank must be large enough and should offer rocky refuge sites in case squabbles occur. A proper assemblage would include three smaller individuals and one larger specimen in a tank of 100 gal. (379 L) or more. All should be added simultaneously. Larger individuals (probably males) have a greater tendency to fight with each other; best to keep only one per tank. Slightly less aggressive than the closely related *A. flavissimus*.

Calloplesiops altivelis (Steindachner, 1903)
Comet (Marine Betta)

Maximum Length: 8.0 in. (20 cm).
Range: Indo-Pacific.
Minimum Aquarium Size: 55 gal. (208 L).
Foods & Feeding: Meaty foods, including marine fish, crustacean flesh, mysid shrimp, and frozen preparations. Feed 2-4 times a week.
Aquarium Suitability Index: 5. ▆
Reef Aquarium Compatibility: Will eat ornamental shrimps and small fishes.
Captive Care: A handsome fish that has a sterling reputation for being very hardy, rarely succumbing to disease or poor water quality. When initially introduced, it is very shy (especially in brightly lit tanks) and may hide for a week or more. Its timid nature can be a problem at feeding time, especially when housed with more-aggressive tankmates. At first it will usually eat only live foods; try feeder fish (preferably those that can live in saltwater, such as mollies or guppies) or live brine shrimp. Can often be switched to frozen preparations when fully acclimated. With time and conditioning, it will spend more time in view, especially in less-intense lighting. Not aggressive toward other species, but may fight with other Comets.

Opistognathus aurifrons (Jordan & Thompson, 1905)
Yellowhead Jawfish (Pearly Jawfish)

Maximum Length: 3.9 in. (10 cm).
Range: Tropical Western Atlantic.
Minimum Aquarium Size: 20 gal. (76 L).
Foods & Feeding: Meaty foods, including chopped marine fish and crustacean flesh, mysid shrimp, or frozen preparations for carnivores. Feed 3 times a day.
Aquarium Suitability Index: 4.
Reef Aquarium Compatibility: Excellent. Possible threat to small, delicate shrimps.
Captive Care: An architect with reef sand and coral rubble, this is a comical and fascinating species for the home aquarium. It must have at least 3.1 in. (8 cm) of mixed substrate, including sand of varying grades and small pieces of shell and/or reef rubble so that it can construct a burrow. Keep with docile tankmates. More than one can be kept—they sometimes do better in colonies, but do not crowd. Will spawn in captivity; the male incubates the eggs in its mouth. A notorious jumper, it will leap from an open tank if frightened; dim tank lights gradually to prevent this. Less likely to jump after it has constructed a burrow (many leap out the first night).

Opistognathus rosenblatti Allen & Robertson, 1991
Bluespotted Jawfish

Maximum Length: 3.9 in. (10 cm).
Range: Tropical Eastern Pacific.
Minimum Aquarium Size: 20 gal. (76 L).
Foods & Feeding: Meaty foods, including chopped marine fish flesh, crustacean flesh, mysid shrimp, and frozen preparations for carnivores. Feed 3 times a day.
Aquarium Suitability Index: 4.
Reef Aquarium Compatibility: Excellent. May attack small, delicate ornamental shrimps.
Captive Care: This spectacular jawfish is less frequently seen in the aquarium trade than some of its Atlantic relatives. It should be kept in a tank with at least 3.1 in. (8 cm) of mixed substrate, including sand of varying grades and small pieces of shell and/or rubble so that it can construct a burrow. Keep with docile tankmates or be sure it is the first fish introduced and that it is given time to establish itself. Normally, only one should be kept per tank as they will fight, sometimes to the death. It is possible to keep a male-female pair in a larger aquarium. This fish is a notorious jumper that will leap from an open tank if frightened.

Opistognathus sp.
Goldspecs Jawfish (Bali Tiger Jawfish)

Maximum Length: 3.9 in. (10 cm).
Range: Western Pacific.
Minimum Aquarium Size: 20 gal. (76 L).
Foods & Feeding: Meaty foods, including chopped marine fish and crustacean flesh, mysid shrimp, or frozen preparations for carnivores. Feed 3 times a day.
Aquarium Suitability Index: 4.
Reef Aquarium Compatibility: Excellent. Possible threat to small shrimps.
Captive Care: This attractive burrowing species makes an interesting display in a tank with at least 3.1 in. (8 cm) of mixed substrate, including sand of varying grades and small pieces of shell and/or coral rubble for construction of a tunnel. A flat rock resting on the sand can also provide a roof for a potential burrow. Can be counted upon to jump from an inadequately covered aquarium. Less likely to jump once it has constructed its burrow. May be kept singly or in pairs. Best kept with docile tankmates. Will only behave aggressively toward fishes that try to enter its burrow.

Opistognathus whitehurstii (Longley, 1931)
Dusky Jawfish

Maximum Length: 3.9 in. (10 cm).
Range: Tropical Western Atlantic.
Minimum Aquarium Size: 20 gal. (76 L).
Foods & Feeding: Meaty foods, including chopped marine fish and crustacean flesh, mysid shrimp, or frozen preparations for carnivores. Feed 3 times a day.
Aquarium Suitability Index: 4.
Reef Aquarium Compatibility: Excellent. Possible threat to small shrimps.
Captive Care: Like the other jawfishes, this unusual species makes for an engaging display in a tank with a deep bed of sand, where it will actively burrow, spitting substrate and hovering above its lair. Provide at least 3.1 in. (8 cm) of mixed substrate, including sand of varying grades and small pieces of shell and/or rubble for construction of a burrow. A flat rock laid on the bottom can also provide a roof for a potential burrow. Aquarium must be covered to prevent jumping. Keep with docile tankmates. Can be kept in pairs or colonies, but they must have enough room to spread out and establish their own territories. Will spawn in captivity.

Amblycirrhitus pinos (Mowbray, 1927)
Redspotted Hawkfish

Maximum Length: 3.7 in. (9.5 cm).
Range: Tropical Atlantic.
Minimum Aquarium Size: 20 gal. (76 L).
Foods & Feeding: Meaty foods, including crustacean flesh, mysid shrimp, and frozen preparations. Feed daily.
Aquarium Suitability Index: 5. ▪
Reef Aquarium Compatibility: Excellent, although it may feed on smaller, more-delicate shrimps.
Captive Care: Lacking a swim bladder and known for their habit of perching—hawklike—on corals or pieces of rock alertly watching and ready to strike prey food items, the hawkfishes are hardy and popular aquarium fishes. This Atlantic species is quite shy when initially introduced, but after it has settled in it may bully newly introduced tankmates. More than one specimen can be kept in a medium to large aquarium if they are introduced simultaneously, are of unequal size, and if adequate hiding places are provided. Will spend most of its time sitting in the open.

Cirrhitichthys aprinus (Cuvier, 1829)
Spotted Hawkfish (Threadfin Hawkfish, Blotched Hawkfish)

Maximum Length: 4.9 in. (12.5 cm).
Range: Western Pacific.
Minimum Aquarium Size: 20 gal. (76 L).
Foods & Feeding: Meaty foods, including marine fish, crustacean flesh, mysid shrimp, and frozen preparations. Feed daily.
Aquarium Suitability Index: 5. ▄▄
Reef Aquarium Compatibility: Excellent, but may eat ornamental shrimps and small fishes.
Captive Care: A hardy but potentially aggressive aquarium inhabitant. Can be kept in male-female pairs. Although not sexually dichromatic, territorial males are larger in body size than the females within their social unit. (They may, however, be smaller than females in other harems.) The greater the disparity in body size between individuals, the more likely they are to be of the opposite sex. Provide with plenty of hiding places. Do not keep with larger, more-aggressive hawkfishes.

Cirrhitichthys falco Randall, 1963
Falco's Hawkfish (Dwarf Hawkfish)

Maximum Length: 2.8 in. (7 cm).
Range: Indo-Pacific.
Minimum Aquarium Size: 20 gal. (76 L).
Foods & Feeding: Meaty foods, including marine fish, crustacean flesh, mysid shrimp, and frozen preparations. Feed daily.
Aquarium Suitability Index: 5. ▉
Reef Aquarium Compatibility: Excellent, but may eat small, ornamental shrimps.
Captive Care: Slightly smaller in size and less of a danger to tank-mates than most other available hawkfishes, this durable species is a great choice for beginning hobbyists. However, it should not be trusted with small, nonaggressive fishes (e.g., dartfishes, small gobies, some anthias, flasher wrasses). In a tank with less-aggressive species, it should be the last fish introduced. Will spend more of its time sitting on the bottom of the tank than on the aquarium decor. Like others in this group of fishes, it can dart with amazing speed to grab food items that catch its ever-alert eye.

Cirrhitichthys oxycephalus (Bleeker, 1855)
Coral Hawkfish (Pixy Hawkfish)

Maximum Length: 3.3 in. (8.5 cm).
Range: Indo-Pacific.
Minimum Aquarium Size: 20 gal. (76 L).
Foods & Feeding: Meaty foods, including marine fish, crustacean flesh, mysid shrimp, and frozen preparations. Feed daily.
Aquarium Suitability Index: 5. ▪
Reef Aquarium Compatibility: Harmless to corals, but will eat ornamental shrimps and harass some other reef aquarium fishes.
Captive Care: Despite its small size, this is a very pugnacious fish that should not be housed with smaller, less-aggressive species. It has been known to pick relentlessly on small dottybacks, grammas, pygmy angelfishes, small butterflyfishes, sand perches, gobies, and dartfishes. The author has even had them attack small Arc-eye Hawkfish (*Paracirrhites arcatus*) introduced after the Coral Hawkfish was a well-established resident. To keep this species with less-pugnacious fishes, it should be the last fish added to the aquarium.

Cirrhitops fasciatus (Bennett, 1828)
Blood Red Hawkfish (Redbar Hawkfish, Banded Hawkfish)

Maximum Length: 5.0 in. (12.7 cm).
Range: Japan, Hawaii, Madagascar, and Mauritius.
Minimum Aquarium Size: 20 gal. (76 L).
Foods & Feeding: Meaty foods, including marine fish, crustacean flesh, mysid shrimp, and frozen preparations. Feed daily.
Aquarium Suitability Index: 5. ■
Reef Aquarium Compatibility: A threat to small fishes and crustaceans.
Captive Care: Although not as commonly available as many hawkfish species, this is a very durable aquarium fish. It is best housed in a system with larger or more-aggressive fishes—such as large angelfishes, larger pseudochromids, larger wrasses, puffers, and triggerfishes. It will greedily eat almost anything, including flake foods. Feed pigment-enriched foods to ensure it maintains it's brilliant coloration.

Cyprinocirrhites polyactis (Bleeker, 1875)
Lyretail Hawkfish (Swallowtail Hawkfish)

Maximum Length: 5.5 in. (14 cm).
Range: Indo-west-Pacific.
Minimum Aquarium Size: 20 gal. (76 L).
Foods & Feeding: Meaty foods, including marine fish, crustacean flesh, mysid shrimp, and frozen preparations. Feed daily.
Aquarium Suitability Index: 5. ■
Reef Aquarium Compatibility: Excellent, but a threat to small, delicate shrimps.
Captive Care: This hawkfish tends to spend most of its time in repose on the reef structure, unless the tank has a considerable amount of water movement, in which case it will often hover in the water column facing into the current. On occasion, will hide near the base and under the tentacles of large anemones (a behavior also seen in the wild) or large-polyped corals (i.e., *Goniopora* spp.). Although not as aggressive as most other hawkfishes, it will often chastise smaller or mild-mannered fishes introduced after it has become established. More than one Lyretail Hawkfish can be kept in a larger aquarium, but all individuals should be introduced simultaneously.

Neocirrhites armatus Castlenau, 1873
Flame Hawkfish

Maximum Length: 3.5 in. (9 cm).
Range: West and South Pacific.
Minimum Aquarium Size: 20 gal. (76 L).
Foods & Feeding: Meaty foods, including marine fishes, crustacean flesh, mysid shrimp, and frozen preparations. Feed daily.
Aquarium Suitability Index: 4.
Reef Aquarium Compatibility: Will eat feather duster worms, hermit crabs, snails, and ornamental shrimps.
Captive Care: With its bold coloration and droll appearance, this is one of the hawkfish species most in demand among aquarists. In reef aquariums, it will sometimes refuge next to the base and under the tentacles of large Magnificent Anemones (*Heteractis magnifica*). The movements of this species within a head of hard coral may facilitate water circulation within the colony and its feces may provide a source of nitrogen for coral tissue growth. Unfortunately, it will sometimes behave aggressively toward other bottom-dwelling fishes. This can be a chronic problem in a smaller aquarium. Will jerk hermit crabs, limpets, and *Turbo* snails out of their shells and eat them; will even knock snails off the glass to attack them.

Oxycirrhites typus Bleeker, 1857
Longnose Hawkfish

Maximum Length: 5.1 in. (13 cm).
Range: Indo-Pacific.
Minimum Aquarium Size: 20 gal. (76 L).
Foods & Feeding: Meaty foods, including marine fishes, crustacean flesh, mysid shrimp, and frozen preparations. Feed daily.
Aquarium Suitability Index: 5. ▪
Reef Aquarium Compatibility: Very good, but a threat to ornamental shrimps and small fishes.
Captive Care: Although one of the best of the hawkfishes for the mini-reef aquarium, it will occasionally eat ornamental shrimps and may attack fishes with elongate bodies, such as firefishes and dart gobies. It has a surprisingly capacious mouth, despite its needlelike snout. A full-grown Longnose Hawkfish will eat smaller fishes. It prefers to perch on gorgonians or similar decor. Can be kept in male-female pairs, but both specimens should be introduced simultaneously. If individuals start fighting they should be separated immediately to prevent serious injury. Tends to be beaten by most other hawkfishes. Has been known to jump out of uncovered aquariums; cover the top of the tank with fiberglass screening or similar material.

Paracirrhites arcatus (Cuvier, 1829)
Arc-eye Hawkfish

Maximum Length: 5.5 in. (14 cm).
Range: Indo-Pacific.
Minimum Aquarium Size: 30 gal. (114 L).
Foods & Feeding: Meaty foods, including marine fishes, crustacean flesh, mysid shrimp, and frozen preparations. Feed daily.
Aquarium Suitability Index: 5. ■
Reef Aquarium Compatibility: Harmless to sessile invertebrates, but will eat ornamental shrimps and small fishes.
Captive Care: A large, rugged hawkfish, this handsome species does best in a community setting with species that are well able to hold their own against potential bullies. It will display hostility toward fishes introduced after it, sometimes even if they are considerably larger. Will not harm corals (except for possible mechanical damage), but will eat small crabs, cleaner, boxer, anemone, and *Saron* shrimps, as well as smaller fishes. A known male and female can be kept in a larger aquarium together, otherwise one individual per community is the best approach.

Paracirrhites forsteri (Schneider, 1801)
Freckled Hawkfish (Forster's Hawkfish, Blackside Hawkfish)

Maximum Length: 8.9 in. (22.5 cm).
Range: Indo-Pacific.
Minimum Aquarium Size: 75 gal. (284 L).
Foods & Feeding: Meaty foods, including chopped fresh or frozen marine fish flesh, shrimp, squid, mysid shrimp, and frozen preparations for carnivores. Feed daily.
Aquarium Suitability Index: 5. ■
Reef Aquarium Compatibility: Not a threat to sessile invertebrates, but will eat ornamental crustaceans and small fishes.
Captive Care: This is a highly predatory species that may appeal to the collector of belligerent larger fishes. It is a voracious fish-eater and is aggressive toward fishes with similar behavior and those introduced after it. Best kept with triggerfishes, large angels, large surgeonfishes, and others that will not be intimidated. Keep only one per tank except in male-female pairs. Appears in different color phases: adults may be light pink, brown, or olive with or without light streaks down the sides; another color phase, originally described as a different species (*Paracirrhites typee*), has a deep maroon body with a yellow tail. In all color morphs, the face is peppered with red or black spots.

Apogon cyanosoma Bleeker, 1853
Orangestriped Cardinalfish

Maximum Length: 3.1 in. (8 cm).
Range: Indo-Pacific.
Minimum Aquarium Size: 30 gal. (144 L).
Foods & Feeding: Meaty foods, including marine fish, crustacean flesh, mysid shrimp, and frozen preparations. Feed daily.
Aquarium Suitability Index: 5.
Reef Aquarium Compatibility: Excellent, but may eat delicate ornamental shrimps.
Captive Care: One of the most ubiquitous cardinalfishes in the marine aquarium trade, in part because it is very colorful and hardy. It is a bolder species than some others in this family, spending much of its time in the open. By its nature, it usually does not move far from cover. Best kept in small groups of five to seven individuals, all of which should be introduced to the tank simultaneously. Can be housed in a shallow- or deep-water reef tank; much less of a threat to small fishes and crustaceans than some of its larger relatives.

Apogon leptacanthus Bleeker, 1856
Threadfin Cardinalfish (Bluestreak Cardinalfish)

Maximum Length: 2.4 in. (6 cm).
Range: Indo-Pacific.
Minimum Aquarium Size: 20 gal. (76 L).
Foods & Feeding: Meaty foods, including marine fish and crustacean flesh, mysid shrimp, and frozen preparations. Feed daily.
Aquarium Suitability Index: 4.
Reef Aquarium Compatibility: Not a threat to other fishes or to ornamental crustaceans.
Captive Care: Although sporadically available in the aquarium trade, this can be a great display animal in a shallow- or deep-water reef aquarium. It can also be a welcome addition to a more-docile fish-only tank or a small-polyped stony coral aquarium. It should be kept in aggregations of five or more individuals, and should not be housed with aggressive tankmates. May be picked on by other, more-aggressive cardinalfishes.

Apogon maculatus (Poey, 1861)
Flamefish

Maximum Length: 4.1 in. (10.5 cm).
Range: Tropical Eastern Atlantic.
Minimum Aquarium Size: 20 gal. (76 L).
Foods & Feeding: Meaty foods, including marine fishes, crustacean flesh, mysid shrimp, and frozen preparations. Feed daily.
Aquarium Suitability Index: 5. ▇
Reef Aquarium Compatibility: May eat delicate ornamental shrimps.
Captive Care: This Caribbean species is one of the most common cardinalfishes in the aquarium trade. It is a great fish for hobbyists at all levels, although it will often spend a considerable amount of time peering from holes and crevices, especially in well-illuminated tanks. Will stake out a small territory in its captive home and chase away any other cardinalfishes that intrude. Keep only one per tank, unless the aquarium is of sufficient size. To keep more than one, add two individuals simultaneously to a tank of 55 gal. (208 L) or larger. Other cardinalfish species are apt to be pestered by this fish in a small tank. Unfortunately, its color often fades after it has been in captivity for some time, especially if it is not fed a varied diet that includes vitamin-enriched and color-enhancing foods.

Apogon compressus
Ochre-striped Cardinalfish
Max. Length: 4.7 in. (12 cm).
Aquarium Suitability: 5. ■

Apogon hartzfeldi
Hartzfeld's Cardinalfish
Max. Length: 3.5 in. (9 cm).
Aquarium Suitability: 5. ■

Apogon novemfasciatus
Ninebanded Cardinalfish
Max. Length: 3.5 in. (9 cm).
Aquarium Suitability: 5. ■

Apogon pseudomaculatus
Twospot Cardinalfish
Max. Length: 4.1 in. (10.5 cm).
Aquarium Suitability: 5. ■

Apogon sealei
Seale's Cardinalfish
Max. Length: 3.1 in. (8 cm).
Aquarium Suitability: 5. ■

Sphaeramia nematoptera
Pajama Cardinalfish
Max. Length: 3.1 in. (8 cm)
Aquarium Suitability: 5. ■

Cheilodipterus quinquelineatus Cuvier, 1828
Fivelined Cardinalfish

Maximum Length: 4.7 in. (12 cm).
Range: Indo-Pacific.
Minimum Aquarium Size: 30 gal. (114 L).
Foods & Feeding: Prefers live foods, such as baby guppies and live grass shrimp, but will usually learn to accept frozen brine shrimp, chopped seafoods, and frozen preparations for carnivores. Feed daily.
Aquarium Suitability Index: 4.
Reef Aquarium Compatibility: Harmless to sessile invertebrates, but will eat small snails, crabs, shrimps, and small fishes.
Captive Care: This is a durable cardinalfish, but one with a greater propensity to eat smaller fishes than many other members of its large family. Will spend most of its time in exposed areas, but rarely moves far from a shelter site, except when presented with food. Juveniles often hang over the tentacles of sea anemones or among the spines of long-spined sea urchins. Feeds both day and night, but actively moves over sand and rubble areas after dark. Keep only one per tank. It is best housed with less-aggressive fishes that roughly match it in length; it should be introduced after more-passive species.

Pterapogon kauderni (Koumans, 1933)
Banggai Cardinalfish (Longfin Cardinalfish)

Maximum Length: 3.0 in. (7.5 cm).
Range: Indonesia.
Minimum Aquarium Size: 20 gal. (76 L).
Foods & Feeding: Meaty foods, including marine fish, crustacean flesh, mysid shrimp, and frozen preparations. Feed daily.
Aquarium Suitability Index: 5.
Reef Aquarium Compatibility: Excellent.
Captive Care: An elegant black-and-silver species only recently brought to the attention of the aquarium world by ichthyologist Dr. Gerald Allen who found them off a remote island in Sulawesi. Males of this hardy species mouthbrood eggs and fry until they are free-swimming, making them relatively easy to breed in the home aquarium. It is risky to keep these fish in groups, except in a larger system. They may behave peacefully when first introduced, but one fish or a pair will often start chasing and nipping conspecifics. In a larger tank, individuals will disperse, which will decrease the number of aggressive encounters, but in small- or medium-sized tanks, subordinate individuals will end up dead or cowering in the corners of the tank. Best housed with other nonaggressive fishes.

Sphaeramia orbicularis (Cuvier, 1828)
Orbiculate Cardinalfish (Polkadot Cardinalfish)

Maximum Length: 3.9 in. (10 cm).
Range: Indo-west-Pacific.
Minimum Aquarium Size: 20 gal. (76 L).
Foods & Feeding: Meaty foods, including marine fish, crustacean flesh, mysid shrimp, and frozen preparations. Feed daily.
Aquarium Suitability Index: 5.
Reef Aquarium Compatibility: Will eat polychaete worms and small fishes.
Captive Care: As hardy as the closely related *Sphaeramia nematoptera* (page 148), but not nearly as chromatically blessed. For this reason, it is often overlooked by marine enthusiasts, but is a good beginner's fish. It is inexpensive, has a peculiar color pattern, will eat most aquarium foods, and is virtually bulletproof. Can, and often should, be kept in small groups, which can prove interesting in their own right. Members of the group will set up a pecking order, with the largest individual being the most dominant. Aggressive exchanges usually consist of the occasional chase or nudge, not all-out warfare.

Hoplolatilus luteus Allen & Kuiter, 1989
Golden Tilefish (Yellow Tilefish)

Maximum Length: 5.5 in. (14 cm).
Range: Flores, Indonesia, and possibly Bali.
Minimum Aquarium Size: 55 gal. (208 L).
Foods & Feeding: Meaty foods, including marine fish, crustacean flesh, mysid shrimp, and frozen preparations. Feed at least 3 times a day.
Aquarium Suitability Index: 3.
Reef Aquarium Compatibility: Excellent, although it will eat small crustaceans.
Captive Care: Like others in the sand tilefish clan, this is a fast swimmer and great jumper that requires ample room and a covered tank. It is one of the more durable and also one of the most aggressive members of the genus. Best kept in groups that are introduced simultaneously; they may chase and nip each other when time has elapsed between the introduction of the first and second fish. May also chase small zooplankton-feeding fishes introduced after them. Can be housed in a deep- or shallow-water reef aquarium. It will jump out of an open tank.

Hoplolatilus starcki Randall & Dooley, 1974
Bluehead Tilefish (Blueface Tilefish, Starck's Tilefish)

Maximum Length: 5.9 in. (15 cm).
Range: Western and South Pacific.
Minimum Aquarium Size: 55 gal. (208 L).
Foods & Feeding: Meaty foods, including marine fish, crustacean flesh, mysid shrimp, and frozen preparations. Feed at least 3 times a day.
Aquarium Suitability Index: 2.
Reef Aquarium Compatibility: Will not harm desirable invertebrates, but does best in a dimly lit tank.
Captive Care: This is an active species that demands space to exercise its swimming abilities. As with other sand tilefishes, this species acclimates more readily if kept with another tilefish: a member of the same species is best, or it can be housed with other sand tilefishes. Debelius and Baensch (1992) report that this species is less social than other tilefishes, maintaining a greater distance between itself and conspecifics and rarely sharing the same hiding place. Juveniles acclimate more readily to captivity than adults. Requires several feedings per day to fuel its fast metabolism. Will acclimate more readily in the low-light conditions of a deep-water reef aquarium. An accomplished jumper, it must be kept in a covered aquarium.

Hoplolatilus chlupatyi
Flashing or Chameleon Tilefish
Max. Length: 5.1 in. (13 cm).
Aquarium Suitability: 2.

Hoplolatilus cuniculus
Green or Pale Tilefish
Max. Length: 5.9 in. (15 cm).
Aquarium Suitability: 2.

Hoplolatilus fourmanoiri
Fourmanoir's Tilefish
Max. Length: 5.5 in. (14 cm).
Aquarium Suitability: 3.

Hoplolatilus fronticinctus
Stocky Tilefish
Max. Length: 7.9 in. (20 cm).
Aquarium Suitability: 2.

Hoplolatilus marcosi
Skunk, Marcos' or Redstripe Tilefish
Max. Length: 4.7 in. (12 cm).
Aquarium Suitability: 2.

Hoplolatilus purpureus
Purple Tilefish
Max. Length: 5.1 in. (13 cm).
Aquarium Suitability: 2.

Gnathanodon speciosus (Forsskål, 1775)
Golden Jack (Pilotfish, Golden Trevally)

Maximum Length: 3.6 ft. (110 cm).
Range: Western Pacific.
Minimum Aquarium Size: 500 gal. (1,893 L).
Foods & Feeding: Meaty foods, including chopped fresh or frozen shrimp, scallop, marine fish flesh, mysid shrimp, and prepared frozen foods for carnivores. Feed 3 times a day.
Aquarium Suitability Index: 2. ◣
Reef Aquarium Compatibility: Not recommended, except for exceptionally large systems. Will eat ornamental crustaceans and small fishes.
Captive Care: Juveniles are a brilliant yellow with black bars, but transform into big, silvery adults with weights up to 33 pounds (15 kg). Although very attractive, this species simply gets too large and is too active to be kept in most home aquariums. They are an appropriate choice for huge systems with plenty of open swimming space, and more than one specimen can be kept in the same aquarium; in fact, they will school. They will also escort larger fishes, especially active shark species. Will eat smaller fishes.

Lutjanus kasmira (Forsskål, 1775)
Bluelined Snapper

Maximum Length: 13.8 in. (35 cm).
Range: Western Pacific.
Minimum Aquarium Size: 135 gal. (511 L).
Foods & Feeding: Meaty foods, including chopped fresh or frozen shrimp, scallop, marine fish flesh, mysid shrimp, and prepared frozen foods for carnivores. Feed to satiation, once a day.
Aquarium Suitability Index: 5. ▮
Reef Aquarium Compatibility: Will eat ornamental crustaceans and any fish it can swallow whole. Adults will also eat mantis shrimps.
Captive Care: This attractively marked species is a voracious carnivore. It is a very aggressive feeder that will intimidate more-passive tankmates and will also pick on smaller and more-peaceful species. In most cases, it should be the last fish introduced to a community tank. Although it sometimes schools in the wild, it is prudent to keep only one specimen per tank, although more than one specimen can be kept in a very large tank (all specimens should be introduced simultaneously). Provide it with a cave or crevices to hide in. Its brilliant colors often fade.

Lutjanus sebae (Cuvier, 1828)
Emperor Snapper (Sebae Snapper)

Maximum Length: 31.5 in. (80 cm).
Range: Western Pacific.
Minimum Aquarium Size: 200 gal. (757 L).
Foods & Feeding: Meaty foods, including chopped fresh or frozen shrimp, scallop, marine fish flesh, mysid shrimp, and prepared frozen foods for carnivores. Feed to satiation, once a day.
Aquarium Suitability Index: 2.
Reef Aquarium Compatibility: Will eat ornamental crustaceans and any fish it can swallow whole. Adults will also eat mantis shrimps.
Captive Care: This eyecatching species will readily acclimate to the home aquarium and is the most commonly available member of this family. It does grow large (outgrowing the majority of home setups), losing its distinctive juvenile pattern to an overall reddish pink color. Provide it with plenty of swimming room as well as suitable hiding places. Juveniles can be intimidated by larger, more-aggressive tankmates, but once acclimated they can become pugnacious. Keep only one adult per tank (although juveniles can be kept together) and do not house with fish tankmates that can be swallowed whole.

Macolor niger (Forsskål, 1775)
Black Snapper (Macolor Snapper)

Maximum Length: 26.0 in. (66 cm).
Range: Indo-Pacific.
Minimum Aquarium Size: 200 gal. (757 L).
Foods & Feeding: Meaty foods, including shaved or chopped fresh or frozen shrimp, scallop, marine fish flesh, mysid shrimp, and prepared frozen foods for carnivores. Juveniles are sometimes finicky and may initially reject all but live foods. Feed 3 times a day.
Aquarium Suitability Index: 2.
Reef Aquarium Compatibility: Will eat polychaete worms, ornamental crustaceans, and small fishes. Needs plenty of swimming room.
Captive Care: The boldly marked juveniles of this species sometimes appear in the aquarium trade, but aquarists should be aware that adults are not nearly as attractive as smaller specimens and require very large aquariums. Avoid keeping them with active food competitors or with aggressive species that will pick on them or nip their long fins. More than one specimen can be housed per tank, although they usually occur singly as juveniles in the wild.

JUVENILE

Symphorichthys spilurus (Günther, 1874)
Threadfin Snapper (Bluelined Sea Bream)

Maximum Length: 23.6 in. (60 cm).
Range: Western Pacific.
Minimum Aquarium Size: 200 gal. (757 L).
Foods & Feeding: Meaty foods, including chopped fresh or frozen shrimp, scallop, marine fish flesh, mysid shrimp, and prepared frozen foods for carnivores. Feed 3 times a day.
Aquarium Suitability Index: 2.
Reef Aquarium Compatibility: Will eat ornamental crustaceans and small fishes. Too large for most reef aquariums.
Captive Care: This glorious fish makes a stunning display animal in a very large home aquarium. Adults are even more attractive than the juveniles, which have a black longitudinal band that gradually fades into an overall pattern of neon-blue bars on a yellow background. It is extremely active and will need plenty of swimming room as well as a hole or cave where it can quickly retreat if threatened. In tanks cluttered with decor, this fish may damage itself if it dashes about when startled. Only one should be kept per aquarium, except in extremely large systems. It will eat smaller fish tankmates.

Anisotremus virginicus (Linnaeus, 1758)
Porkfish

Maximum Length: 15.7 in. (40 cm).
Range: Western Atlantic.
Minimum Aquarium Size: 135 gal. (511 L).
Foods & Feeding: Meaty foods, including chopped shrimp, marine fish flesh, mysid shrimp, and prepared frozen foods for carnivores. Feed 2-3 times a day.
Aquarium Suitability Index: 4.
Reef Aquarium Compatibility: Not recommended. Will eat small prey, including snails, polychaete worms, hermit crabs, ornamental shrimps, and serpent stars.
Captive Care: This is one of the flashy grunts, a group of fishes known for the sounds produced by the grinding of their pharyngeal teeth and esteemed more for the table than the aquarium. Juveniles do appear in the pet trade and are peaceful in a community setting. Small individuals can be kept in groups and will clean other fishes. They may be intimidated by more-aggressive species, and should be kept with less-pugnacious tankmates; plan to add adults first if they are to be housed in a more-aggressive community tank. Provide with plenty of swimming room and a cave or ledge for refuge.

Plectorhinchus albovittatus (Rüppell, 1838)
Twostriped Sweetlips

Maximum Length: 11.8 in. (30 cm).
Range: Indo-Pacific.
Minimum Aquarium Size: 75 gal. (284 L).
Foods & Feeding: Meaty foods, including chopped shrimp, scallop, marine fish flesh, mysid shrimp, and prepared frozen foods for carnivores. Feed 2-3 times a day.
Aquarium Suitability Index: 4.
Reef Aquarium Compatibility: Will eat small snails, polychaete worms, ornamental crustaceans (including cleaner species), and serpent stars. Will consume some noxious worms, like smaller fireworms.
Captive Care: This is one of the more durable of the sweetlips, although the cute black-and-white juveniles lose all but two stripes and most of their color intensity as they mature. A voracious predator, it will feed on a wide range of invertebrates and can successfully compete with species with a similar nature once fully acclimated to aquarium life. Keep only one per tank. Will sift mouthfuls of substrate, which can help keep the upper layers of the aquarium sand clean. Provide with plenty of swimming space and some good hiding places.

Plectorhinchus chaetodonoides Lacépède, 1800
Harlequin Sweetlips (Clown Sweetlips)

Maximum Length: 28.3 in. (72 cm).
Range: Indo-Pacific.
Minimum Aquarium Size: 200 gal. (757 L).
Foods & Feeding: Difficult to feed as juveniles. May require live shrimp or black worms to catalyze a feeding response. Some can be enticed into taking meaty foods, including finely chopped fresh or frozen shrimp, scallop, marine fish flesh, mysid shrimp, and prepared frozen foods for carnivores. Feed 2-3 times a day.
Aquarium Suitability Index: 2. ◣
Reef Aquarium Compatibility: Will eat small snails, polychaete worms, ornamental crustaceans (including cleaner species), and serpent stars.
Captive Care: Juveniles of this delicate species exhibit gorgeous camouflage patterns and an unusual swimming behavior: paddling with oversized pectoral fins and undulating their bodies. Juveniles tend to starve in captivity and must not be kept with aggressive tankmates, which will harass them or snap up all the food before they have a chance to feed. Will eat worms and crustaceans in live sand, which may keep the fish alive until it starts taking introduced foods. Juveniles can be housed together, but adults get very large.

Plectorhinchus orientalis Bloch, 1793
Oriental Sweetlips

Maximum Length: 33.9 in. (86 cm).
Range: Indo-Pacific.
Minimum Aquarium Size: 200 gal. (757 L).
Foods & Feeding: Juveniles are often difficult to feed and may require live shrimp or black worms to initiate feeding. Some will eat only live foods; others can be enticed into taking finely chopped fresh or frozen shrimp, scallop, marine fish flesh, mysid shrimp, and prepared frozen rations for carnivores. Feed 2-3 times a day.
Aquarium Suitability Index: 2. ▰
Reef Aquarium Compatibility: Will eat small snails, polychaete worms, ornamental crustaceans (including cleaner species), and serpent stars. Will consume some noxious worms, like smaller fireworms.
Captive Care: The sweetlips are Indo-Pacific relatives of the Atlantic grunts, and juveniles regularly appear in aquarium stores. This species can be a challenge to feed and must be kept with nonaggressive tankmates that will not pick on it or snap up all the food. Will eat worms and crustaceans in live sand, which may keep the fish alive until it starts taking introduced foods. Juveniles can be housed together; adults get very large. Peaceful with other species.

Scolopsis bilineatus Bloch, 1793
Twoline Spinecheek

Maximum Length: 9.1 in. (23 cm).
Range: Indo-Pacific.
Minimum Aquarium Size: 75 gal. (284 L).
Foods & Feeding: Meaty foods, including finely chopped fresh or frozen shrimp, scallop, marine fish flesh, mysid shrimp, and prepared frozen rations for carnivores. Feed 2-3 times a day.
Aquarium Suitability Index: 4.
Reef Aquarium Compatibility: Will eat small snails, worms, and ornamental crustaceans. Will take in mouthfuls of sand, sort out edible materials, and spit out the remainder, keeping the sand bed stirred.
Captive Care: Sometimes known as sea breams and widely sold in Asian food markets, this is one of a group of fishes not particularly popular in the aquarium trade. Still, this species is both hardy and interesting to watch. Only one should be kept per tank, and it should not be housed with aggressive tankmates. Its aquarium should have a 2-in. (5-cm) sand substrate with limited decor and plenty of open bottom space.

Pentapodus sp.
Blue Whiptail (Banana Fish)

Maximum Length: 7.9 in. (20 cm).
Range: Western and South Pacific.
Minimum Aquarium Size: 75 gal. (284 L).
Foods & Feeding: Meaty foods, including pieces of fresh shrimp, scallop, and marine fish flesh impaled on a feeding stick. Feed 2-3 times a day.
Aquarium Suitability Index: 4.
Reef Aquarium Compatibility: Will eat small snails, worms, and ornamental crustaceans. Will take in mouthfuls of sand, sort out edible materials, and spit out the remainder, keeping the sand bed stirred.
Captive Care: This is easily the most common representative of the sea breams (Family Nemipteridae) in the aquarium trade because of its bright blue coloration. Only one should be kept per tank, and it should not be housed with aggressive tankmates. Its tank should have a 2-in. (5-cm) layer of sand substrate with limited decor and plenty of open bottom space. This fish is a strong jumper and will leap out of open aquariums.

Equetus lanceolatus (Linnaeus, 1758)
Jackknife Fish

Maximum Length: 9.8 in. (25 cm).
Range: Tropical Western Atlantic.
Minimum Aquarium Size: 100 gal. (379 L).
Foods & Feeding: Can be difficult to feed. May require live foods, such as vitamin-enriched brine shrimp, grass shrimp, black worms, and baby livebearers (e.g., guppies or mollies) to induce a feeding response. A productive refugium and live sand can help provide natural foods. In time, some specimens can be switched to finely chopped shrimp, scallop, and marine fish flesh. Feed 2-3 times a day.
Aquarium Suitability Index: 2.
Reef Aquarium Compatibility: Will eat polychaete worms, ornamental crustaceans, and small fishes. Sometimes eats smaller fireworms.
Captive Care: This is a graceful and unusual fish that must be housed with its own kind or with other very peaceful species if it is to acclimate to aquarium life. Avoid keeping it with food competitors. More than one can be kept per tank, although as they grow they may squabble, especially if space is limited. Secretive and shy, it will need plenty of suitable hiding places and does best in aquariums situated in low-traffic areas.

Pareques acuminatus (Bloch & Schneider, 1801)
Highhat

Maximum Length: 9.1 in. (23 cm).
Range: Tropical Western Atlantic.
Minimum Aquarium Size: 100 gal. (379 L).
Foods & Feeding: Can be difficult to feed. May require live foods, such as vitamin-enriched brine shrimp, grass shrimp, and black worms to induce a feeding response. A productive refugium and live sand can help provide natural foods. In time, some specimens can be switched to finely chopped shrimp, scallop, and marine fish flesh. Feed 2-3 times a day.
Aquarium Suitability Index: 3.
Reef Aquarium Compatibility: Will eat polychaete worms, ornamental crustaceans, and small fishes. May eat small fireworms.
Captive Care: An appropriate fish for a Caribbean biotope system, and hardier than its close relative, *Equetus lanceolatus* (page 166). However, it does need to be housed on its own or with other very peaceful species if it is to acclimate to aquarium life. Secretive and shy, it will need plenty of suitable caves or shaded hiding places to feel secure in the aquarium. More than one can be kept per tank, although as they grow they may quarrel, especially in smaller tanks.

Parupeneus barberinoides (Bleeker, 1852)
Dash-and-Dot Goatfish (Bicolor Goatfish,
Half-and-Half Goatfish, Swarthy-headed Goatfish)

Maximum Length: 9.8 in. (25 cm).
Range: Indo-Pacific.
Minimum Aquarium Size: 55 gal. (208 L).
Foods & Feeding: Demands frequent feeding. Offer meaty foods, including fresh and frozen seafoods, live grass shrimp, and frozen prepared foods. Feed juveniles at least 4 times a day.
Aquarium Suitability Index: 3.
Reef Aquarium Compatibility: Will eat worms and crustaceans. Good at stirring the substrate, but will decimate infaunal invertebrate populations.
Captive Care: Equipped with barbels that they use to grub in the soft substrate for food, goatfishes are active and appealing but less than simple to care for in most aquariums. They need plenty of swimming space and should be housed with nonaggressive tankmates. Goatfishes are often infected with intestinal worms and will often do better if given a deworming treatment when first purchased. Juveniles must be fed multiple times daily as they have a high metabolism and are likely to lose weight if fed less frequently.

Parupeneus cyclostomus (Lacépède, 1801)
Yellowsaddle Goatfish (Yellow Goatfish)

Maximum Length: 20.0 in. (50 cm).
Range: Indo-Pacific.
Minimum Aquarium Size: 135 gal. (511 L).
Foods & Feeding: Demands frequent feeding. Offer meaty foods, including fresh and frozen seafoods, live grass shrimp, and frozen prepared foods. Feed juveniles at least 4 times a day.
Aquarium Suitability Index: 3.
Reef Aquarium Compatibility: Will eat worms, crustaceans, and small fishes.
Captive Care: This is a nervous fish that should be provided with plenty of swimming space, several good hiding places, and nonaggressive tankmates. Unlike other goatfishes, this species does not grub in the substrate for food and is thus not an appropriate choice as a sand-stirrer for reef aquariums. Adults will outgrow the average home aquarium. Juveniles of this species will spend much of their time swimming beneath their tankmates, especially long, slender fishes like wrasses and tilefishes. They have an active metabolism and must be fed several times a day.

Parupeneus multifasciatus (Quoy & Gaimard, 1824)
Manybar Goatfish (Multibarred Goatfish)

Maximum Length: 12.0 in. (30 cm).
Range: Indo-Pacific.
Minimum Aquarium Size: 75 gal. (284 L).
Foods & Feeding: Meaty foods, including fresh and frozen seafoods, live grass shrimp, and frozen prepared foods. Feed juveniles at least 4 times a day.
Aquarium Suitability Index: 3.
Reef Aquarium Compatibility: Will eat worms, crustaceans, and small fishes.
Captive Care: This sizable species should be provided with plenty of swimming space, several good hiding places, and nonaggressive tank-mates. It will grub in the substrate, which aids in keeping it stirred and clean. Larger individuals will eat other fishes: one individual owned by the author ate three juvenile Striped Eel Catfish (*Plotosus lineatus*)—venomous spines and all. Juveniles are likely to lose weight if fed less than 4 times a day.

Pseudupeneus maculatus (Bloch, 1793)
Spotted Goatfish

Maximum Length: 11.0 in. (28 cm).
Range: Tropical Western Atlantic.
Minimum Aquarium Size: 75 gal. (284 L).
Foods & Feeding: Meaty food, including chopped fresh and frozen seafoods, live grass shrimp, and frozen carnivore rations. A well-established bed of live sand in the aquarium may provide a source of natural prey. Feed 3 times daily. (Feed juveniles at least 4 times a day, as they have a high metabolism and are likely to lose weight if fed less frequently.)
Aquarium Suitability Index: 3.
Reef Aquarium Compatibility: Harmless to corals, but will eat worms, crustaceans, and small bottom-dwelling fishes.
Captive Care: A typical goatfish in its habit of grubbing in the sand with its barbels, this species is often followed by wrasses in the wild waiting to steal prey items stirred into the water column from the substrate. In the aquarium, it requires plenty of swimming space and open bottom for its rooting activities and also needs several good hiding places. House with nonaggressive tankmates.

Chaetodon auriga Forsskål, 1775
Threadfin Butterflyfish (Auriga Butterflyfish)

Maximum Length: 9.0 in. (23 cm).
Range: Indo-Pacific.
Minimum Aquarium Size: 75 gal. (284 L).
Foods & Feeding: Varied diet, including marine fish, crustacean flesh, mysid shrimp, and frozen preparations. Feed at least 3 times daily.
Aquarium Suitability Index: 4.
Reef Aquarium Compatibility: Not recommended. Will eat a wide variety of corals and desirable invertebrates.
Captive Care: This is a bold, attractive species and one of the best butterflyfishes for the home aquarium. It will accept a wide variety of aquarium foods, but should be provided with a varied diet. It is one of the more-aggressive members of the family, often chasing conspecifics and species with similar color patterns. To keep more than one, add them to a larger tank simultaneously. Does very well with live rock aquascaping, but is not safe with corals. Although it can be employed to clean live rock of *Aiptasia* spp. or glass anemones, it will also feed on some of the more-desirable invertebrates living on the rock, such as fanworms. The author has had this species "clean" other fishes in captivity.

Chaetodon burgessi Allen & Starck, 1973
Burgess' Butterflyfish

Maximum Length: 5.5 in. (14 cm).
Range: Western Pacific.
Minimum Aquarium Size: 55 gal. (208 L).
Foods & Feeding: Varied diet, including marine fish, crustacean flesh, mysid shrimp, and frozen preparations. Feed at least 3 times daily.
Aquarium Suitability Index: 4.
Reef Aquarium Compatibility: Can be kept with mushroom anemones and certain soft corals (e.g., *Litophyton* spp., *Cladiella* spp.), and possibly with small-polyped stony corals. Large-polyped varieties are susceptible to being picked on, and tubeworms will be eaten. Great for ridding a tank of *Aiptasia* spp. anemones.
Captive Care: A prized deep-water species, this is actually one of the more-durable butterflyfishes, well suited to the home aquarium. It will feed on most captive fare, including flake foods, but should be provided with a varied, enriched diet to ensure good health and color fidelity. Not aggressive toward other fishes, and more than one individual can be housed in the same aquarium. Because it is accustomed to deep-water conditions, it is best housed in a dimly lit tank.

Chaetodon capistratus Linnaeus, 1758
Foureye Butterflyfish

Maximum Length: 5.9 in. (15 cm).
Range: Western Tropical Atlantic.
Minimum Aquarium Size: 55 gal. (208 L).
Foods & Feeding: Difficult to feed. Most specimens are reluctant to take food in captivity. Try vitamin-enriched live brine shrimp, clam on the half shell, or mashed squid or shrimp on a bleached stony coral skeleton. Once eating, offer crustacean flesh, mysid shrimp, and frozen preparations for carnivores. It has a small mouth, so its food must be finely chopped. Feed at least 3 times daily.
Aquarium Suitability Index: 1. ▉▉▉
Reef Aquarium Compatibility: Not suitable. It will eat stony coral and gorgonian polyps.
Captive Care: This handsome but delicate fish is best kept with peaceful species and fishes that will not compete with it for food, at least until it is eating normal aquarium fare. A male-female pair can be kept together, but members of the same sex may quarrel. Usually indifferent toward its tankmates, with the possible exception of other butterflyfishes. Juveniles have two eyespots on the back of the body and dorsal fin until they reach about 1 in. (3 cm) in length.

Chaetodon collare Bloch, 1787
Collare Butterflyfish (Pakistan Butterflyfish)

Maximum Length: 6.3 in. (16 cm).
Range: Indian Ocean.
Minimum Aquarium Size: 55 gal. (208 L).
Foods & Feeding: Varied diet, including marine fish, crustacean flesh, mysid shrimp, and frozen preparations. Feed at least 3 times daily.
Aquarium Suitability Index: 3.
Reef Aquarium Compatibility: Can be housed with certain soft corals but should not be kept with stony corals. Will nip at many of the sessile invertebrates that grow on live rock.
Captive Care: A richly pigmented and distinctive species, this butterflyfish can do well in the home aquarium but may require special selection and acclimation. It eats coral polyps in the wild, and individuals vary in their willingness to accept substitute foods, with smaller specimens often proving more difficult to feed than medium-sized fish (over 3 in. [8 cm]). Often shuns food for several days in a new aquarium. Is best kept singly, as conspecifics often behave aggressively toward each other. To keep two individuals together, add them to a larger tank simultaneously. Adults should be provided with plenty of swimming room.

Chaetodon ephippium Cuvier, 1831
Saddled Butterflyfish (Saddleback Butterflyfish)

Maximum Length: 9.0 in. (23 cm).
Range: Indo-Pacific.
Minimum Aquarium Size: 100 gal. (379 L).
Foods & Feeding: Varied diet, including marine fish, crustacean flesh, mysid shrimp, and frozen preparations. Feed at least 3 times daily.
Aquarium Suitability Index: 3.
Reef Aquarium Compatibility: Can be housed with certain soft corals but should not be kept with stony corals. Will nip at many of the sessile invertebrates that grow on live rock.
Captive Care: Regarded by some as a challenging species, the Saddleback Butterfly varies in its suitability to aquarium life, depending in part on the age of the individual selected. Smaller specimens are less likely to feed in captivity than medium-sized individuals (over 4 in. [10 cm] in total length), while large specimens require plenty of swimming space and optimal water quality to thrive in captivity. Will often acclimate more readily if kept in an aquarium with lush filamentous algae growth. Only one specimen should be housed per tank, unless a male-female pair is acquired. Typically not bothered by moderately pugnacious species.

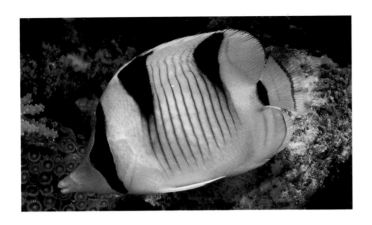

Chaetodon falcula Bloch, 1793
Falcula Butterflyfish (Saddleback Butterflyfish)

Maximum Length: 7.8 in. (20 cm).
Range: Indian Ocean.
Minimum Aquarium Size: 75 gal. (284 L).
Foods & Feeding: Varied diet, including meaty foods—marine fish, crustacean flesh, mysid shrimp, krill, and frozen preparations. Feed 2-3 times a day.
Aquarium Suitability Index: 3.
Reef Aquarium Compatibility: Smaller individuals (under 3.1 in. [8 cm]) can be kept in a reef aquarium with soft corals, but will become more destructive as they grow larger. Will pick at stony corals, sea anemones, and mushroom anemones.
Captive Care: This is a bright, attractive butterflyfish, a favorite of many aquarists and more durable than some of its relatives. Acclimated individuals will actively compete for food with other aggressive feeders, more than many of the other butterflyfishes. However, some individuals may be reluctant to feed on normal aquarium fare. It is possible to induce finicky individuals to begin feeding by offering them inexpensive anemones to pick at. Resembles the closely related *C. ulietensis*, page 193.

Chaetodon fremblii Bennett, 1829
Bluestripe Butterflyfish

Maximum Length: 5.1 in. (13 cm).
Range: Hawaiian Islands.
Minimum Aquarium Size: 55 gal. (208 L).
Foods & Feeding: Varied diet, including marine fish, crustacean flesh, mysid shrimp, and frozen preparations. Feed at least 3 times daily.
Aquarium Suitability Index: 4.
Reef Aquarium Compatibility: Can be kept in a reef aquarium that contains only soft corals, such as *Lemnalia, Litophyton, Sinularia flexibilis*, and *Dendronephthya*, but is likely to pick on both small- and larger-polyped stony corals.
Captive Care: Endemic to Hawaiian waters, this is an unusual and beautiful species when seen with its colors at full intensity. Unfortunately, it often adopts its fright, or nocturnal, color pattern during the day when held in captivity, and takes on a dirty yellow or blotchy color overall, with blue lines. It is a moderately hardy but shy butterflyfish that will eat most aquarium foods offered. Can be kept singly or in pairs, but should not be kept with overly aggressive tankmates, as it is likely to hide and may get little to eat.

Chaetodon kleinii Bloch, 1790
Klein's Butterflyfish (Brown Butterflyfish,
Corallicola Butterflyfish, Blacklip Butterflyfish)

Maximum Length: 5.5 in. (14 cm).
Range: Indo-Pacific.
Minimum Aquarium Size: 55 gal. (208 L).
Foods & Feeding: Varied diet, including marine fish, crustacean flesh,
mysid shrimp, and frozen preparations. Feed at least 3 times daily.
Aquarium Suitability Index: 5. ■
Reef Aquarium Compatibility: Can be kept in a reef aquarium if it is well
fed and coral tankmates are selected carefully. Best kept with some
of the more-noxious soft corals, but will eat leather coral polyps.
Captive Care: This is perhaps the most durable member of the butterflyfish family and an excellent beginner's butterflyfish. Will accept almost any food offered once it has acclimated, although it
should be fed a varied diet for good health and coloration. Can be
kept with other butterflyfishes, including members of its own species
if they are introduced simultaneously. It may also be housed with
moderately aggressive fishes, as long as it is introduced before its
more-belligerent tankmates.

Chaetodon lineolatus Cuvier, 1831
Lined Butterflyfish

Maximum Length: 11.8 in. (30 cm).
Range: Indo-Pacific.
Minimum Aquarium Size: 100 gal. (379 L).
Foods & Feeding: Meaty foods, including vitamin-enriched live brine shrimp, clam on the half shell, crustacean flesh, mysid shrimp, and frozen preparations for carnivores. Feed at least 3 times daily.
Aquarium Suitability Index: 3.
Reef Aquarium Compatibility: Not suitable. It eats both stony and soft coral polyps, as well as sea anemones and mushroom anemones.
Captive Care: Dinner-plate-sized adults of this species are the largest of all butterflyfishes and require a large tank with plenty of swimming room. The hardiness of this species varies: some specimens readily accept most foods, while others are finicky and need special attention. Most individuals begin feeding if kept in a well-maintained aquarium and provided with a wide range of first foods. Smaller- to medium-sized fish (2 to 6 in. [5 to 15 cm]) tend to acclimate more quickly to captive life. Once settled, it is an aggressive feeder that can be kept with more-pugnacious tankmates. Keep only one per tank and do not house with similarly colored butterflyfishes.

Chaetodon lunula (Lacépède, 1803)
Raccoon Butterflyfish

Maximum Length: 7.9 in. (20 cm).
Range: Indo-Pacific.
Minimum Aquarium Size: 75 gal. (284 L).
Foods & Feeding: Varied diet, including marine fish, crustacean flesh, mysid shrimp, and frozen preparations. Feed at least 3 times daily.
Aquarium Suitability Index: 4.
Reef Aquarium Compatibility: Unsafe with most corals and desirable invertebrates, with the exception of well-armored crustaceans.
Captive Care: This is a robust species that will greedily attack and eat even large, stinging sea anemones. On the reef it feeds primarily at night, but is also active during "light-time" hours in the aquarium. Occasionally, very small and very large individuals may have trouble acclimating to captivity. If a specimen is reluctant to feed, place a small anemone in the tank—most individuals cannot resist nibbling on these invertebrates. More than one adult can be kept in the same large tank, but they will chase each other, and other members of their family, on occasion—usually without damage. It is peaceful with nonrelated fish species. Similar to *C. fasciatus*, the Red Sea Raccoon Butterflyfish.

Chaetodon melannotus Bloch & Schneider, 1801
Blackback Butterflyfish (Melannotus Butterflyfish)

Maximum Length: 5.9 in. (15 cm).
Range: Indo-west-Pacific.
Minimum Aquarium Size: 55 gal. (208 L).
Foods & Feeding: Varied diet, including marine fish, crustacean flesh, mysid shrimp, and frozen preparations. Feed at least 3 times daily.
Aquarium Suitability Index: 4.
Reef Aquarium Compatibility: Not recommended. Naturally preys on soft corals but may also nip at stony corals in captivity.
Captive Care: This is a desirable butterflyfish and one that typically adapts easily to life in the home aquarium. It will accept a wide range of aquarium foods and and has a rather bold disposition. Unless acquired as pair, this species is best kept singly, as it is more likely to chase conspecifics than many other butterflyfish species. However, it is rarely aggressive toward other members of its family, except for those with similar coloration. Offer vitamin-enriched and color-enhancing foods to maintain the most brilliant coloration. Provide plenty of suitable shelter sites and ample swimming space.

Chaetodon mertensii Cuvier, 1831
Merten's Butterflyfish (Pearlscale Butterflyfish)

Maximum Length: 4.9 in. (12.5 cm).
Range: Western and South Pacific.
Minimum Aquarium Size: 55 gal. (208 L).
Foods & Feeding: Varied diet, including marine algae and *Spirulina*, as well as meaty foods. Feed at least 3 times daily.
Aquarium Suitability Index: 3.
Reef Aquarium Compatibility: Can be kept in a reef tank with some of the more-noxious soft corals.
Captive Care: This is a fairly hardy butterflyfish, acclimating quickly to aquarium life if kept in peaceful surroundings. Marine algae comprises a large part of its natural diet, making it relatively easy to feed. Some of the dried and frozen preparations that incorporate marine seaweeds or the blue-green algae *Spirulina* make good staple foods, although these may be rejected by newly acquired individuals. May behave aggressively toward conspecifics and other members of the "*xanthurus* complex," which includes *C. xanthurus*, page 196; the Redback Butterflyfish (*C. paucifasciatus*); and this species. All have similar care and feeding requirements and are best kept with nonaggressive tankmates.

Chaetodon milliaris Quoy & Gaimard, 1824
Lemon Butterflyfish (Milletseed Butterflyfish)

Maximum Length: 5.1 in. (13 cm).
Range: Hawaiian Islands and Johnston Atoll.
Minimum Aquarium Size: 75 gal. (284 L).
Foods & Feeding: Varied diet, including marine fish, crustacean flesh, mysid shrimp, and frozen preparations. Feed 2-3 times daily.
Aquarium Suitability Index: 4.
Reef Aquarium Compatibility: Feeds mainly on zooplankton in the wild; will occasionally pick at large-polyped stony corals in the aquarium.
Captive Care: One of the most common Hawaiian butterflyfishes, this species is relatively easy to keep and one of the better members of the genus for beginners. Will eat most foods; should be offered a varied diet that includes fresh, finely chopped seafood. Is especially partial to live brine shrimp and fish roe. Should be provided with plenty of swimming room and nonaggressive tankmates. Can be kept singly, in pairs, or in small groups, but all individuals should be introduced simultaneously. A peaceful species, it will not bother other fishes, including its close relatives. Unfortunately, its brilliant yellow attire tends to fade in captivity. A diet including vitamin-enriched and color-enhancing foods may be beneficial.

Chaetodon pelewensis Kner, 1868
Dot-and-Dash Butterflyfish

Maximum Length: 5.0 in. (12.5 cm).
Range: Western Pacific.
Minimum Aquarium Size: 55 gal. (208 L).
Foods & Feeding: Feed marine fish, crustacean flesh, mysid shrimp, and frozen preparations. Feed at least 3 times daily.
Aquarium Suitability Index: 3.
Reef Aquarium Compatibility: Not suitable for the reef aquarium, although most individuals will coexist with stinging anemones and mushroom anemones.
Captive Care: Although it feeds on coral polyps in the wild, this species will typically accept substitute foods, including finely chopped, fresh or frozen seafoods, live brine shrimp, live black worms, and frozen preparations. Has a relatively small mouth, so its food must be finely chopped. Smaller individuals may even have trouble ingesting adult brine shrimp. It can be kept with other butterflyfishes, including members of its own species. To keep more than one individual, add both to the aquarium simultaneously. Similar to *C. punctatofasciatus*, page 187, but this species has slanting, rather than vertical, body bars.

Chaetodon plebius Cuvier, 1831
Bluespot Butterflyfish

Maximum Length: 5.9 in. (15 cm).

Range: Eastern Indian Ocean, Western and South Pacific.

Minimum Aquarium Size: 55 gal. (208 L).

Foods & Feeding: Difficult to feed. It feeds almost entirely on *Acropora* corals in the wild and is reluctant to accept substitutes in captivity. Try vitamin-enriched live brine shrimp, clam on the half shell, or mashed squid or shrimp on a bleached stony coral skeleton. Once the individual is feeding, offer crustacean flesh, mysid shrimp, and frozen preparations for carnivores at least 3 times daily.

Aquarium Suitability Index: 1.

Reef Aquarium Compatibility: Not suitable for the majority of reef aquariums. Will eat stony coral polyps, but may be kept with certain soft corals.

Captive Care: Adults develop distinctive blue flashes on their sides, but this pretty species does not have a good record of adapting to captivity. (Some sources suggest it is easy to keep and will even accept flake food, but this is far from a common experience.) More than one adult can be kept per tank, if they are introduced at the same time. Will tolerate other chaetodontids in its tank.

Chaetodon punctatofasciatus Cuvier, 1831
Spotbanded Butterflyfish (Punctato Butterflyfish)

Maximum Length: 4.7 in. (12 cm).
Range: Indo-Pacific.
Minimum Aquarium Size: 55 gal. (208 L).
Foods & Feeding: Varied diet, including both meaty foods and vegetable matter, such as marine algae and *Spirulina*. Feed at least 3 times daily.
Aquarium Suitability Index: 3.
Reef Aquarium Compatibility: Not suitable for the reef aquarium; usually ignores stinging anemones and mushroom anemones.
Captive Care: A relatively hardy species that will accept most types of fish foods, including finely chopped seafoods, baby brine shrimp, frozen preparations, and flake foods. Because a good deal of its diet includes algae, it should be fed a frozen preparation that includes marine algae or *Spirulina* algae. Has a relatively small mouth and may have trouble ingesting larger pieces of food, including adult brine shrimp. Can be shy initially; does best if housed with peaceful tankmates and can be kept in pairs in larger tanks and with other butterflyfishes. Similar to *C. pelewensis*, page 185, but this species has vertical, rather than slanting, body bars.

Chaetodon quadrimaculatus Gray, 1831
Fourspot Butterflyfish

Maximum Length: 6.4 in. (16 cm).
Range: Western and South Pacific.
Minimum Aquarium Size: 75 gal. (284 L).
Foods & Feeding: Varied diet, including meaty foods and frozen prepa-
rations. Feed at least 3 times daily.
Aquarium Suitability Index: 2-3.
Reef Aquarium Compatibility: Not recommended. Feeds on small-
polyped stony corals, especially *Pocillopora* spp. in the wild.
Captive Care: Not to be confused with the similarly named Foureye
Butterflyfish (*C. capistratus*), page 174, this is a Pacific species that
is generally considered a difficult-to-keep fish. Tends to be shy and
is often reluctant to feed, especially if initially housed with boisterous
tankmates. Requires a peaceful community tank with several suitable
hiding places. Some individuals will rapidly acclimate under these
conditions, while others will take more coaxing to catalyze a feeding
response. Live foods, pieces of live rock with some encrusting invertebrates and algae on them, or a tank with a lush growth of filamentous algae will assist in their acclimation.

Chaetodon rafflesi Bennett, 1830
Latticed Butterflyfish

Maximum Length: 5.9 in. (15 cm).
Range: Indo-Pacific.
Minimum Aquarium Size: 75 gal. (284 L).
Foods & Feeding: Feed marine fish, crustacean flesh, mysid shrimp, and frozen preparations. Feed at least 3 times daily.
Aquarium Suitability Index: 3.
Reef Aquarium Compatibility: Not recommended. Cannot be trusted with most stony or soft corals, zoanthids, or anemones.
Captive Care: Brightly colored with a distinctive crosshatch pattern suggested by its common name, this species is relatively easy to maintain if kept in a peaceful community tank with numerous hiding places. Will usually accept fresh, chopped seafoods and frozen brine shrimp soon after being introduced, but reluctant individuals may have to be tempted with live brine shrimp or black worms. Can be kept in pairs and with other butterflyfish species. When sleeping or stressed, this species becomes darker and exhibits a dark blotch on the anterior part of the body. Will often display this color pattern during the day for some time after it is initially placed in its new home, but even so it will feed and behave normally.

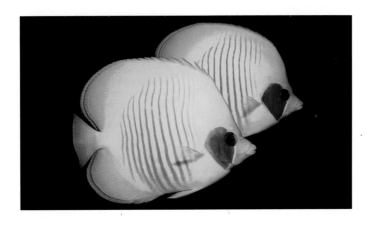

Chaetodon semilarvatus Cuvier, 1831
Golden Butterflyfish (Semilarvatus Butterflyfish)

Maximum Length: 9.1 in. (23 cm).
Range: Red Sea and Gulf of Aden.
Minimum Aquarium Size: 100 gal. (379 L).
Foods & Feeding: Individuals vary in their willingness to feed. Offer live black worms, clam on the half shell, live or frozen mysid shrimp, or vitamin-enriched brine shrimp to induce a feeding response. Once they are eating, vary the diet, and include frozen preparations for herbivores. Feed at least 3 times daily.
Aquarium Suitability Index: 3.
Reef Aquarium Compatibility: Not suitable for a reef aquarium that contains stony corals, although it can be kept with some soft corals, such as *Sinularia* spp.
Captive Care: A majestic Red Sea endemic, this beautiful species can be a bold, relatively hardy aquarium fish if acquired as a healthy, younger specimen. Smaller individuals acclimate more readily and are more likely to accept substitute foods, while larger fish sometimes refuse aquarium fare or are quite finicky. It grows to a large size and needs plenty of swimming room. Best kept with peaceful species. Can be kept in pairs or in small groups.

Chaetodon speculum Cuvier, 1831
Speculum Butterflyfish (Ovalspot Butterflyfish)

Maximum Length: 5.9 in. (15 cm).
Range: Eastern Indian and Western Pacific.
Minimum Aquarium Size: 55 gal. (208 L).
Foods & Feeding: Difficult to feed. Relies heavily on stony coral polyps and coral mucus in the wild. Try vitamin-enriched live brine shrimp, clam on the half shell, black mussels, or mashed squid or shrimp on a bleached stony coral skeleton. Once eating, it can be fed a varied diet of crustacean flesh, mysid shrimp, and frozen preparations for carnivores. Feed at least 3 times daily.
Aquarium Suitability Index: 1. ▨
Reef Aquarium Compatibility: Not suitable for reef aquariums with stony corals, but may be kept with certain soft corals.
Captive Care: One of the many colorful butterflyfishes that feed almost exclusively on corals in the wild and are reluctant to accept substitute foods in captivity. This is particularly true for very small juveniles and large adults. Even individuals that pick at live foods rarely get enough to eat. This species has a greater chance of surviving if kept with nonaggressive tankmates, which should include one of the hardier butterflyfish species to encourage feeding behavior.

Chaetodon tinkeri Schultz, 1951
Tinker's Butterflyfish

Maximum Length: 5.9 in. (15 cm).
Range: Hawaiian, Johnston, Marshall, and Cook Islands.
Minimum Aquarium Size: 75 gal. (284 L).
Foods & Feeding: Varied diet, including marine fish, crustacean flesh, mysid shrimp, and frozen preparations. Feed at least 3 times daily.
Aquarium Suitability Index: 4.
Reef Aquarium Compatibility: Will eat tubeworms and may nip polyps off some soft corals, gorgonians, and large-polyped stony corals.
Captive Care: A resident of the deep reef, this uniquely attractive fish is collected by specialists who demand and receive a premium for their efforts. Will readily accept most foods if water parameters are suitable and it is not being bullied by established tank residents. Tends to be quite bold, spending most of its time in the open, but should have several suitable hiding places. Not overly aggressive, but may quarrel with members of its own kind or with closely related species. Sometimes available in pairs. Best kept in a dimly lit tank, but specimens can acclimate to the higher illumination levels of a shallow-water reef aquarium. Some aquarists suggest keeping it in a lower temperature range of 70-75°F (21-24°C).

Chaetodon ulietensis Cuvier, 1831
Doublesaddle Butterflyfish (False Falcula Butterflyfish)

Maximum Length: 5.9 in. (15 cm).
Range: Indo-Pacific.
Minimum Aquarium Size: 75 gal. (284 L).
Foods & Feeding: Varied diet, including meaty foods and vegetable matter. Feed at least 3 times daily.
Aquarium Suitability Index: 4. ◣
Reef Aquarium Compatibility: Not an acceptable addition to the reef aquarium, as it will eat tubeworms, mushroom corals, anemones, and stony corals.
Captive Care: This a commendable and hardy butterflyfish species. Although it can be shy initially, it will settle down and eat most foods offered if provided with places to hide and relatively peaceful tankmates. Once it is adjusted, it will become an aggressive feeder that can compete with most other fish species. Smaller specimens are to be preferred, as large adults may be reluctant to feed initially. They can be kept together in larger tanks and will tolerate the presence of other members of the family. Can be mistaken for the related and similar-looking *C. falcula*, page 177.

Chaetodon unimaculatus Bloch, 1787
Teardrop Butterflyfish

Maximum Length: 7.8 in. (20 cm).
Range: Indo-Pacific.
Minimum Aquarium Size: 75 gal. (284 L).
Foods & Feeding: Varied diet, including both meaty foods and vegetable matter. Feed at least 3 times daily.
Aquarium Suitability Index: 3.
Reef Aquarium Compatibility: Perhaps the most destructive species of butterflyfish to house in a reef aquarium. Will eat corals, anemones, mushroom anemones, and may even pick at crustaceans.
Captive Care: Named for a curious marking that resembles a bluish teardrop running down its side, this is a potentially large, omnivorous butterflyfish that readily accepts most foods offered in captivity. It is moderately hardy, and reportedly does especially well if kept in a tank full of filamentous algae. Can be kept with members of its own species or with other butterflyfishes in larger tanks, and is able to hold its own with more-boisterous tankmates.

Chaetodon vagabundus Linnaeus, 1758
Vagabond Butterflyfish

Maximum Length: 9 in. (23 cm).
Range: Indo-Pacific.
Minimum Aquarium Size: 100 gal. (379 L).
Foods & Feeding: Feed marine fish, crustacean flesh, mysid shrimp, and frozen preparations. Feed at least 3 times daily.
Aquarium Suitability Index: 4.
Reef Aquarium Compatibility: Not recommended. Will make short work of stony corals and many soft coral species. Will also nip at the tentacles and bases of larger stinging anemones and will pick at mushroom anemones.
Captive Care: Handsome and common on many Indo-Pacific reefs, this is one of the hardiest of butterflyfish species. As a larger fish, it needs plenty of swimming room and will accept a wide range of aquarium fare, including chopped fresh or frozen seafood, brine shrimp, frozen preparations, and flake food. Feed enriched foods to retain its intense colors. Will also pick filamentous algae off the substrate or aquarium glass. Can be kept in pairs or with other butterflyfish species and will hold its own with many more-aggressive tankmates once it is fully acclimated to its new home.

Chaetodon xanthurus Bleeker, 1857
Yellowtail Butterflyfish (Crowned Pearlscaled Butterflyfish)

Maximum Length: 5.5 in. (14 cm).

Range: Western Pacific.

Minimum Aquarium Size: 55 gal. (208 L).

Foods & Feeding: Feed marine fish, crustacean flesh, mysid shrimp, and frozen preparations. Feed at least 3 times daily.

Aquarium Suitability Index: 3.

Reef Aquarium Compatibility: Can be kept in a reef aquarium with some of the more-noxious soft corals.

Captive Care: This is a moderately hardy aquarium fish that will usually accept a wide range of substitute foods. May refuse to feed if housed with pugnacious tankmates or in a poorly maintained aquarium. More than one individual can be kept in the same tank if both are introduced simultaneously; may also share tank space with other butterflyfishes. If individuals engage in interspecific aggression, they are more likely to do so with species of similar coloration. Part of the "*xanthurus* complex," which includes *C. mertensii*, page 183; the Redback Butterflyfish (*C. paucifasciatus*); and this species. All have similar care and feeding requirements.

Butterflies to Avoid *Obligate Corallivores*

The butterflyfishes shown below and on the following page are among the most frustrating species available to marine aquarists. Many are exquisitely beautiful, but all share a specialized diet of live coral polyps that cannot be duplicated in the typical home aquarium. Because they are so dependent on this food supply, they are collectively known as obligate corallivores (see *Chaetodon plebius*, page 186, and *C. speculum*, page 191). Occasionally, a young specimen learns to accept substitute aquarium foods, but this is the rare exception. These fishes should be left on the reef.

Chaetodon austriacus
Exquisite Butterflyfish
Max. Length: 5.1 in. (13 cm).
Aquarium Suitability: 1.

Chaetodon baronessa
Eastern Triangle Butterflyfish
Max. Length: 5.9 in. (15 cm).
Aquarium Suitability: 1.

Chaetodon bennetti
Bennett's Butterflyfish
Max. Length: 7 in. (18 cm).
Aquarium Suitability: 1.

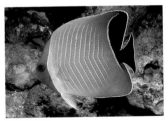

Chaetodon larvatus
Orangeface or Larvatus Butterflyfish
Max. Length: 4.7 in. (12 cm).
Aquarium Suitability: 1.

Chaetodon lunulatus
Pacific Redfin Butterflyfish
Max. Length: 4.7 in. (12 cm).
Aquarium Suitability: 1.

Chaetodon meyeri
Meyer's Butterflyfish
Max. Length: 7.0 in. (18 cm).
Aquarium Suitability: 1.

Chaetodon octofasciatus
Eightbanded Butterflyfish
Max. Length: 4.7 in. (12 cm).
Aquarium Suitability: 1.

Chaetodon ornatissimus
Ornate or Clown Butterflyfish
Max. Length: 7.1 in. (18 cm).
Aquarium Suitability: 1.

Chaetodon rainfordi
Rainford's Butterflyfish
Max. Length: 6.0 in. (15 cm).
Aquarium Suitability: 2.

Chaetodon trifasciatus
Indian Ocean Redfin Butterflyfish
Max. Length: 6.0 in. (15 cm).
Aquarium Suitability: 1.

Chelmon rostratus (Linnaeus, 1758)
Copperbanded Butterflyfish (Beaked Coralfish)

Maximum Length: 7.9 in. (20 cm).
Range: Indo-west-Pacific.
Minimum Aquarium Size: 75 gal. (284 L).
Foods & Feeding: Live foods may be required, such as live freshwater clams or black mussels that have had their shells broken open. Offer marine fish, crustacean flesh, mysid shrimp, and frozen carnivore preparations. Feed 2-3 times daily.
Aquarium Suitability Index: 2-3.
Reef Aquarium Compatibility: Generally safe with soft corals and small-polyped stony corals. An occasional specimen may nip at large-polyped stony corals, certain soft corals, and zoanthids. Most will eat glass anemones (*Aiptasia* spp.) and polychaete worms.
Captive Care: This is an appealing long-nosed species that, unfortunately, has an uneven survival record in captivity. Many aquarists have found it difficult to keep with specimens varying in their hardiness. Some settle into their new home within several days and begin eating fresh and frozen foods, while others may refuse to feed or accept only live foods. Will behave aggressively toward conspecifics, unless partnered in a male-female pair.

Forcipiger flavissimus Jordan & McGregor, 1898
Yellow Longnose Butterflyfish (Forceps Fish)

Maximum Length: 8.7 in. (22 cm).
Range: Indo-Pacific.
Minimum Aquarium Size: 75 gal. (284 L).
Foods & Feeding: Varied diet, including meaty foods, crustacean flesh, mysid shrimp, and frozen preparations. Feed at least 3 times daily.
Aquarium Suitability Index: 4.
Reef Aquarium Compatibility: In most cases, these fish seem to ignore corals, but they have been reported to feed on stony and soft coral polyps in the wild. Will also eat tubeworms and nip at sea urchin tube feet.
Captive Care: A marine aquarium icon, this is a hardy fish that will usually begin feeding within hours of being placed in captivity. Consistently does better if kept in a peaceful community tank, but can be housed with moderately aggressive tankmates if it is acclimated to the tank first. When harassed by other fishes, it will direct its long, stout dorsal spines toward the aggressor. Keep singly, as it will often behave aggressively toward members of its own species. Similar to the less-common _F. longirostris_, page 201, which has a longer, thinner beak or snout.

Forcipiger longirostris (Broussonet, 1782)
Big Longnose Butterflyfish

Maximum Length: 8.7 in. (22 cm).
Range: Indo-Pacific.
Minimum Aquarium Size: 75 gal. (284 L).
Foods & Feeding: Varied diet, including small meaty foods, crustacean flesh, mysid shrimp, and frozen preparations. Feed at least 3 times daily.
Aquarium Suitability Index: 3.
Reef Aquarium Compatibility: Excellent.
Captive Care: With an even more elongated snout than its more-common counterpart, *F. flavissimus,* page 200, this species presents more of a challenge to aquarists because its tiny mouth limits it to small food items. One way to provide appropriate living foods is to keep it in a reef tank or a fish-only tank partially filled with live rock that supports a population of natural prey organisms, such as amphipods. Keep only one per tank, except in the case of a male-female pair. House with more-passive species. It may quarrel with some other butterflyfish species, especially *F. flavissimus.* This species has an all-brown color morph, not uncommon in certain parts of its range, such as the Kona Coast of Hawaii.

Hemitaurichthys polylepis (Bleeker, 1857)
Pyramid Butterflyfish

Maximum Length: 7.0 in. (18 cm).
Range: Indo-Pacific.
Minimum Aquarium Size: 100 gal. (379 L).
Foods & Feeding: Varied diet, including marine fish, crustacean flesh, mysid shrimp, and frozen preparations. Feed at least 3 times daily.
Aquarium Suitability Index: 4.
Reef Aquarium Compatibility: Not a threat to sessile invertebrates. Can be housed in a shallow- or deep-water reef tank if the aquarist is willing to feed it frequently.
Captive Care: Exotic in appearance, this is an easily kept aquarium fish that will accept a wide range of aquarium fare, including finely chopped seafood, frozen or live brine shrimp, frozen preparations, and even flake food. Its optimal tank will have plenty of swimming space. Can be kept singly, in pairs, or in small groups if the aquarium is large enough. More likely to acclimate to its new home if it is not pestered by its tankmates, although once it has fully adjusted to life in captivity, moderately aggressive fishes can be introduced to its tank.

Prognathodes aculeatus (Poey, 1860)
Caribbean Longnose Butterflyfish
(Atlantic Longnose Butterflyfish, Rosy Butterflyfish)

Maximum Length: 3.9 in. (10 cm).
Range: Tropical Western Atlantic.
Minimum Aquarium Size: 55 gal. (208 L).
Foods & Feeding: Meaty foods, including marine fish, crustacean flesh, mysid shrimp, and frozen preparations. Feed at least 3 times a day.
Aquarium Suitability Index: 3-4.
Reef Aquarium Compatibility: Will eat feather duster worms and may occasionally nip at large-polyped stony corals and gorgonians. May not adapt well to intense lighting systems.
Captive Care: Although Caribbean butterflyfishes are often regarded as difficult to keep, this is one of the most durable members of the family, readily accepting most foods offered. (Some hobbyists report unexplained long-term survival problems.) Only one of these fish should be kept per tank, as they often display aggression toward conspecifics. However, it will not normally bother other species—with the possible exception of other butterflyfishes. When attacked by another fish, it usually does not flee, but instead directs its stout spines toward its aggressor. It is best kept in a deep-water reef tank.

Heniochus diphreutes (Jordan, 1903)
Schooling Bannerfish

Maximum Length: 7.1 in. (18 cm).
Range: Indo-Pacific.
Minimum Aquarium Size: 100 gal. (379 L).
Foods & Feeding: Varied diet, including meaty foods such as vitamin-enriched brine shrimp, crustacean flesh, and mysid shrimp, as well as frozen preparations for herbivores. Feed at least 3 times daily.
Aquarium Suitability Index: 5.
Reef Aquarium Compatibility: Not a threat to sessile invertebrates, but do not confuse it with the similar-looking Longfin Bannerfish (*H. acuminatus*), page 206, which can be destructive in a reef tank. The Schooling Bannerfish has a more-rounded breast, less-protruding snout, and the middle black band ends at the corner of the anal fin.
Captive Care: The genus *Heniochus* includes a couple of commendable aquarium butterflyfishes. This sturdy, bold species schools readily in captivity, but it should be provided with plenty of swimming room. Young individuals will do best if kept with peaceful tankmates. All individuals of a captive group should be added to the tank at the same time, and its members will form a dominance hierarchy. It will sometimes engage in cleaning behavior with other fishes.

Heniochus varius (Cuvier, 1829)
Humphead Bannerfish

Maximum Length: 7.9 in. (20 cm).
Range: Western and South Pacific.
Minimum Aquarium Size: 75 gal. (284 L).
Foods & Feeding: Varied diet, including meaty foods such as vitamin-enriched brine shrimp, crustacean flesh, and mysid shrimp, as well as frozen preparations for herbivores. Feed at least 3 times daily.
Aquarium Suitability Index: 3.
Reef Aquarium Compatibility: Will nip at some sessile invertebrates, including stony coral polyps. Can be housed in a shallow- or deep-water reef tank, if the aquarist is prepared to feed it frequently enough.
Captive Care: A hump on the forehead and a curved horn over each eye make adults of this species highly unusual specimens. Although it takes time to adjust to aquarium foods, this species will often acclimate to captivity, doing best when housed with small, peaceful fishes. If it is harassed by tankmates or the activities of the aquarist, it will not acclimate. Provide a rocky aquascape with overhangs or caves where it can take shelter. May be kept in pairs, provided both are introduced simultaneously.

Heniochus acuminatus
Longfin Bannerfish
Max. Length: 9.8 in. (25 cm).
Aquarium Suitability: 5.

Heniochus chrysostomus
Pennant Bannerfish
Max. Length: 7.1 in. (18 cm).
Aquarium Suitability: 3.

Heniochus intermedius
Red Sea Bannerfish
Max. Length: 7.1 in. (18 cm).
Aquarium Suitability: 4.

Heniochus monoceros
Masked Bannerfish
Max. Length: 9.1 in. (23 cm).
Aquarium Suitability: 4.

Heniochus pleurotaenia
Phantom or Indian Bannerfish
Max. Length: 6.7 in. (17 cm).
Aquarium Suitability: 3.

Heniochus singularis
Singular Bannerfish
Max. Length: 9.8 in. (25 cm).
Aquarium Suitability: 4.

Apolemichthys trimaculatus (Lacépède, 1831)
Flagfin Angelfish (Threespot Angelfish)

Maximum Length: 9.8 in. (25 cm).
Range: Indo-Pacific.
Minimum Aquarium Size: 75 gal. (284 L).
Foods & Feeding: Difficult to feed. This a sponge-eater that often fails to adapt to aquarium fare. Try feeding it sponge-containing frozen angelfish rations, vitamin-enriched brine shrimp, and mysid shrimp as well as plentiful plant material, including frozen preparations for herbivores and marine algae. Feed at least 3 times a day.
Aquarium Suitability Index: 2. ◣
Reef Aquarium Compatibility: Not recommended. May nip at sessile invertebrates, including stony and soft corals, and clam mantles.
Captive Care: This beautiful fish usually fares poorly in the home aquarium. Chances of keeping it successfully are increased in a reef-type system with plenty of invertebrate-encrusted live rock. Younger specimens tend to acclimate better, and individuals from areas other than the Philippines tend to have greater rates of survival. It is usually not overly aggressive toward unrelated species, but may fight with close relatives. Only one should be housed per tank. Can be quite shy at first and should have a choice of good hiding places.

Apolemichthys xanthurus (Bennett, 1832)
Indian Yellowtail Angelfish

Maximum Length: 7.9 in. (20 cm).
Range: Indian Ocean.
Minimum Aquarium Size: 75 gal. (284 L).
Foods & Feeding: Varied diet, including meaty foods, marine algae, and occasional meals of frozen, sponge-containing preparations for angelfishes. Feed 2-4 times a day.
Aquarium Suitability Index: 5.
Reef Aquarium Compatibility: Some risk as it may nip at sessile invertebrates, including stony and soft corals, and clam mantles.
Captive Care: Although its color is somewhat subdued, this is a great aquarium species that readily acclimates to captive conditions. Sponges form a large part of its natural diet, but it can be switched rather easily to other aquarium fare. This species can be aggressive toward closely related forms or fishes introduced after it is established, and will prove too boisterous for a peaceful community tank. Keep only one specimen per aquarium.

Centropyge argi Woods & Kanazawa, 1951
Cherub Angelfish (Atlantic Pygmy Angelfish)

Maximum Length: 3.1 in. (8 cm).
Range: Tropical Western Atlantic.
Minimum Aquarium Size: 30 gal. (114 L).
Foods & Feeding: Varied diet, including frozen preparations that contain marine or *Spirulina* algae, as well as mysid shrimp and/or finely shaved fresh or frozen shrimp. Feed at least 3 times a day, unless in an aquarium with healthy microalgae growth.
Aquarium Suitability Index: 4.
Reef Aquarium Compatibility: Will occasionally nip at large-polyped stony corals, some soft corals, and clam mantles.
Captive Care: Tiny but feisty, this vividly colored little angelfish is hardy, interesting, and will spawn in the home aquarium. Beware, though—once settled into an aquarium, it can become a tyrant that will harass more-docile fishes and even kill other pygmy angelfishes, especially in a smaller tank. A male and female, or two or more females, can be kept together as long as the tank is large enough (at least 50 gal. [189 L]) and they are introduced simultaneously. Males, on the other hand, will fight, often to the death, if kept in the same aquarium.

Centropyge aurantia Randall & Wass, 1974
Golden Angelfish

Maximum Length: 3.9 in. (10 cm).
Range: Western and South Pacific.
Minimum Aquarium Size: 55 gal. (208 L).
Foods & Feeding: Varied diet, including vitamin-enriched brine shrimp, finely-chopped crustacean flesh, mysid shrimp, and frozen preparations for herbivores. Keep in a well-established tank with microalgae growth. Feed at least 2-3 times daily.
Aquarium Suitability Index: 3.
Reef Aquarium Compatibility: May nip at both large-polyped and small-polyped stony corals. Will not bother most soft corals, with the possible exception of *Xenia*.
Captive Care: This is a lovely fish with a cryptic nature, making it difficult to catch and somewhat of a prize in the aquarium trade. Unfortunately, some specimens are captured with drugs, and the quality of individuals available to hobbyists varies greatly. Some readily acclimate and thrive, but many die within 2-4 months, possibly due to the damage resulting from cyanide exposure. Place in a well-established tank with ample live rock for grazing and shelter. Keep with less-aggressive tankmates and no other *Centropyge* species.

Centropyge bicolor (Bloch, 1787)
Bicolor Angelfish (Oriole Angelfish)

Maximum Length: 5.9 in. (15 cm).
Range: Indo-west-Pacific.
Minimum Aquarium Size: 55 gal. (208 L).
Foods & Feeding: Varied diet, including frozen preparations that contain *Spirulina* algae, as well as mysid shrimp and/or finely shaved fresh or frozen shrimp. Feed at least 2-3 times a day, unless in an aquarium with healthy microalgae growth.
Aquarium Suitability Index: 3.
Reef Aquarium Compatibility: Add with caution; will often nip large-polyped stony corals, soft corals, zoanthids, and tridacnid clams.
Captive Care: Once thought difficult to keep alive in captivity, this beautiful species can do very well if it was net-collected (cyanide-affected specimens are, fortunately, becoming less common) and if kept in a system furnished with live rock, which affords constant grazing opportunities. Is not overly aggressive toward other fishes, and more than one individual can be kept in a medium-sized tank if all are added simultaneously.

Centropyge bispinosa (Günther, 1860)
Coral Beauty (Twospined Angelfish, Dusky Angelfish)

Maximum Length: 3.9 in. (10 cm).
Range: Indo-Pacific.
Minimum Aquarium Size: 30 gal. (114 L).
Foods & Feeding: Varied diet, containing *Spirulina* and marine algae, as well as mysid shrimp and other high-quality meaty fare. Feed 2-3 times a day and, ideally, provide live rock for constant grazing.
Aquarium Suitability Index: 4.
Reef Aquarium Compatibility: Will occasionally nip at large-polyped stony corals and clam mantles.
Captive Care: This is a favorite member of the genus *Centropyge*, and for good reasons: it is hardy, brilliantly colored, readily available, and inexpensive. It is typically not as aggressive as many of the other members of the genus, but individuals may assert their dominance in smaller aquariums, especially after they have become established. The larger the reef tank, the less likely the fish is to keep picking at a particular sessile invertebrate until it is irreparably damaged.

Centropyge eibli Klausewitz, 1963
Eibl's Angelfish (Orangelined Angelfish)

Maximum Length: 5.9 in. (15 cm).
Range: Indo-west-Pacific.
Minimum Aquarium Size: 30 gal. (114 L).
Foods & Feeding: Varied diet, containing *Spirulina* and marine algae, as well as mysid shrimp and other high-quality meaty fare. Feed 2-3 times a day and, ideally, provide live rock for constant grazing.
Aquarium Suitability Index: 4.
Reef Aquarium Compatibility: Add with caution; may nip at large-polyped stony corals and tridacnid clam mantles. May also eat some soft coral polyps and nip at zoanthids.
Captive Care: A lovely fish that typically adapts quickly to aquarium living if provided with ample hiding places and relatively peaceful tankmates. Will do best in a tank with live rock and abundant microalgae growth. It is one of the larger dwarf angelfishes, and although not terribly pugnacious, it may display aggression toward smaller fishes, especially in more-confined quarters. Sometimes crossbreeds with *C. vroliki*; the resulting progeny occasionally appear in aquarium stores.

Centropyge fisheri (Snyder, 1904)
Fisher's Angelfish

Maximum Length: 2.4 in. (6 cm).
Range: Hawaiian Islands and Johnston Atoll.
Minimum Aquarium Size: 20 gal. (76 L).
Foods & Feeding: Varied diet, containing *Spirulina* and marine algae, as well as mysid shrimp and other high-quality meaty fare. Feed 2-3 times a day and, ideally, provide live rock for constant grazing.
Aquarium Suitability Index: 4.
Reef Aquarium Compatibility: May nip at large-polyped stony corals and tridacnid clam mantles, although it is less of a threat than some of its larger congeners. May also eat some soft coral polyps and nip at zoanthids.
Captive Care: This smaller angelfish is a good choice for the community aquarium. It frequents areas with coral rubble in its natural environment, and will spend much of its time peering from a hiding place or dashing from one reef crevice to another. Feeds heavily on diatoms growing on the aquarium glass, rock, or other decor. Can be aggressive toward docile tankmates in a smaller aquarium, but is less pugnacious than many of its relatives.

Centropyge flavissima (Cuvier, 1831)
Lemonpeel Angelfish

Maximum Length: 5.5 in. (14 cm).
Range: Indo-Pacific.
Minimum Aquarium Size: 20 gal. (76 L).
Foods & Feeding: Varied diet, containing *Spirulina* and marine algae, as well as mysid shrimp and other high-quality meaty fare. Feed 2-3 times a day and, ideally, provide live rock for constant grazing.
Aquarium Suitability Index: 3.
Reef Aquarium Compatibility: Notorious for nipping large-polyped stony corals and tridacnid clam mantles. May also eat some soft coral polyps and nip at zoanthids.
Captive Care: With its brilliant yellow coloration and blue-ringed eyes, this is a fish many aquarists would like to keep, but it is not one of the most durable members of the genus. Will usually do best in an aquarium aquascaped with live rock or that has profuse microalgae growth. It can become aggressive once it has become established, especially toward other members of its genus. It is possible to keep a pair (male-female) or even a trio (one male-two females) in a larger tank with plenty of hiding places. Hybrids of this fish and *C. vroliki* are sometimes available.

Centropyge heraldi Woods & Schultz, 1953
Herald's Angelfish (False Lemonpeel Angelfish)

Maximum Length: 3.9 in. (10 cm).
Range: Western and South Pacific.
Minimum Aquarium Size: 20 gal. (76 L).
Foods & Feeding: Varied diet, containing *Spirulina* and marine algae, as well as mysid shrimp and other high-quality meaty fare. Feed 2-3 times a day and, ideally, provide live rock for constant grazing.
Aquarium Suitability Index: 3.
Reef Aquarium Compatibility: May nip at large-polyped stony corals, zoanthids, and tridacnid clam mantles. May also eat some soft coral polyps.
Captive Care: Like *C. flavissima*, this species can be difficult to feed and will slowly waste away in aquariums that fail to provide ample opportunities for its constant picking and grazing. It will do best if housed in a tank with live rock and/or profuse microalgae growth. Usually not aggressive toward fish tankmates, with the possible exception of related dwarf angelfish species. A male-female pair can be housed together in a medium-sized aquarium (75 gal. [284 L]).

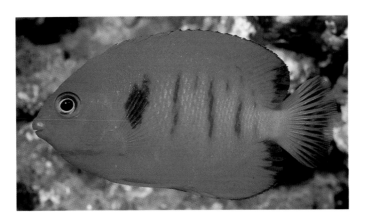

Centropyge loricula (Günther, 1874)
Flame Angelfish

Maximum Length: 3.9 in. (10 cm).
Range: Western, South, and Central Pacific.
Minimum Aquarium Size: 20 gal. (76 L).
Foods & Feeding: Varied diet, containing *Spirulina* and marine algae, as well as mysid shrimp and other high-quality meaty fare. Feed 2-3 times a day and, ideally, provide live rock for constant grazing.
Aquarium Suitability Index: 4.
Reef Aquarium Compatibility: May nip at large-polyped stony corals, zoanthids, and tridacnid clam mantles. May also eat some soft coral polyps.
Captive Care: A flashy and justifiably popular species, this dwarf angelfish has long been considered a durable aquarium choice. (Sadly, in recent years some individuals have failed to survive more than a month; the reason for these mortalities is not known, although collection or shipping problems are suspected by some observers.) Can be aggressive toward members of its own genus, as well as toward fishes with similar shape or behavior if they are introduced after it has become established. To fit into a relatively peaceful community setting, it should be the last fish introduced.

Centropyge potteri (Jordan & Metz, 1912)
Potter's Angelfish

Maximum Length: 5.1 in. (13 cm).
Range: Hawaiian Islands and Johnston Atoll.
Minimum Aquarium Size: 20 gal. (76 L).
Foods & Feeding: Varied diet, containing *Spirulina* and marine algae, as well as mysid shrimp and other high-quality meaty fare. Feed 2-3 times a day and, ideally, provide live rock for constant grazing.
Aquarium Suitability Index: 4.
Reef Aquarium Compatibility: May attack some soft corals and nip at large-polyped stony corals, zoanthids, and tridacnid clam mantles.
Captive Care: A distinctive Hawaiian endemic species, this is a popular fish that is reasonably hardy if placed in an an appropriate aquarium setting. It should be provided with plenty of hiding places, preferably in live rock, which will also afford a natural substrate where it can forage for algae and tiny invertebrate life forms. It may behave aggressively toward congeners and fishes introduced after it has become established, especially in smaller tanks. It can be reluctant to feed initially, and may starve in new or barren tanks, but will usually accept frozen preparations after a few days and will pick at diatoms on the glass and decor.

Centropyge tibicen (Cuvier, 1831)
Keyhole Angelfish (Melas Angelfish)

Maximum Length: 7.5 in. (19 cm).
Range: Eastern Indian Ocean and Western Pacific.
Minimum Aquarium Size: 20 gal. (76 L).
Foods & Feeding: Varied diet, containing *Spirulina* and marine algae, as well as mysid shrimp and other high-quality meaty fare. Feed 2-3 times a day and, ideally, provide live rock for constant grazing.
Aquarium Suitability Index: 4.
Reef Aquarium Compatibility: May attack some soft corals and nip at large-polyped stony corals, zoanthids, and tridacnid clam mantles.
Captive Care: Bold and growing larger than other *Centropyge* angelfishes, this is a durable aquarium fish that will accept a wide range of aquarium foods. It may behave pugnaciously toward other pygmy angelfishes and fishes added to the tank after it has become established. Will browse on filamentous algae and diatoms growing on the aquarium decor. Large males often have a pleasing bluish hue.

Centropyge acanthops
African Flameback Angelfish
Max. Length: 2.8 in. (7 cm).
Aquarium Suitability: 4.

Centropyge ferrugata
Rusty Angelfish
Max. Length: 3.9 in. (10 cm).
Aquarium Suitability: 3.

Centropyge flavicauda
Whitetail Pygmy Angelfish
Max. Length: 3.1 in. (8 cm).
Aquarium Suitability: 4.

Centropyge nox
Midnight Angelfish
Max. Length: 3.5 in. (9 cm).
Aquarium Suitability: 3.

Centropyge shepardi
Shepard's Pygmy Angelfish
Max. Length: 3.5 in. (9 cm).
Aquarium Suitability: 4.

Centropyge vroliki
Halfblack or Pearlscale Angelfish
Max. Length: 3.5 in. (9 cm).
Aquarium Suitability: 4.

Chaetodontoplus caeruleopunctatus (Bleeker, 1853)
Bluespotted Angelfish

Maximum Length: 5.5 in. (14 cm).
Range: Eastern Indian Ocean and Western Pacific.
Minimum Aquarium Size: 55 gal. (208 L).
Foods & Feeding: Varied diet, containing *Spirulina* and marine algae, as well as mysid shrimp and other high-quality meaty fare. Feed at least 3 times a day, unless in an aquarium with healthy microalgae growth.
Aquarium Suitability Index: 4.
Reef Aquarium Compatibility: May eat some soft corals and nip at large-polyped stony corals, zoanthids, and tridacnid clam mantles.
Captive Care: Speckled with tiny blue dots, this small angelfish is unique in appearance and part of a genus highly prized by aquarists. Will usually adapt to aquarium life if kept with nonaggressive tankmates and provided with numerous hiding places into which it can retreat if threatened. It is secretive and usually not overly aggressive. Will browse on filamentous algae and diatoms growing on the aquarium decor. As with the other angelfishes, it is best placed in a well-established aquarium.

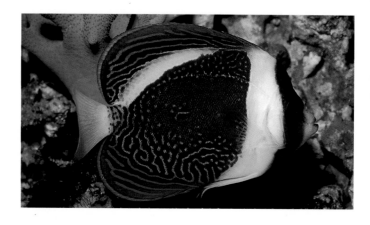

Chaetodontoplus duboulayi (Bleeker, 1853)
Scribbled Angelfish

Maximum Length: 9.8 in. (25 cm).

Range: Australia and Papua New Guinea.

Minimum Aquarium Size: 100 gal. (379 L).

Foods & Feeding: Varied diet, containing *Spirulina* and marine algae, as well as mysid shrimp and other high-quality meaty fare. Feed at least 3 times a day, unless in an aquarium with healthy microalgae growth.

Aquarium Suitability Index: 4.

Reef Aquarium Compatibility: May eat some soft corals and nip at large-polyped stony corals, zoanthids, and tridacnid clam mantles. Adults are a greater threat than juveniles.

Captive Care: This is a treasured species and a good aquarium fish, acclimating readily if provided with lots of swimming room, some good hiding places, and no overly aggressive tankmates during the acclimation phase. Once it has adjusted to aquarium life, it can become quite boisterous. Will browse on filamentous algae and diatoms growing on the aquarium decor.

Chaetodontoplus melanosoma (Bleeker, 1853)
Black Velvet Angelfish (Gray Poma)

Maximum Length: 6.7 in. (17 cm).
Range: Eastern Indian Ocean and Western Pacific.
Minimum Aquarium Size: 55 gal. (208 L).
Foods & Feeding: Varied diet, containing *Spirulina* and marine algae, as well as mysid shrimp and other high-quality meaty fare. Feed at least 3 times a day, unless in an aquarium with healthy microalgae growth.
Aquarium Suitability Index: 4.
Reef Aquarium Compatibility: May eat some soft corals and nip at large-polyped stony corals, zoanthids, and tridacnid clam mantles. Adults are a greater threat than juveniles.
Captive Care: One of the more-affordable members of this genus and a handsome fish with subtle colors. Will usually adapt to aquarium life if kept with nonaggressive tankmates and provided with plenty of hiding places. It is usually not overly aggressive. Will browse on filamentous algae and diatoms growing on the aquarium decor.

Chaetodontoplus mesoleucus (Bleeker, 1853)
Vermiculated Angelfish (Singapore Angelfish)

Maximum Length: 6.7 in. (17 cm).
Range: Western Pacific.
Minimum Aquarium Size: 55 gal. (208 L).
Foods & Feeding: Feed frozen preparations that contain *Spirulina* algae, as well as mysid shrimp and/or finely shaved fresh or frozen shrimp. Feed at least 3 times a day, unless in an aquarium with healthy microalgae growth. It will browse on filamentous algae and diatoms growing on the aquarium decor.
Aquarium Suitability Index: 3-4.
Reef Aquarium Compatibility: Poses a moderate risk to large-polyped stony corals. May also eat some soft coral polyps and nip at zoanthids.
Captive Care: Butterflylike in appearance, and somewhat of an enigma for aquarists, this species is a challenge to keep. Some individuals adapt quickly to aquarium life, while others hide constantly and never feed. Provide a quietly situated aquarium with lots of hiding places and nonaggressive tankmates, and the chances of success are increased. Live rock and a good crop of macroalgae (such as *Caulerpa*) or microalgae may also facilitate acclimation.

Genicanthus lamarck (Lacépède, 1802)
Lamarck's Angelfish

Maximum Length: 9.1 in. (23 cm).
Range: Indo-west-Pacific.
Minimum Aquarium Size: 100 gal. (379 L).
Foods & Feeding: Varied diet, including *Spirulina* and marine algae, finely shaved fresh or frozen shrimp, frozen brine shrimp, *Mysis* shrimp and other meaty prepared foods. Feed 2-3 times a day.
Aquarium Suitability Index: 4.
Reef Aquarium Compatibility: One of the best angelfishes for reef aquariums, because it poses no threat to stony or soft corals.
Captive Care: Elegant and interesting, this reef-safe angelfish readily adapts to life in captivity, accepting aquarium fare and acclimating to the conditions found in a well-maintained tank. These fish are active and spend most daylight hours swimming about in mid-water; they need plenty of swimming room. They are not overly aggressive, but may chase small, docile planktivores, such as anthias, fairy wrasses, flasher wrasses, and fire gobies. Will usually ignore other fish species, including other members of the angelfish family. Can be kept in pairs or in small aggregations in larger tanks; keep only one male per aquarium.

MAIN PHOTO, FEMALE; INSET, MALE

Genicanthus melanospilos (Bleeker, 1857)
Blackspot Angelfish

Maximum Length: 7.1 in. (18 cm).
Range: Western Pacific.
Minimum Aquarium Size: 100 gal. (379 L).
Foods & Feeding: Feed a varied diet, including finely shaved fresh or frozen shrimp, frozen brine shrimp, *Mysis* shrimp, and frozen preparations containing *Spirulina* algae. Feed at least 3 times a day. Will browse on filamentous algae and diatoms growing in the aquarium.
Aquarium Suitability Index: 3.
Reef Aquarium Compatibility: One of the best angelfishes for reef aquariums because it poses no threat to stony or soft corals.
Captive Care: Dramatic differences between males and females make an interesting display of sexual dimorphism. This species readily adapts to aquarium conditions and foods. These fish are constantly active, and they need plenty of swimming space. Not overly aggressive, but may chase small, docile planktivores, while ignoring other fish species, including other angelfishes. Males may fight with other *Genicanthus* spp., especially those similar in coloration. Can be kept in pairs or in small aggregations in larger tanks; keep only one male per aquarium.

MAIN PHOTO, MALE; INSET, FEMALE

Genicanthus watanabei (Yasuda & Tominaga, 1970)
Watanabe's Angelfish

Maximum Length: 5.9 in. (15 cm).
Range: Western and South Pacific.
Minimum Aquarium Size: 100 gal. (379 L).
Foods & Feeding: Varied diet, including meaty foods, such as vitamin-enriched brine shrimp, finely-chopped crustacean flesh, and mysid shrimp, as well as frozen preparations for herbivores. Feed at least 3 times daily.
Aquarium Suitability Index: 2.
Reef Aquarium Compatibility: Excellent, especially for deep-water reef tanks.
Captive Care: This a lovely fish, ideally suited to the reef aquarium. Sadly, most specimens in the aquarium trade suffer from swim bladder damage and should be avoided. Healthy individuals will readily acclimate if housed in a peaceful community tank. Keep singly or in a male-female pair, but two males will fight. Males have a deeper blue on the back, with 8 to 13 black stripes on the body, a yellow stripe on the body and caudal peduncle, black stripes on the anal fin, and blue caudal lobes. Typically adjusts more rapidly if housed in a dimly lit tank, and thus is better suited to a deep-water reef tank.

Holacanthus bermudensis Jordan & Rutter, 1898
Blue Angelfish

Maximum Length: 15.0 in. (38 cm).
Range: Tropical Eastern Atlantic.
Minimum Aquarium Size: 180 gal. (681 L).
Foods & Feeding: A sponge-feeder, but can be switched to aquarium foods, including ample vegetable matter, meaty fare, and occasionally, special angelfish rations containing marine sponges. Feed 3 times a day.
Aquarium Suitability Index: 4.
Reef Aquarium Compatibility: Will nip at sessile invertebrates, including stony and soft corals and clam mantles.
Captive Care: An attractive and durable aquarium fish that makes a good choice for newer aquarists interested in the larger angelfishes. True to the general rule for angelfishes, larger juveniles and subadults acclimate more readily than very small or very large specimens. Needs plenty of swimming room, as well as suitable hiding places. Prone to being combative with its tankmates. Do not try to house with other large angelfishes. The juvenile form looks quite different (see page 245). This species will crossbreed with *H. ciliaris.*

Holacanthus ciliaris (Linnaeus, 1758)
Queen Angelfish

Maximum Length: 17.7 in. (45 cm).
Range: Tropical Atlantic.
Minimum Aquarium Size: 180 gal. (681 L).
Foods & Feeding: A sponge-feeder, but can be switched to aquarium foods, including ample vegetable matter, meaty fare, and occasionally, special angelfish rations containing marine sponges. Feed 3 times a day.
Aquarium Suitability Index: 4.
Reef Aquarium Compatibility: Not recommended. Will nip at most sessile invertebrates, including corals and tridacnid clams.
Captive Care: Considered among the most attractive of all coral reef fishes, this is a rugged aquarium species. The drawbacks to keeping one of these Caribbean beauties include its size and pugnacious disposition. Large juveniles and subadults are especially aggressive, often picking on newly introduced fishes or closely related species. It is imperative to place it in a large aquarium outfitted with numerous hiding places and to add it to a community tank last. The juvenile form looks quite different (see page 245).

Holacanthus passer Valenciennes, 1846
Passer Angelfish (King Angelfish)

Maximum Length: 14.2 in. (36 cm).
Range: Tropical Eastern Pacific.
Minimum Aquarium Size: 100 gal. (379 L).
Foods & Feeding: A sponge-feeder, but can be switched to aquarium foods, including ample vegetable matter, meaty fare, and occasionally, special angelfish rations containing marine sponges. Feed 3 times a day.
Aquarium Suitability Index: 4.
Reef Aquarium Compatibility: Not recommended. Will nip at sessile invertebrates, including stony and soft corals and tridacnid clams.
Captive Care: A very hardy aquarium inhabitant, but like many other angelfishes, it can be very belligerent. May be kept with other fishes in a large tank if it is the last one introduced. Select tankmates carefully: squirrelfishes, groupers, snappers, damselfishes, hawkfishes, surgeonfishes, eels, and triggerfishes are appropriate. Avoid more-passive tankmates, like anthias, batfishes, tilefishes, and butterflyfishes or even sedentary predators—it is likely to pick at them. The author has observed them biting the venomous dorsal spines off lionfishes. Adult males have yellow pelvic fins; females have white pelvic fins.

Holacanthus tricolor (Bloch, 1795)
Rock Beauty Angelfish

Maximum Length: 7.9 in. (20 cm).
Range: Tropical Western Atlantic.
Minimum Aquarium Size: 100 gal. (379 L).
Foods & Feeding: A sponge-feeder that often has difficulty switching to aquarium foods. Try feeding vegetable matter, meaty fare, and occasionally, special angelfish rations containing marine sponges. Feed 3 times a day.
Aquarium Suitability Index: 2-3.
Reef Aquarium Compatibility: Will nip at sessile invertebrates, including stony and soft corals and tridacnid clam mantles.
Captive Care: Unlike other *Holacanthus* angelfishes, the adult Rock Beauty will usually perish without its normal sponge-dominated diet. It may eat and look good for many months, when suddenly its color will begin to fade, it will lose weight, and a dark area may appear on top of its head. An occasional specimen will thrive, especially if it is offered a marine-sponge food formulation, but most will perish. Young Rock Beauties will do better in the aquarium than adults but present another problem: they feed, in part, on the slime of other fishes and will persistently chase their tankmates and nip at them.

Paracentropyge multifasciata (Smith & Radcliffe, 1911)
Multibarred Angelfish (Manybanded Angelfish)

Maximum Length: 4.7 in. (12 cm).
Range: Eastern Indian, Western, and South Pacific Oceans.
Minimum Aquarium Size: 55 gal. (208 L).
Foods & Feeding: Difficult to feed. Varied diet, including vitamin-enriched brine shrimp, finely-chopped crustacean flesh, mysid shrimp, as well frozen preparations for angelfishes and herbivores. It might also feed on microalgae, detritus, and live sponges growing on live rock. Feed at least 3 times daily.
Aquarium Suitability Index: 2.
Reef Aquarium Compatibility: May nip at large-polyped stony corals. Will not bother most soft corals.
Captive Care: Typically found in deeper habitats, this is a shy species that often has difficulty acclimating to aquarium life. Most individuals are reluctant to eat in captivity. It will adapt more readily in an aquarium with reduced light levels and should be provided with numerous rocky hiding places. It should not be housed with aggressive species. Best kept singly or in a male-female pair. Juveniles have a distinct, large ocellus (eyespot) on the posterior portion of the dorsal fin.

Paracentropyge venusta (Yasuda & Tominaga, 1969)
Venusta Angelfish (Purple Masked Angelfish)

Maximum Length: 4.7 in. (12 cm).
Range: Western Pacific.
Minimum Aquarium Size: 55 gal. (208 L).
Foods & Feeding: Difficult to feed. Varied diet, including vitamin-enriched brine shrimp, finely-chopped crustacean flesh, mysid shrimp, as well as frozen preparations for angelfishes and herbivores. It might also feed on microalgae, detritus, and live sponges growing on live rock. Feed at least 3 times daily.
Aquarium Suitability Index: 2.
Reef Aquarium Compatibility: Can be kept in the reef aquarium, but may nip at large-polyped stony corals and clam mantles.
Captive Care: This is an attractive and prized species, but often difficult to keep. Many individuals are reluctant to accept aquarium foods. A prospective purchase should be active, feeding, and have a full-looking stomach. Provide with plenty of suitable hiding places, including rocky caves and overhangs, and house with nonaggressive fishes. Best kept singly, in a male-female pair or a harem (one male and several females). Because it is a cave dweller in the wild, it will often spend more time in the open if housed in a dimly lit tank.

Pomacanthus annularis (Bloch, 1787)
Blue-ring Angelfish (Annularis Angelfish)

Maximum Length: 11.8 in. (30 cm).
Range: Indo-west-Pacific.
Minimum Aquarium Size: 100 gal. (379 L).
Foods & Feeding: Varied diet, including ample vegetable matter, meaty fare, and occasionally, special angelfish rations containing marine sponges. May require live foods, such as brine shrimp, mysid shrimp, or fresh, finely chopped seafoods (e.g., squid, scallop, shrimp) to induce feeding. Feed at least 3 times a day.
Aquarium Suitability Index: 3.
Reef Aquarium Compatibility: Will nip at sessile invertebrates, including stony and soft corals, and tridacnid clam mantles.
Captive Care: In its full adult coloration, a spectacular fish. Usually quite shy when first introduced, spending much of its time hiding behind the decor or racing for cover whenever anyone approaches. It must have several suitable caves or hiding places. Once it acclimates, it is an aggressive feeder and recognizes the aquarist as a source of food. It may even begin to bully some tankmates, such as butterflyfishes, other angelfishes, spadefishes, and batfishes. Juveniles look quite different (see page 245).

Pomacanthus arcuatus (Linnaeus, 1758)
Gray Angelfish

Maximum Length: 19.7 in. (50 cm).
Range: Western Atlantic.
Minimum Aquarium Size: 180 gal. (681 L).
Foods & Feeding: Varied diet, including *Spirulina* and marine algae, as well as mysid shrimp or frozen shrimp and high-quality angelfish preparations. Feed at least 3 times a day.
Aquarium Suitability Index: 4.
Reef Aquarium Compatibility: Not recommended. Will nip at sessile invertebrates, including stony and soft corals, and clam mantles.
Captive Care: Although its color is less spectacular than that of many other pomacanthids, this is a handsome and hardy species for the larger aquarium. Juveniles are black with yellow stripes, page 245, and very similar to juvenile *P. paru*, page 246. However, the juvenile *P. arcuatus*'s caudal fin (tail) is squared off and the posterior margin is white or transparent; the juvenile *P. paru*'s is rounded, with a yellow border that forms an oval. May be shy at first, but will quickly become a bold member of the aquarium community. Smaller specimens will pick crustacean parasites and dead tissue from tankmates and may pester slow-moving species, such as boxfishes.

Pomacanthus asfur (Forsskål, 1775)
Asfur Angelfish (Arabian Angelfish)

Maximum Length: 15.7 in. (40 cm).
Range: Red Sea and Gulf of Aden.
Minimum Aquarium Size: 135 gal. (511 L).
Foods & Feeding: Varied diet, including ample vegetable matter, meaty fare, and occasionally, special angelfish rations containing marine sponges. May require live foods, such as brine shrimp, mysid shrimp, or fresh, finely chopped seafoods (e.g, squid, scallop, shrimp) to induce feeding. Feed at least 3 times a day.
Aquarium Suitability Index: 3.
Reef Aquarium Compatibility: Will nip at large-polyped stony corals, some soft corals (e.g., *Xenia*), and tridacnid clam mantles. Can usually be kept with small-polyped stony corals and more-noxious soft corals.
Captive Care: A Red Sea beauty that is no longer forbiddingly rare and expensive. One of the shyest members of the genus, it may take several days to a week before it begins feeding, especially if housed in a tank without adequate shelter. Although not usually overly aggressive, some individuals may pester newly introduced fishes, more-passive tankmates, and especially other angelfishes. Only one should be kept per tank. Juveniles look quite different (see page 245).

Pomacanthus imperator (Bloch, 1787)
Emperor Angelfish

Maximum Length: 15.0 in. (38 cm).
Range: Indo-Pacific.
Minimum Aquarium Size: 135 gal. (511 L).
Foods & Feeding: Varied diet, including *Spirulina* and marine algae, as well as mysid shrimp or frozen shrimp and high-quality angelfish preparations. Feed at least 3 times a day.
Aquarium Suitability Index: 3.
Reef Aquarium Compatibility: Will nip at large-polyped stony corals, some soft corals (e.g., *Xenia*), and tridacnid clam mantles. Can usually be kept with small-polyped stony corals and more-noxious soft corals.
Captive Care: One of the truly dazzling members of this genus. Juveniles and small adults are good aquarium inhabitants, although larger individuals are sometimes poor feeders and are susceptible to a variety of parasites. Adults are also prone to color loss and may develop head and lateral line erosion. Be forewarned: when juveniles transform into adult colors they may not attain the same brilliance as in the wild. The transition may not be quite complete or the final adult color may be pale (see page 245). A varied diet including vitamin-enriched and color-enhancing foods should be offered.

Pomacanthus maculosus (Forsskål, 1775)
Yellowbar Angelfish (Maculosus Angelfish, Map Angelfish)

Maximum Length: 11.8 in. (30 cm).
Range: Red Sea and East Africa
Minimum Aquarium Size: 100 gal. (379 L).
Foods & Feeding: Varied diet, including ample vegetable matter, meaty fare and, occasionally, special angelfish rations containing marine sponges. Feed at least 3 times a day.
Aquarium Suitability Index: 5. ■
Reef Aquarium Compatibility: Will nip at large-polyped stony corals, some soft corals (e.g., *Xenia*), and tridacnid clam mantles. Can usually be kept with small-polyped stony corals and more-noxious soft corals.
Captive Care: A great "first" large angelfish, being bold, beautiful—no two are patterned alike—and the easiest member of the genus to maintain in captivity. Feeds greedily on a wide variety of aquarium fare, and it cannot be trusted with most reef aquarium invertebrates. May behave aggressively toward passive tankmates, fishes introduced after it has been in a tank for some time, or other angelfishes. Grows large; only one should be housed per aquarium. Is more reliably hardy than its Red Sea counterpart, *P. asfur*. Juveniles have a white tail (see page 246) unlike *P. asfur*, which has a yellow tail.

Pomacanthus navarchus (Cuvier, 1831)
Bluegirdled Angelfish (Majestic Angelfish)

Maximum Length: 11.8 in. (30 cm).
Range: Eastern Indian Ocean and Western Pacific.
Minimum Aquarium Size: 100 gal. (379 L).
Foods & Feeding: Varied diet, including _Spirulina_ and marine algae, as well as mysid shrimp or frozen shrimp and high-quality angelfish preparations. Feed at least 3 times a day.
Aquarium Suitability Index: 3.
Reef Aquarium Compatibility: Will nip at large-polyped stony corals, some soft corals (e.g., _Xenia_), and tridacnid clam mantles. Can usually be kept with small-polyped stony corals and more-noxious soft corals.
Captive Care: Flamboyant in looks but retiring in personality, this species is not particularly difficult to maintain, but is shy. Juveniles are very reclusive, spending most of their time hiding. Adults are also shy, but will make more forays into the open. Both are easily startled and need one or more "bolt" holes to dart into when frightened. Can become quite aggressive, especially toward related species or similarly shaped fishes introduced after it has become established. Large adults are more difficult to acclimate than juveniles or smaller adults. Has been reported to live more than 21 years in captivity.

Pomacanthus paru (Bloch, 1787)
French Angelfish

Maximum Length: 15.0 in. (38 cm).
Range: Tropical Atlantic.
Minimum Aquarium Size: 135 gal. (511 L).
Foods & Feeding: Varied diet, including ample vegetable matter, meaty fare and, occasionally, special angelfish rations containing marine sponges. Feed at least 3 times a day.
Aquarium Suitability Index: 4.
Reef Aquarium Compatibility: Not recommended. Will eat or nip at most sessile invertebrates.
Captive Care: A favorite of Caribbean divers and snorkelers, this species is a relatively hardy fish that makes a fine display animal in larger aquariums. Like many angelfish species, tiny juveniles typically do not acclimate to captive life or foods. Juveniles are cleaners and will sometimes pester less-mobile species (e.g., boxfishes). Juveniles are very similar to juvenile *P. arcuatus* (see page 245), but are distinguished by a tail that is rounded and more fully pigmented. Adults become large and will often aggressively dominate their aquarium domain.

Pomacanthus semicirculatus (Cuvier, 1831)
Koran Angelfish (Semicircular Angelfish, Halfcircled Angelfish)

Maximum Length: 15.0 in. (38 cm).
Range: Indo-Pacific.
Minimum Aquarium Size: 135 gal. (511 L).
Foods & Feeding: Varied diet, including *Spirulina* and marine algae, as well as mysid shrimp or frozen shrimp and high-quality angelfish preparations. Feed at least 3 times a day.
Aquarium Suitability Index: 4.
Reef Aquarium Compatibility: Not recommended. Will nip at sessile invertebrates, including stony and soft corals, and clam mantles.
Captive Care: An excellent aquarium fish that is commonly available and often thrives in a well-maintained tank. Eats a wide variety of aquarium fare, including algae—even slime algae or cyanobacteria—growing on the aquarium glass and decor. Juvenile specimens display a blue, black, and white pattern typical of a number of Indo-Pacific angelfishes, and are distinguished by semicircular white rings radiating outward from the tail (see page 246). A juvenile can be very pugnacious and should be the last fish introduced to a tank. Has been reported to live more than 20 years in captivity.

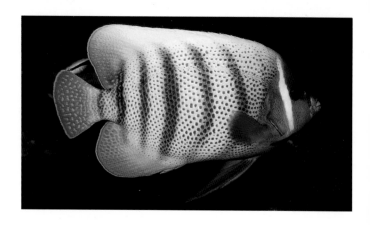

Pomacanthus sexstriatus (Cuvier, 1831)
Sixbanded Angelfish

Maximum Length: 18.1 in. (46 cm).
Range: Eastern Indian Ocean and Western Pacific.
Minimum Aquarium Size: 180 gal. (681 L).
Foods & Feeding: Varied diet, including *Spirulina* and marine algae, as well as mysid shrimp or frozen shrimp and high-quality angelfish preparations. Feed at least 3 times a day.
Aquarium Suitability Index: 3.
Reef Aquarium Compatibility: Not recommended. Will nip at sessile invertebrates, including stony and soft corals, and clam mantles.
Captive Care: This is a relatively hardy aquarium species, but one that grows to a substantial size and requires an extra-large tank if it is to be properly maintained. Often seen in pairs in the wild, where it is well known for producing underwater grunting sounds in warning when approached by divers (Steene, 1977). Alert aquarists may notice these sounds when keeping this and other large angelfishes. Has been reported to live over 21 years in captivity. Provide this species with appropriate hiding places in which it can dart when startled. Juveniles look quite different (see page 246).

Pomacanthus xanthometopon (Bleeker, 1853)
Blueface Angelfish (Yellowface Angelfish)

Maximum Length: 15.0 in. (38 cm).
Range: Indo-west-Pacific.
Minimum Aquarium Size: 135 gal. (511 L).
Foods & Feeding: Varied diet, including *Spirulina* and marine algae, as well as mysid shrimp or frozen shrimp and high-quality angelfish preparations. Feed at least 3 times a day.
Aquarium Suitability Index: 4.
Reef Aquarium Compatibility: Not recommended. Will nip at sessile invertebrates, including stony and soft corals, and clam mantles.
Captive Care: A gorgeous fish for more-experienced aquarists, this moderately hardy species should be provided with plenty of swimming space, as well as a number of suitable hiding places. Often shy initially, but if not bullied by tankmates or in a high-traffic area, it will become bolder. Does not tend to be as aggressive as some of its relatives, but may chase close relatives. Its reputation for being a poor survivor may be a carryover from the days of heavy cyanide use by Filipino collectors. Beware of specimens that seem dazed, uninterested in food or their surroundings, or that show signs of wasting. Juveniles look quite different (see page 246).

Pomacanthus zonipectus (Gill, 1862)
Cortez Angelfish

Maximum Length: 18.1 in. (46 cm).
Range: Tropical Eastern Pacific.
Minimum Aquarium Size: 180 gal. (681 L).
Foods & Feeding: Sponges are its natural diet, but can be switched to aquarium foods. Offer both meaty and algae-based foods, as well as occasional feedings of special angelfish rations that contain marine sponges. Feed at least 2 times a day.
Aquarium Suitability Index: 4.
Reef Aquarium Compatibility: Not recommended. May nip at various corals and anemones and will eat sponges and tunicates.
Captive Care: This native of the far-eastern Pacific appears only sporadically in the aquarium trade. The small juveniles, which are black with alternating curved yellow and blue lines (see page 246), are highly sought after, but they mature into rather drably colored adults. Keep only one per tank. Juveniles tend to be territorial and should not be housed with other *Pomacanthus* spp. juveniles, especially young *P. arcuatus* or *P. paru* angelfishes, which are similar in color (see pages 245 and 246). Juveniles may engage in cleaning behavior.

Holacanthus bermudensis (juv.)
Blue Angelfish
Aquarium Suitability: 4.
Adult: page 228.

Holacanthus ciliaris (juv.)
Queen Angelfish
Aquarium Suitability: 4.
Adult: page 229.

Pomacanthus annularis (juv.)
Bluering Angelfish
Aquarium Suitability: 3.
Adult: page 234.

Pomacanthus arcuatus (juv.)
Gray Angelfish
Aquarium Suitability: 4.
Adult: page 235.

Pomacanthus asfur (juv.)
Asfur Angelfish
Aquarium Suitability: 3.
Adult: page 236.

Pomacanthus imperator (juv.)
Emperor Angelfish
Aquarium Suitability: 3.
Adult: page 237.

Pomacanthus maculosus (juv.)
Yellowbar Angelfish
Aquarium Suitability: 5.
Adult: page 238.

Pomacanthus paru (juv.)
French Angelfish
Aquarium Suitability: 4.
Adult: page 240.

Pomacanthus semicirculatus (juv.)
Koran Angelfish
Aquarium Suitability: 4.
Adult: page 241.

Pomacanthus sexstriatus (juv.)
Sixbanded Angelfish
Aquarium Suitability: 3.
Adult: page 242.

Pomacanthus xanthometopon (juv.)
Blueface Angelfish
Aquarium Suitability: 4.
Adult: page 243.

Pomacanthus zonipectus (juv.)
Cortez Angelfish
Aquarium Suitability: 4.
Adult: page 244.

Pygoplites diacanthus (Boddaert, 1772)
Regal Angelfish

Maximum Length: 9.8 in. (25 cm).
Range: Indo-Pacific.
Minimum Aquarium Size: 100 gal. (379 L).
Foods & Feeding: Individuals vary in their willingness to accept captive fare. Offer chopped fresh shrimp, squid, scallop, or marine fish flesh, as well as frozen, prepared foods for angelfishes and herbivores. Feed at least 3 times a day.
Aquarium Suitability Index: 2-3.
Reef Aquarium Compatibility: Will nip at large-polyped stony corals, some soft corals (e.g., *Xenia*), and tridacnid clam mantles. Can usually be kept with small-polyped stony corals and more-noxious soft corals.
Captive Care: A glorious fish whose hardiness is somewhat dependent on collection site. Indian Ocean and Red Sea specimens (with an orange rather than a blue "chest") are more likely to adapt to captivity than those from the Pacific—perhaps owing to better collection and handling. Provide with plenty of good hiding places. Make sure it has fully acclimated before mixing with aggressive tankmates. Keep singly, unless in a mated pair.

MALE IN SPAWNING COLORS

Abudefduf saxatilis (Linnaeus, 1758)
Sergeant Major

Maximum Length: 5.9 in. (15 cm).
Range: Tropical Atlantic.
Minimum Aquarium Size: 55 gal. (208 L).
Foods & Feeding: Varied diet, including meaty food items, such as frozen mysid shrimp, vitamin-enriched brine shrimp, and finely chopped table shrimp, as well as frozen preparations for herbivores. Feed 2-3 times a day.
Aquarium Suitability Index: 5. ▪▪
Reef Aquarium Compatibility: Usually not a threat, although some may eat zoanthids. Will graze on some algae.
Captive Care: This is one species of a circumtropical genus of damselfishes commonly known as sergeants and not particularly prized by aquarists.They are so hardy as to be highly recommended for breaking in new aquariums, but tend to become large, pugnacious, and less colorful as they mature. Juveniles can be kept in schools in medium-sized aquariums. Adults are often very aggressive toward conspecifics and other fishes and should not be kept with peaceful species. They are, however, ideal in communities of bellicose fishes. Provide with suitable hiding places. Will spawn in captivity.

Amphiprion clarkii (Bennett, 1830)
Clark's Anemonefish (Clark's Clownfish, "Sebae" Clownfish)

Maximum Length: 5.5 in. (14 cm).
Range: Indo-Pacific.
Minimum Aquarium Size: 30 gal. (114 L).
Foods & Feeding: Varied diet, including meaty food items, such as frozen mysid shrimp, vitamin-enriched brine shrimp, and finely chopped table shrimp, as well as frozen preparations for herbivores. Feed 2-3 times a day.
Aquarium Suitability Index: 5.
Reef Aquarium Compatibility: Ideal for the reef aquarium. An occasional specimen may wallow in the polyps of large-polyped stony corals, which could irritate the polyps and cause them to close. May eat small, ornamental shrimps.
Captive Care: One of the most common and durable anemonefishes in the aquarium trade, where it is often misidentified as the Sebae Clownfish (*A. sebae*). Hardy even for beginning aquarists, feeds on almost anything, and is fairly disease-resistant. Best acquired as juveniles and kept in pairs or singly; adults will fight each other (unless they are a mated pair) and will attack other anemonefishes and passive tankmates. Adopts almost all common sea anemones as a host.

JUVENILE WITH WHITE HEAD BAR

Amphiprion ephippium (Bloch, 1790)
Red Saddleback Anemonefish (Fire Anemonefish)

Maximum Length: 4.7 in. (12 cm).

Range: Eastern Indian Ocean.

Minimum Aquarium Size: 30 gal. (114 L).

Foods & Feeding: Varied diet, including meaty food items, such as frozen mysid shrimp, vitamin-enriched brine shrimp, and finely chopped table shrimp, as well as frozen preparations for herbivores. Feed at least 2 times a day.

Aquarium Suitability Index: 5. ▮

Reef Aquarium Compatibility: Ideal for the reef aquarium. If a host anemone is not present, an occasional specimen may wallow in the polyps of a large-polyped stony coral, which may irritate them and cause them to close.

Captive Care: A colorful and durable aquarium inhabitant, this is an aggressive fish that will punish other anemonefishes and smaller, more-passive tankmates. Will also fight among themselves. Best kept singly or in mated pairs and only with larger or more-pugnacious species. Associates with the Bubbletip (*Entacmaea quadricolor*) and Leathery (*Heteractis crispa*) Sea Anemones.

JUVENILE WITH CENTRAL BODY BAR

Amphiprion frenatus Brevoort, 1856
Tomato Anemonefish (Tomato Clownfish)

Maximum Length: 5.5 in. (14 cm).
Range: Western Pacific.
Minimum Aquarium Size: 30 gal. (114 L).
Foods & Feeding: Varied diet, including meaty food items, such as frozen mysid shrimp, vitamin-enriched brine shrimp, and finely chopped table shrimp, as well as frozen preparations for herbivores. Feed at least 2 times a day
Aquarium Suitability Index: 5. ■
Reef Aquarium Suitability: Ideal for the reef aquarium. An occasional specimen may wallow in the polyps a of large-polyped stony coral, which can irritate them and cause them to close. Will occasionally pull feather dusters from their tubes.
Captive Care: Bold and colorful, this species is extremely hardy, and captive-bred individuals are almost invincible. It can also prove to be very belligerent when it begins to mature, striking out at peaceful tankmates, especially other anemonefishes. Should be kept singly or in mated pairs; never house with other anemonefishes. Associates with the Bubbletip (*Entacmaea quadricolor*) and Leathery (*Heteractis crispa*) Sea Anemones, although it will thrive without them.

Amphiprion melanopus Bleeker, 1852
Red and Black Anemonefish (Cinnamon Clownfish)

Maximum Length: 4.7 in. (12 cm).
Range: Western and South Pacific.
Minimum Aquarium Size: 30 gal. (114 L).
Foods & Feeding: Varied diet, including meaty food items, such as frozen mysid shrimp, vitamin-enriched brine shrimp, and finely chopped table shrimp, as well as frozen preparations for herbivores. Feed at least 2 times a day.
Aquarium Suitability Index: 5. █
Reef Aquarium Compatibility: Ideal for the reef aquarium. An occasional specimen may wallow in the polyps of a large-poiyped stony coral, which can irritate them and cause them to close.
Captive Care: A robust species that fares well in the home aquarium, particularly captive-bred specimens. Like its close relatives (*A. frenatus, A. ephippium*) it can be belligerent, often fighting with other anemonefishes and picking on more-passive tankmates. A larger tank will reduce aggression. As with most anemonefishes, two juveniles will typically grow into a pair; keep adults singly or in mated pairs. Associates with the Bubbletip (*Entacmaea quadricolor*) and Leathery (*Heteractis crispa*) Sea Anemones, but does not require one.

Amphiprion nigripes Regan, 1908
Maldives Anemonefish (Blackfinned Anemonefish)

Maximum Length: 4.3 in. (11 cm).
Range: Indian Ocean.
Minimum Aquarium Size: 20 gal. (76 L).
Foods & Feeding: Varied diet, including smaller, meaty food items, such as frozen mysid shrimp, vitamin-enriched brine shrimp, and finely chopped table shrimp, as well as frozen preparations for herbivores. Feed at least 2 times a day.
Aquarium Suitability Index: 3-4.
Reef Aquarium Compatibility: Excellent.
Captive Care: A relative rarity among the anemonefishes, this species typically does well in captivity if healthy specimens can be obtained. Unfortunately, it often ships poorly from its native waters, and captive-bred stock is a much safer acquisition. In nature, it lives among the tentacles of the Magnificent Sea Anemone (*Heteractis magnifica*), typically in small groups. Can be very aggressive toward conspecifics. When keeping in groups, provide plenty of room or be sure there is "enough anemone" (you many need more than one). Rarely aggressive toward other anemonefishes, with the possible exception of similar species; may be picked on by others in this genus.

Amphiprion ocellaris Cuvier, 1830
Ocellaris Anemonefish (False Clown Anemonefish,
False Percula Clownfish)

Maximum Length: 3.5 in. (9 cm).
Range: Eastern Indian Ocean and Western Pacific.
Minimum Aquarium Size: 20 gal. (76 L).
Foods & Feeding: Varied diet, including meaty food items, such as frozen mysid shrimp, vitamin-enriched brine shrimp, and finely chopped table shrimp, as well as frozen preparations for herbivores. Feed at least 2 times a day.
Aquarium Suitability Index: 4-5.
Reef Aquarium Compatibility: Excellent.
Captive Care: Vivid coloration and an endearing personality make this an all-time favorite among coral reef fishes. Wild-caught specimens have a dubious reputation for hardiness, but captive-raised individuals almost always fare well in the aquarium. Can be kept in groups, but one individual will eventually dominate and may pick on the others, especially if space and shelter are limited. Rarely aggressive toward other anemonefish species. Associates with *Heteractis magnifica*, *Stichodactyla gigantea*, and *S. mertensii* anemones in the wild, although it does fine without a host anemone in captivity.

Amphiprion percula (Lacépède, 1802)
Percula Anemonefish (Clown Anemonefish,
Percula Clownfish)

Maximum Length: 3.1 in. (8 cm).
Range: Western Pacific.
Minimum Aquarium Size: 20 gal. (76 L).
Foods & Feeding: Varied diet, including meaty food items, such as frozen mysid shrimp, vitamin-enriched brine shrimp, and finely chopped table shrimp, as well as frozen preparations for herbivores. Feed at least 2 times a day.
Aquarium Suitability Index: 4.
Reef Aquarium Compatibility: Ideal for the reef aquarium. An occasional specimen may wallow in the polyps of a large-polyped stony coral, causing them to retract in irritation.
Captive Care: An exquisite fish that is a joy to keep. Very similar to *A. ocellaris*, although the white body bars in this species are often edged in jet black. Associates with *Heteractis magnifica*, *H. crispa*, or *Stichodactyla mertensii* anemones. Tends to be more aggressive toward conspecifics than *A. ocellaris*. House singly or in pairs; two juveniles will usually mature into a mated pair. Adult females are larger than their mates (also true for *A. ocellaris*).

Amphiprion perideraion Bleeker, 1855
Pink Skunk Anemonefish (Pink Skunk Clownfish,
Pink Anemonefish)

Maximum Length: 3.9 in. (10 cm).
Range: Indo-west-Pacific.
Minimum Aquarium Size: 20 gal. (76 L).
Foods & Feeding: Varied diet, including meaty food items, such as
frozen mysid shrimp, vitamin-enriched brine shrimp, and finely
chopped table shrimp, as well as frozen preparations for herbivores.
Feed at least 2 times a day.
Aquarium Suitability Index: 3-4.
Reef Aquarium Compatibility: Excellent.
Captive Care: A pretty and much-liked species that is more easily in-
timidated by boisterous tankmates than most of the anemonefishes.
In groups, these fish can be aggressive amongst themselves and need
plenty of room and hiding places. They are rarely aggressive toward
other anemonefishes, with the possible exception of closely related
species. Lives in several anemone species in the wild (including *Heteractis crispa*, *Macrodactyla doreensis*, and *Stichodactyla gigantea*), but
seems to prefer the Magnificent Sea Anemone (*Heteractis magnifica*).
In captivity, will thrive and spawn without a host.

Amphiprion polymnus (Linnaeus, 1758)
Saddleback Anemonefish (Saddleback Clownfish)

Maximum Length: 5.1 in. (13 cm).
Range: Eastern Indian Ocean and Western Pacific.
Minimum Aquarium Size: 30 gal. (114 L).
Foods & Feeding: Varied diet, including meaty food items, such as frozen mysid shrimp, vitamin-enriched brine shrimp, and finely chopped table shrimp, as well as frozen preparations for herbivores. Feed at least 2 times a day.
Aquarium Suitability Index: 3.
Reef Aquarium Compatibility: Excellent.
Captive Care: Somewhat rare in the aquarium trade, this species varies greatly in its ability to acclimate when imported from the wild. Some settle quickly and eat almost anything; others sulk in the corners and refuse food. The latter usually become infected with the common anemonefish parasites and quickly perish. Captive-bred specimens, when available, are a much more reliable choice. Usually inoffensive and can be kept in small groups. Most likely to adopt Haddon's Sea Anemone (*Stichodactyla haddoni*) in the aquarium; may do better if an anemone is present. On the reef, a pair and juveniles of varying sizes are typically found in a single anemone.

Amphiprion sandaracinos Allen, 1972
Orange Skunk Anemonefish

Maximum Length: 5.5 in. (14 cm).
Range: Western Pacific.
Minimum Aquarium Size: 30 gal. (114 L).
Foods & Feeding: Varied diet, including meaty food items, such as frozen mysid shrimp, vitamin-enriched brine shrimp, and finely chopped table shrimp, as well as frozen preparations for herbivores. Feed at least 2 times a day.
Aquarium Suitability Index: 4.
Reef Aquarium Compatibility: Excellent.
Captive Care: A beautiful anemonefish that does well in smaller aquariums. Wild-caught specimens not uncommonly suffer from clownfish disease (*Brooklynella hostilis),* most easily recognized by copious slime that sloughs off the fish's body. Choose captive-bred specimens when possible. Larger females can be very aggressive toward conspecifics or closely related species. Best kept in pairs with a host sea anemone. Usually inhabits Merten's Carpet Anemone (*Stichodactyla mertensii*) and the Leathery Sea Anemone (*Heteractis crispa*) in the wild, but will acclimate to others in captivity. May behave aggressively toward similar species (e.g., *A. perideraion*).

Chromis atripectoralis Welander & Schultz, 1951
Blackaxil Chromis (Green Chromis)

Maximum Length: 4.3 in. (11 cm).
Range: Indo-Pacific.
Minimum Aquarium Size: 55 gal. (208 L).
Foods & Feeding: Varied diet, including meaty items, such as frozen mysid shrimp, and vitamin-enriched brine shrimp, as well as herbivore flakes and frozen preparations. Feed at least 3 times a day.
Aquarium Suitability Index: 4.
Reef Aquarium Compatibility: Excellent.
Captive Care: The chromises are bright, active fishes that can, and should, be kept in groups in the aquarium. A shoal of six or more fish makes an interesting display. A dominant individual may occasionally bicker with subordinate members, but this is not usually a problem if the group is large enough. Lone individuals tend to be easily harassed by tankmates and often fail to thrive. Chromises tend to spend their time in the upper part of the water column, often inciting reclusive species to spend more time in the open. This species is very similar to, and often sold as, the Blue Green Chromis (*Chromis viridis*), page 260, but the Blackaxil has black at the inner bases of its pectoral fins. Offer enriched foods to prevent color loss.

Chromis cyanea
Blue Chromis
Max. Length: 5.1 in. (13 cm).
Aquarium Suitability: 4.

Chromis insolatus
Sunshine or Olive Chromis
Max. Length: 6.3 in. (16 cm).
Aquarium Suitability: 4.

Chromis retrofasciata
Blackbar Chromis
Max. Length: 2.0 in. (5 cm).
Aquarium Suitability: 4.

Chromis scotti
Purple Chromis
Max. Length: 3.9 in. (10 cm).
Aquarium Suitability: 4.

Chromis vanderbilti
Vanderbilt's Chromis
Max. Length: 2.4 in. (6 cm).
Aquarium Suitability: 4.

Chromis viridis
Blue Green Chromis
Max. Length: 3.5 in. (9 cm).
Aquarium Suitability: 4.

Chrysiptera cyanea (Quoy & Gaimard, 1824)
Blue Damselfish (Blue Devil)

Maximum Length: 3.1 in. (8 cm).
Range: Western Pacific.
Minimum Aquarium Size: 30 gal. (114 L).
Foods & Feeding: Varied diet, including meaty items, such as frozen mysid shrimp and vitamin-enriched brine shrimp, as well as herbivore flakes and frozen preparations. Feed at least 3 times a day.
Aquarium Suitability Index: 5. ▮
Reef Aquarium Compatibility: Excellent. Grazes on some algae.
Captive Care: This little electric-blue fish has probably attracted more hobbyists to marine aquariums than any other. It is colorful, inexpensive, and hardy, but can also become aggressive as it matures, especially larger males. May pick on more-peaceful tankmates, such as cardinalfishes, gobies, firefishes, blennies, etc. A male and female can be kept in a smaller tank, while a group can be kept in a medium-sized aquarium aquascaped with plenty of nooks and crannies for hiding. Best to keep only one male per tank, unless housed in a large aquarium. Will readily spawn in captivity. Males from some Indonesian waters have a blue tail with a dark border; in other geographic areas the tail is bright orange. The female's tail is clear.

Chrysiptera parasema (Fowler, 1918)
Yellowtail Blue Damselfish (Yellowtail Demoiselle)

Maximum Length: 2.8 in. (7 cm).
Range: Western Pacific.
Minimum Aquarium Size: 20 gal. (76 L).
Foods & Feeding: Varied diet, including meaty items, such as frozen mysid shrimp and vitamin-enriched brine shrimp, as well as herbivore flakes and frozen preparations. Feed at least 3 times a day.
Aquarium Suitability Index: 5.
Reef Aquarium Compatibility: Excellent.
Captive Care: This little beauty is one of the less-aggressive members of this genus and a classic choice for beginning aquarists. Can be kept in small groups in a medium-sized tank with plenty of hiding places. A male-female pair can be kept in a smaller tank and will often spawn. This damsel feeds on zooplankton and algae and is also ideal for the reef aquarium; will ignore invertebrate tankmates and will pick at filamentous algal growths. Should not be kept with highly aggressive species, including more-pugnacious damselfishes.

Chrysiptera talboti (Allen, 1975)
Talbot's Demoiselle

Maximum Length: 2.4 in. (6 cm).
Range: Indo-Pacific.
Minimum Aquarium Size: 20 gal. (76 L).
Foods & Feeding: Varied diet, including meaty items, such as frozen mysid shrimp and vitamin-enriched brine shrimp, as well as herbivore flakes and frozen preparations. Feed at least 3 times a day.
Aquarium Suitability Index: 5. ▪
Reef Aquarium Compatibility: Excellent.
Captive Care: This is an attractive little fish, tinged with canary yellow colors, and one of the more mild-mannered damsels. Although it should not be housed in a smaller tank with peaceful species, it can be kept with less-aggressive fishes in a medium to large tank. Keep one specimen per tank, unless the aquarium is large, or a pair is obtained or created by raising juveniles together. Provide it with plenty of shelter sites, especially if housed with more-aggressive fishes.

Chrysiptera taupou (Jordan & Seale, 1906)
South Seas Devil Damselfish (Fiji Blue Devil)

Maximum Length: 2.4 in. (6 cm).
Range: South Pacific.
Minimum Aquarium Size: 20 gal. (76 L).
Foods & Feeding: Varied diet, including meaty items, such as frozen mysid shrimp and vitamin-enriched brine shrimp, as well as herbivore flakes and frozen preparations. Feed at least 3 times a day.
Aquarium Suitability Index: 5. ▪
Reef Aquarium Compatibility: Ideal for the reef aquarium; will not harm any invertebrate tankmates and will eat some algae.
Captive Care: The jewel-like colors of this species are matched only by its intense aggressiveness. Keep only one per tank, unless a known pair is obtained, and do not place with docile species. It will pick on other damselfishes unless they match it in belligerence. The best setting for this fish is in a moderately aggressive community tank, with fishes such as larger dottybacks, angelfishes, triggerfishes, puffers, and others that can easily keep it at bay. Mature males have a blue spinous dorsal fin; in mature females, it is yellow.

Dascyllus aruanus (Linnaeus, 1758)
Humbug Dascyllus (Striped Damselfish)

Maximum Length: 3.1 in. (8 cm).
Range: Indo-Pacific.
Minimum Aquarium Size: 20 gal. (76 L).
Foods & Feeding: Varied diet, including meaty items, such as frozen mysid shrimp and vitamin-enriched brine shrimp, as well as herbivore flakes and frozen preparations. Feed at least 3 times a day.
Aquarium Suitability Index: 5. ■
Reef Aquarium Compatibility: Will not harm sessile invertebrate tankmates and will eat some algae. Larger specimens may eat small crustaceans just after molting.
Captive Care: Little humbugs are cute as juveniles and hardy enough to be used in starting new aquariums, but they grow into real terrors in the community tank. Young specimens can be kept in groups, but as adults they will fight, unless they are a male-female pair. Will also fight with other damselfishes and will pick on docile tankmates. Best kept in a moderately aggressive community tank with fishes such as eels, triggerfishes, larger dottybacks, angelfishes, and puffers. Provide suitable hiding places, especially for juveniles.

Dascyllus melanurus (Bleeker, 1854)
Blacktail Dascyllus (Striped Damselfish)

Maximum Length: 3.1 in. (8 cm).
Range: Western Pacific.
Minimum Aquarium Size: 20 gal. (76 L).
Foods & Feeding: Varied diet, including meaty items, such as frozen mysid shrimp and vitamin-enriched brine shrimp, as well as herbivore flakes and frozen preparations. Feed at least 3 times a day.
Aquarium Suitability Index: 5.
Reef Aquarium Compatibility: Ideal for the reef aquarium; will not harm sessile invertebrates and will eat some algae. Larger specimens may eat small crustaceans just after molting.
Captive Care: A group of juveniles of this boldly marked species makes an interesting display, but unfortunately they mature into hellions, especially in smaller aquariums with placid tankmates. Very similar to *D. aruanus*, page 265, but with an added black patch on the tail. Adults will quarrel among themselves and also pester tankmates, unless they are larger and/or equally feisty. Should never be kept with docile tankmates. Best housed in a moderately aggressive community tank with fishes like larger dottybacks, angelfishes, and puffers. Provide suitable hiding places, especially for juveniles.

Dascyllus reticulatus (Richardson, 1846)
Reticulate Dascyllus

Maximum Length: 3.1 in. (8 cm).
Range: Indo-Pacific.
Minimum Aquarium Size: 20 gal. (76 L).
Foods & Feeding: Varied diet, including meaty items, such as frozen mysid shrimp and vitamin-enriched brine shrimp, as well as herbivore flakes and frozen preparations. Feed at least 3 times a day.
Aquarium Suitability Index: 5. ▩
Reef Aquarium Compatibility: Excellent.
Captive Care: Not beautiful, but an extremely hardy reef fish. Like other members of the genus, it changes from a likable, sociable juvenile into a belligerent adult that can disrupt an entire community tank. Young specimens may be kept in groups, but adults will fight, unless they are a male-female pair. Will also battle with other damselfishes and pick on docile tankmates. Best kept in a moderately aggressive community tank with fishes like larger dottybacks, angelfishes, and puffers. Provide suitable hiding places, especially for juveniles. Ideal for reef aquariums without small, timid fishes; will eat filamentous algae and won't harm invertebrate tankmates.

Dascyllus trimaculatus (Rüppell, 1828)
Threespot Dascyllus (Domino Damselfish)

Maximum Length: 5.5 in. (14 cm).
Range: Indo-Pacific.
Minimum Aquarium Size: 55 gal. (208 L).
Foods & Feeding: Varied diet, including meaty items, such as frozen mysid shrimp and vitamin-enriched brine shrimp, as well as herbivore flakes and frozen preparations. Feed at least 3 times a day.
Aquarium Suitability Index: 5.
Reef Aquarium Compatibility: Ideal for the reef aquarium; will not harm any invertebrate tankmates and will eat some algae.
Captive Care: A popular fish for conditioning new aquariums because it is able to tolerate water conditions that will kill other species. Juveniles are striking in color, and a group makes an interesting display. Unfortunately, they grow to become a threat to each other and to tankmates that are less aggressive or similar in size. Their presence can make life difficult or impossible for mild-mannered community species. Adults can be kept in male-female pairs or singly. House in a moderately aggressive community tank with fishes like larger dottybacks, angelfishes, and puffers. In the wild, juveniles will shelter in sea anemones.

MAIN PHOTO, ADULT; INSET, JUVENILE

Microspathodon chrysurus (Cuvier & Valenciennes, 1830)
Yellowtail Damselfish (Jewel Damselfish)

Maximum Length: 8.3 in. (21 cm).
Range: Tropical Western Atlantic.
Minimum Aquarium Size: 55 gal. (208 L).
Foods & Feeding: Varied diet, including meaty items, such as frozen mysid shrimp and vitamin-enriched brine shrimp, as well as herbivore flakes and frozen preparations. Feed at least 3 times a day.
Aquarium Suitability Index: 5. ▪
Reef Aquarium Compatibility: Ideal for the reef aquarium; will not harm any invertebrate tankmates and will eat some algae. Larger specimens may eat smaller crustaceans.
Captive Care: Bejeweled with sparkling blue dots in a rich black body, juveniles of this common Western Atlantic species are difficult for aquarists to resist. Typical of others in this genus, they become less spectacular as they grow, in this case changing to brown, with smaller blue spots and a yellow tail. Juveniles can be combative with smaller, more-peaceful tankmates, but adults are even more aggressive and can inflict damage on a wider range of tankmates. Only one specimen should be kept per tank, whether juvenile or adult. House with larger, aggressive fishes.

Neoglyphidodon crossi
Cross's Damselfish
Max. Length: 5.1 in. (13 cm).
Aquarium Suitability: 5.

Neoglyphidodon melas
Black Damselfish
Max. Length: 6.3 in. (16 cm).
Aquarium Suitability: 5.

Neoglyphidodon nigroris
Behn's Damselfish
Max. Length: 5.1 in. (13 cm).
Aquarium Suitability: 5.

Neoglyphidodon oxyodon
Javanese or Neon Damselfish
Max. Length: 5.9 in. (15 cm).
Aquarium Suitability: 5.

Destined for Drabness *Neoglyphidodon* spp.

In a perfect reversal of the tale of the ugly duckling that turns into a beautiful swan, damselfishes of this genus can be a surprising disappointment to the aquarist. These species all start life as colorful—even dazzling—juveniles (as in the photographs above), but they gradually transform into big, drab, nasty adults. Mature specimens of most of these species are brown or black (Behn's Damselfish retains some yellow on the posterior part of the body, otherwise it is brown). Large individuals can easily terrorize an entire aquarium.

Neopomacentrus azysron (Bleeker, 1877)
Yellowtail Demoiselle

Maximum Length: 3.1 in. (8 cm).
Range: Indo-west-Pacific.
Minimum Aquarium Size: 20 gal. (76 L).
Foods & Feeding: Varied diet, including meaty items, such as frozen mysid shrimp and vitamin-enriched brine shrimp, as well as herbivore flakes and frozen preparations. Feed at least 3 times a day.
Aquarium Suitability Index: 5.
Reef Aquarium Compatibility: Ideal for the reef aquarium; will not harm any invertebrate tankmates and will eat some algae.
Captive Care: Sleeker and much less blue than the similarly named Yellowtail Damselfish (*Chrysiptera parasema*), page 262, this is a durable damsel that is not as aggressive as many of its relatives. More than one adult can be kept in a medium-sized aquarium, although all specimens should be introduced simultaneously. It is less likely to harass its tankmates, although diminutive, peaceful species may be in some danger of being picked on in smaller tanks. In turn, it may be the target of more-aggressive tankmates, including other damselfishes. An aquascape with plenty of hiding places will provide a ready retreat from such encounters.

Plectroglyphidodon lacrymatus (Quoy & Gaimard, 1824)
Jewel Damselfish

Maximum Length: 3.9 in. (10 cm).
Range: Indo-Pacific.
Minimum Aquarium Size: 55 gal. (208 L).
Foods & Feeding: Varied diet, including meaty items, such as frozen mysid shrimp and vitamin-enriched brine shrimp, as well as herbivore flakes and frozen preparations. Feed at least 3 times a day.
Aquarium Suitability Index: 5.
Reef Aquarium Compatibility: Harmless to corals and most sessile invertebrates. Larger specimens may eat smaller crustaceans.
Captive Care: Typical of many rather plain damselfishes that appear in the aquarium trade from time to time. Juveniles will usually survive even difficult aquarium conditions, and they can be counted upon to be extremely durable. Unfortunately, they also become very aggressive as they gain size. Only one should be kept per tank, except in male-female pairs. Do not attempt to keep with peaceful tankmates—or even with other damselfishes, unless in a larger tank with equally belligerent species. Should be housed with other aggressive species. Provide with plenty of hiding places.

Pomacentrus alleni Burgess, 1981
Allen's Damselfish

Maximum Length: 2.4 in. (6 cm).
Range: Indian Ocean.
Minimum Aquarium Size: 55 gal. (208 L).
Foods & Feeding: Varied diet, including meaty items, such as frozen mysid shrimp and vitamin-enriched brine shrimp, as well as herbivore flakes and frozen preparations. Feed at least 3 times a day.
Aquarium Suitability Index: 4.
Reef Aquarium Compatibility: Excellent.
Captive Care: Regarded by some as the most beautiful of the damselfishes, this species is named in honor of Dr. Gerald R. Allen, the ichthyologist recognized as the world authority on the Family Pomacentridae. It is also one of the more-peaceful species and a wonderful aquarium fish. Can be kept in groups and housed with relatively docile tankmates. In fact, it will often perish in a tank with more-aggressive fishes. Provide with plenty of shelter sites. Ideal for the reef aquarium, being harmless to invertebrate tankmates and nibbling filamentous algae if it appears. Other species in this genus, page 274, have similar personalities and care requirements.

Pomacentrus auriventris
Goldbelly Damselfish
Max. Length: 2.8 in. (7 cm).
Aquarium Suitability: 5.

Pomacentrus caeruleus
Caerulean Damselfish
Max. Length: 3.1 in. (8 cm).
Aquarium Suitability: 5.

Pomacentrus coelestis
Neon Damselfish
Max. Length: 3.5 in. (9 cm).
Aquarium Suitability: 5.

Pomacentrus moluccensis
Lemon Damselfish
Max. Length: 2.8 in. (7 cm).
Aquarium Suitability: 5.

Pomacentrus pavo
Pavo or Blue Damselfish
Max. Length: 4.3 in. (11 cm).
Aquarium Suitability: 5.

Pomacentrus vaiuli
Princess Damselfish
Max. Length: 3.5 in. (9 cm).
Aquarium Suitability: 5.

Premnas biaculeatus (Bloch, 1790)
Maroon Anemonefish (Maroon Clownfish,
Spinecheek Anemonefish)

Maximum Length: 6.3 in. (16 cm).
Range: Eastern Indian Ocean to Western Pacific.
Minimum Aquarium Size: 30 gal. (114 L).
Foods & Feeding: Varied diet, including meaty items, such as frozen mysid shrimp and vitamin-enriched brine shrimp, as well as herbivore flakes and frozen preparations. Feed at least 2 times a day.
Aquarium Suitability Index: 5.
Reef Aquarium Compatibility: Excellent.
Captive Care: This boldly beautiful anemonefish is alone in its genus, with cheek spines unlike those of its *Amphiprion* spp. relatives. It is also one of the largest and most aggressive anemonefishes and should never be housed with other anemonefishes or small, peaceful fish species. Keep singly or in mated pairs. Highly sexually dimorphic, with females sometimes over three times the length of males. Readily acclimates and accepts a wide array of aquarium fare. Its cheek spines are easily entangled in aquarium nets; use a specimen container if capture is necessary. In nature, a male-female pair will inhabit one Bubbletip Sea Anemone (*Entacmaea quadricolor*).

Anampses caeruleopunctatus Rüppell, 1828
Bluespotted Wrasse

Maximum Length: 16.5 in. (42 cm).
Range: Indo-Pacific.
Minimum Aquarium Size: 100 gal. (379 L).
Foods & Feeding: Difficult to feed. Offer live foods such as black worms and adult brine shrimp to induce a feeding response. Live rock, or a tank with a healthy amphipod population, can help maintain weight while it adjusts to frozen aquarium foods. In time, some specimens will accept frozen _Mysis_ shrimp, brine shrimp, or finely chopped fresh or frozen table shrimp. Feed at least 3 times a day.
Aquarium Suitability Index: 2-3.
Reef Aquarium Compatibility: Will feed on fanworms, ornamental crustaceans, and pick at small tridacnid clams.
Captive Care: Also known as tamarin wrasses, _Anampses_ spp. have a poor survival record in captivity. They tend to ship poorly and usually refuse food when first acquired. Keep with nonaggressive fishes and provide at least 1 in. (2.5 cm) of fine sand. Several females can be kept in the same tank, or one or more females can be housed with a single male. Males are rarely available, but a female may transform into a male. Will jump from uncovered tanks.

Anampses chrysocephalus (female)
Redtail Tamarin Wrasse
Max. Length: 6.7 in. (17 cm).
Aquarium Suitability: 2.

Anampses chrysocephalus (male)
Psychedelic Wrasse
Max. Length: 6.7 in. (17 cm).
Aquarium Suitability: 2.

Anampses geographicus
Geographic Wrasse
Max. Length: 12 in. (31 cm).
Aquarium Suitability: 3.

Anampses lineatus
Lined or White-dashed Wrasse
Max. Length: 4.7 in. (12 cm).
Aquarium Suitability: 2.

Anampses meleagrides
Yellowtail Wrasse
Max. Length: 8.7 in. (22 cm).
Aquarium Suitability: 2.

Anampses neoguinaicus
New Guinea Wrasse
Max. Length: 5.9 in. (15 cm).
Aquarium Suitability: 2.

Bodianus anthioides (Bennett, 1830)
Lyretail Hogfish

Maximum Length: 8.2 in. (21 cm).
Range: Indo-Pacific.
Minimum Aquarium Size: 75 gal. (284 L).
Foods & Feeding: Meaty foods, including fresh or frozen seafoods, frozen or live brine shrimp, mysid shrimp, live black worms, flake food, live grass shrimp. Feed at least 3 times a day.
Aquarium Suitability Index: 4.
Reef Aquarium Compatibility: Not recommended. Juveniles can be kept in the reef tank, but as they grow they will become a threat to crustaceans, worms, snails, and small clams.
Captive Care: The hogfishes are commendable, generally robust wrasses that readily adapt to aquarium life. Adults are quite active and need plenty of swimming space. Small juveniles may not survive in a competitive community tank; to increase their chances of survival, house with docile fish species and provide ample hiding places. Juveniles will often clean other fishes in captivity. This species is one of the least aggressive hogfishes, but is best kept with moderately aggressive tankmates. Larger Lyretail Hogfish often blow jets of water at the sand surface from their mouths to uncover buried prey.

Bodianus bimaculatus Allen, 1973
Twinspot Hogfish (Twospot Slender Hogfish, Yellow Hogfish)

Maximum Length: 3.9 in. (10 cm).
Range: Indo-west-Pacific.
Minimum Aquarium Size: 20 gal. (76 L).
Foods & Feeding: Meaty foods, including fresh or frozen seafoods, frozen or live brine shrimp, mysid shrimp, live black worms, flake food, live grass shrimp. Feed at least 3 times a day.
Aquarium Suitability Index: 4.
Reef Aquarium Compatibility: One of the best hogfishes for the reef aquarium. Although it can be acclimated to the brighter conditions of the shallow reef tank, it does best in deep-water reef tanks.
Captive Care: This is great aquarium fish that readily adjusts to life in captivity. Its diminutive size makes it an ideal hogfish for the aquarist with a smaller tank. Juveniles do best if housed with nonaggressive tankmates, but as this species grows, it will become more boisterous and may bully smaller, more-docile fish species, such as seahorses, pipefishes, flasher wrasses, leopard wrasses, and dartfishes. House singly unless the tank is large (100 gal. [379 L] or larger), in which case, introduce all individuals at the same time.

Bodianus diana (Lacépède, 1801)
Diana's Hogfish (Spotted Hogfish)

Maximum Length: 9.8 in. (25 cm).
Range: Indo-west-Pacific.
Minimum Aquarium Size: 55 gal. (208 L).
Foods & Feeding: Meaty foods, including fresh or frozen seafoods, frozen or live brine shrimp, mysid shrimp, live black worms, flake food, live grass shrimp. Feed at least 3 times a day.
Aquarium Suitability Index: 4.
Reef Aquarium Compatibility: Not recommended. Will not bother corals but will eat a wide range of motile invertebrates (e.g., snails, crabs, shrimps).
Captive Care: Hardy and a greedy feeder, this is a solitary fish in nature and is one of the least sociable members of the genus, often behaving aggressively toward newly introduced fishes or more-docile tankmates. Adults may even nip persistently at juvenile morays. Will eat any smaller fish that can be ingested whole. Juveniles can be housed in a shallow- or deep-water reef aquarium, but they will begin to prey upon small bivalves, clams, worms, and crustaceans as they grow.

Bodianus rufus (Linnaeus, 1758)
Spanish Hogfish

Maximum Length: 15.7 in. (40 cm).
Range: Tropical Western Atlantic.
Minimum Aquarium Size: 180 gal. (681 L).
Foods & Feeding: Meaty foods, including fresh or frozen seafoods, frozen or live brine shrimp, mysid shrimp, live black worms, flake food, live grass shrimp. Feed at least 2 times a day.
Aquarium Suitability Index: 4.
Reef Aquarium Compatibility: Not recommended. Juveniles can be kept in the reef tank, but as they mature they will become a threat to crustaceans, worms, snails, and clams.
Captive Care: An attractive and rugged fish, this Caribbean hogfish can be shy and retiring when first introduced to the aquarium, but within a day or two it will become bold and boisterous. Adolescent and adult individuals should not be kept with docile fish species, as they are likely to bully them. This is an active species that fits in well with moderately aggressive tankmates; larger specimens require plenty of swimming room. Juveniles will often clean other fishes in captivity, although they are not as dependent as some of the obligatory cleaners on parasites or fish slime for survival.

Bodianus axillaris
Axilspot Hogfish
Max. Length: 7.9 in. (20 cm).
Aquarium Suitability: 4.

Bodianus bilunulatus
Saddleback or Hawaiian Hogfish
Max. Length: 21.7 in. (55 cm).
Aquarium Suitability: 4.

Bodianus bilunulatus (juv.)
Saddleback or Hawaiian Hogfish
Max. Length: 21.7 in. (55 cm).
Aquarium Suitability: 4.

Bodianus loxozonus
Blackfin Hogfish
Max. Length: 18.5 in. (47 cm).
Aquarium Suitability: 4.

Bodianus mesothorax
Coral or Mesothorax Hogfish
Max. Length: 7.5 in. (19 cm).
Aquarium Suitability: 4.

Bodianus pulchellus
Spotfin or Cuban Hogfish
Max. Length: 5.9 in. (15 cm).
Aquarium Suitability: 4.

Cheilinus oxycephalus Bleeker, 1853
Snooty Maori Wrasse

Maximum Length: 6.7 in. (17 cm).
Range: Indo-west-Pacific.
Minimum Aquarium Size: 55 gal. (208 L).
Foods & Feeding: Meaty foods, including fresh or frozen seafoods, frozen or live brine shrimp, mysid shrimp, live black worms, flake food, live grass shrimp. Feed at least 3 times a day.
Aquarium Suitability Index: 4.
Reef Aquarium Compatibility: Safe with corals, but will eat small fishes, ornamental crustaceans, and many other desirable motile invertebrates (including snails and serpent stars) as well as pests, such as bristleworms and small mantis shrimps.
Captive Care: One of a group of wrasses whose facial patterns suggest the decorative skin art of the Maori people of New Zealand and give them their common name. This is a secretive and rather sensitive species; good hiding places and less-aggressive tankmates are a prerequisite for successful acclimation. If it settles in and feeds well, it will thrive. It tends to be less aggressive than its congeners, so it can be kept with less-pugnacious species, but should not be added to an aquarium with small, passive fishes.

Choerodon fasciatus (Günther, 1867)
Harlequin Tuskfish

Maximum Length: 9.8 in. (25 cm).
Range: Indo-west-Pacific.
Minimum Aquarium Size: 55 gal. (208 L).
Foods & Feeding: Meaty foods, including chopped, fresh or frozen seafoods, frozen preparations for carnivores, frozen or live brine shrimp, mysid shrimp, live black worms, even small feeder fish. Feed at least 3 times a day.
Aquarium Suitability Index: 4.
Reef Aquarium Compatibility: Not recommended. Will not bother corals but will eat a wide range of motile invertebrates (e.g., snails, crabs, shrimps).
Captive Care: This magnificent fish makes a wonderful addition to the aggressive community tank. Juveniles are less bold than more-mature specimens and will spend time hiding until they gain size and competitive confidence. Adults, especially, may behave aggressively toward newly introduced fishes and docile tankmates. Keep with larger angelfishes, boisterous wrasses, surgeonfishes, sociable triggers, puffers, and the like. Keep only one per tank. Specimens from the Great Barrier Reef tend to be more colorful.

MALE

Cirrhilabrus cyanopleura (Bleeker, 1851)
Bluehead Fairy Wrasse (Yellowflanked Fairy Wrasse, Purplehead "Parrotfish")

Maximum Length: 5.1 in. (13 cm).
Range: Eastern Indian Ocean and Western Pacific.
Minimum Aquarium Size: 55 gal. (208 L).
Foods & Feeding: Meaty foods, including vitamin-enriched mysid shrimp, vitamin-enriched brine shrimp, and high-quality frozen preparations. Feed at least 3 times a day.
Aquarium Suitability Index: 4.
Reef Aquarium Compatibility: Excellent.
Captive Care: This is a great reef fish that displays a range of attractive color patterns. Like others in its genus, it is not a threat to ornamental invertebrates and does well if properly acclimated. Sometimes ships poorly, so do not be too hasty about taking a new specimen home. Does best with less-aggressive tankmates and numerous places to hide. Often kept in a small groups of one male and up to four females, but solitary specimens can also thrive. More than one male can be kept in a spacious tank (180 gal. [681 L] or larger), but they should be introduced simultaneously. May behave aggressively toward other fairy wrasses and zooplankton feeders.

MALE

Cirrhilabrus luteovittatus Randall, 1988
Yellowstreaked Fairy Wrasse (Yellowband Wrasse)

Maximum Length: 4.7 in. (12 cm).
Range: Western Pacific.
Minimum Aquarium Size: 55 gal. (208 L).
Foods & Feeding: Meaty foods, including vitamin-enriched mysid shrimp or brine shrimp and frozen preparations. Feed at least 3 times a day.
Aquarium Suitability Index: 3.
Reef Aquarium Compatibility: Excellent, but prefers dim lighting.
Captive Care: Large males of this species are eyecatching, but often prove much more difficult to acclimate than the less-colorful females. Once adjusted, however, they are equally hardy. Provide with plenty of swimming space and do not place two males in the same tank, unless the tank is very large. This fish prefers a dimly lit aquarium, making it difficult to acclimate to a shallow-water reef tank. Females are olive and purplish blue overall, with two rows of red spots from the pectoral fin base to the caudal fin. Males are maroon overall, with a dark bar at the base of the pectoral fin, a bright yellow streak on the flank, and blue stripes on the dorsal and anal fins, which intensify during courtship.

MALE

Cirrhilabrus rubriventralis Springer & Randall, 1974
Longfin Fairy Wrasse (Social Wrasse)

Maximum Length: 2.9 in. (7.5 cm).
Range: Indian Ocean and Red Sea.
Minimum Aquarium Size: 30 gal. (114 L).
Foods & Feeding: Meaty foods, including vitamin-enriched mysid shrimp, vitamin-enriched brine shrimp, and high-quality frozen preparations. Feed at least 3 times a day.
Aquarium Suitability Index: 4.
Reef Aquarium Compatibility: Excellent.
Captive Care: Known by its scarlet ventral and anal fins, this is a popular species among marine aquarists, and for good reason—it's beautiful and reasonably hardy. It is a great reef fish that is not a threat to ornamental invertebrates. Specimens may become quite aggressive after living in a tank for a while, chasing and nipping other small wrasses, nonaggressive anthias, and even tobies (a.k.a. sharpnose puffers). To keep more than one specimen, choose one male and several females. However, it is possible to place two males in the same aquarium if the tank is spacious with ample hiding places. Will jump from open aquariums.

MALE

Cirrhilabrus scottorum Randall & Pyle, 1989
Scott's Fairy Wrasse

Maximum Length: 5.1 in. (13 cm).
Range: Western, South, and Central Pacific.
Minimum Aquarium Size: 55 gal. (208 L).
Foods & Feeding: Meaty foods, including vitamin-enriched mysid shrimp or brine shrimp, and high-quality frozen preparations. Feed at least 3 times a day.
Aquarium Suitability Index: 4.
Reef Aquarium Compatibility: Excellent. A good choice for a shallow- or deep-water reef tank.
Captive Care: Extraordinary coloration and hardiness make this a favorite among reef aquarists. Large males are most frequently available because they ship well and are in demand, but smaller specimens tend to acclimate more readily. A new individual should be given plenty of hiding places. Once acclimated, it will become less reclusive and can be quite boisterous, feeding greedily. Do not attempt to house two males together unless the tank is extremely large. Females should be introduced before, or at least at the same time as, the male. Large males will behave aggressively toward other fairy wrasses introduced after them. Notorious for jumping from open aquariums.

Cirrhilabrus exquisitus (male)
Exquisite Fairy Wrasse
Max. Length: 4.7 in. (12 cm).
Aquarium Suitability: 4.

Cirrhilabrus lubbocki (male)
Lubbock's Fairy Wrasse
Max. Length: 3.1 in. (8 cm).
Aquarium Suitability: 4.

Cirrhilabrus punctatus (male)
Finespotted Fairy Wrasse
Max. Length: 5.1 in. (13 cm).
Aquarium Suitability: 3.

Cirrhilabrus rubripinnis (male)
Redfin Fairy Wrasse
Max. Length: 3.1 in. (8 cm).
Aquarium Suitability: 4.

Cirrhilabrus rubromarginatus (male)
Redmargin Fairy Wrasse
Max. Length: 5.5 in. (14 cm).
Aquarium Suitability: 3.

Cirrhilabrus solorensis (male)
Redheaded or Solar Fairy Wrasse
Max. Length: 5.1 in. (13 cm).
Aquarium Suitability: 4.

Coris aygula Lacépède, 1801
Twinspot Coris (Clown Coris)

Maximum Length: 47.2 in. (120 cm) reported, although few exceed 21.7 in. (55 cm).
Range: Indo-Pacific.
Minimum Aquarium Size: 180 gal. (681 L).
Foods & Feeding: Meaty foods, including fresh or frozen seafoods, frozen or live brine shrimp, mysid shrimp, live black worms, flake food, live grass shrimp. Feed at least 3 times a day.
Aquarium Suitability Index: 4.
Reef Aquarium Compatibility: Not recommended. An opportunistic predator that will eat snails, mollusks, hermit crabs, crabs, shrimps, and sea urchins. Larger individuals are adept at flipping over a wide range of corals and live rock.
Captive Care: From cute, bright little juveniles, this species transforms into formidable dark green, bulbous-headed adults that require plenty of swimming space and large tankmates that cannot be bullied or eaten. Tiny juveniles are difficult to keep because of their high caloric requirements, and individuals greater than 2 in. (5 cm) are preferable. *Coris* spp. wrasses require a layer of fine sand 2-4 in. (5-10 cm) deep in which to bury themselves at night.

Coris frerei Playfair & Günther, 1867
Formosan Coris (Queen Coris)

Maximum Length: 23.6 in. (60 cm).
Range: Indian Ocean.
Minimum Aquarium Size: 135 gal. (511 L).
Foods & Feeding: Meaty foods, including fresh or frozen seafoods, frozen or live brine shrimp, mysid shrimp, live black worms, flake food, live grass shrimp. Feed at least 3 times a day.
Aquarium Suitability Index: 4.
Reef Aquarium Compatibility: Not recommended. An opportunistic predator that will eat snails, mollusks, hermit crabs, crabs, shrimps, and sea urchins. Larger individuals are adept at flipping over a wide range of corals and live rock.
Captive Care: This is an interesting fish that will thrive in the home aquarium, with spectacular transformations of coloration as it grows. Typically not aggressive toward other fishes, although larger individuals may harass smaller tankmates. Juveniles can be housed together, but may fight as they become larger. Large wild adults do not ship well, and tiny juveniles are difficult to feed; subadult individuals greater than 2.0 in. (5 cm) are preferable. Provide a layer of fine sand 2-4 in. (5-10 cm) deep where they can bury at night.

MAIN PHOTO, ADULT; INSET, JUVENILE

Coris gaimard (Quoy & Gaimard, 1824)
Yellowtail Coris (Red Coris)

Maximum Length: 13.7 in. (35 cm).

Range: Indo-Pacific.

Minimum Aquarium Size: 100 gal. (379 L).

Foods & Feeding: Meaty foods, including fresh or frozen seafoods, frozen or live brine shrimp, mysid shrimp, live black worms, flake food, live grass shrimp. Feed at least 3 times a day.

Aquarium Suitability Index: 4.

Reef Aquarium Compatibility: Not recommended. An opportunistic predator that will eat snails, mollusks, hermit crabs, crabs, shrimps, and sea urchins. Larger individuals may rearrange aquascaping. May eat pyramidellid snails (which are parasites of tridacnid clams).

Captive Care: Flashy juveniles morph into eyecatching adults in this aquarium-hardy species. They are typically not aggressive toward other fishes, although larger individuals may harass smaller tank-mates. Tiny juveniles are difficult to keep because of their high caloric requirements, and subadult individuals greater than 2.0 in. (5 cm) are preferable. *Coris* spp. wrasses require a layer of fine sand 2-4 in. (5-10 cm) deep in which to bury themselves at night. Large adults should be provided plenty of swimming space.

MALE

Gomphosus varius (Lacépède, 1801)
Bird Wrasse (Green Bird Wrasse, Brown Bird Wrasse)

Maximum Length: 11.0 in. (28 cm).
Range: Indo-Pacific.
Minimum Aquarium Size: 100 gal. (379 L).
Foods & Feeding: Meaty foods, including vitamin-enriched mysid shrimp and brine shrimp and frozen preparations. Feed at least 3 times a day.
Aquarium Suitability Index: 5.
Reef Aquarium Compatibility: Will eat worms, including troublesome fireworms, as well as ornamental crustaceans and small clams.
Captive Care: This unusual beaked wrasse is very hardy and wonderfully active in the aquarium. It needs plenty of unobstructed swimming room as well as suitable rocky hiding places. (It does not bury in the substrate after dark.) Keep only one male per tank; a male and a female should be introduced simultaneously or add the female first. Males are green; females are brown. Can become aggressive toward its tankmates, especially smaller fishes. It will grasp an elongate prey fish in its jaws and bash it against the substrate until it breaks into bite-sized pieces. The Bird Wrasse is a proficient jumper and will leap out of an open tank.

Halichoeres chloropterus (Bloch, 1791)
Green Wrasse (Pastel Green Wrasse, Green "Coris")

Maximum Length: 7.4 in. (19 cm).
Range: Western Pacific.
Minimum Aquarium Size: 55 gal. (208 L).
Foods & Feeding: Meaty foods, including fresh or frozen seafoods, frozen or live brine shrimp, mysid shrimp, live black worms, flake food, live grass shrimp. Feed at least 3 times a day.
Aquarium Suitability Index: 4.
Reef Aquarium Compatibility: Safe with corals, but a potential threat to fanworms, small snails, and ornamental shrimps. Will feed on fireworms, pyramidellid snails (which are parasites of tridacnid clams), and flatworms.
Captive Care: This is a lovely green aquarium fish that generally proves to be durable if it survives the shipping process. Although smaller specimens usually cause little trouble in the community tank, larger individuals have been known to pick on small, more-passive wrasses, like flasher wrasses and some of the more-diminutive fairy wrasses. May be kept in groups. Provide with a 2 in. (5 cm) layer of fine sand in which it will sleep and escape when chased. Like others in this genus, it is very prone to jumping from open aquariums.

Halichoeres chrysus Randall, 1981
Golden Wrasse (Canary Wrasse, Yellow "Coris")

Maximum Length: 4.7 in. (12 cm).
Range: Eastern Indian Ocean to Central Pacific.
Minimum Aquarium Size: 30 gal. (114 L).
Foods & Feeding: Meaty foods, including fresh or frozen seafoods, frozen or live brine shrimp, mysid shrimp, live black worms, flake food, live grass shrimp. Feed at least 3 times a day.
Aquarium Suitability Index: 4.
Reef Aquarium Compatibility: Safe with corals, but a potential threat to fanworms, small snails, and ornamental shrimps. Will feed on fireworms, flatworms, and pyramidellid snails (which are parasites of tridacnid clams).
Captive Care: A great beginner's fish for smaller aquariums, as well as an especially attractive addition to a larger reef tank when kept in aggregations of 4-5 individuals. It is nonaggressive and can be housed with docile species, such as leopard wrasses, flasher wrasses, firefishes, and razor gobies. This species may clean other fishes in captivity and this should not be confused with aggressive behavior. Provide with a 2 in. (5 cm) layer of fine sand on the aquarium bottom where it will bury at night or when frightened. Will jump from open tanks.

Halichoeres hortulanus
Checkerboard Wrasse
Max. Length: 10.6 in. (27 cm).
Aquarium Suitability: 4.

Halichoeres iridis
Orangehead, Iridis, or Radiant Wrasse
Max. Length: 4.5 in. (11.5 cm).
Aquarium Suitability: 4.

Halichoeres marginatus
Dusky Wrasse
Max. Length: 6.7 in. (17 cm).
Aquarium Suitability: 3.

Halichoeres melanurus
Tailspot or Neon Wrasse
Max. Length: 4.7 in. (12 cm).
Aquarium Suitability: 4.

Halichoeres ornatissimus
Ornate Wrasse
Max. Length: 6.7 in. (17 cm).
Aquarium Suitability: 4.

Halichoeres scapularis
Zigzag Wrasse
Max. Length: 7.9 in. (20 cm)
Aquarium Suitability: 4.

Hemigymnus melapterus (Bloch, 1791)
Blackedge Thicklip Wrasse (Half-and-Half Wrasse)

Maximum Length: 19.7 in. (50 cm).
Range: Indo-Pacific.
Minimum Aquarium Size: 180 gal. (681 L).
Foods & Feeding: Can be difficult to feed; even when it does eat it tends to waste away. Does best in a tank with live rock. Offer vitamin-enriched live brine shrimp and frozen mysid shrimp. Feed 3-5 times a day.
Aquarium Suitability Index: 2.
Reef Aquarium Compatibility: Will eat ornamental crustaceans, fanworms, and small clams.
Captive Care: Dramatically colored juveniles are commonly available in the aquarium trade. This is unfortunate, because most do not survive captivity. It will often refuse to eat anything but its natural prey and even if it does survive, adults are too large and active for most home aquariums. Keep one per tank and do not house with more-aggressive species unless in a very large tank. Needs plenty of swimming room. Will take mouthfuls of substrate, sift out the edibles, and spit the remainder out, helping to keep a sand bed well stirred.

Hologymnosus doliatus Lacépède, 1801
Candycane Wrasse (Longface Wrasse, Pastel Ringwrasse)

Maximum Length: 15.0 in. (38 cm).
Range: Indo-Pacific.
Minimum Aquarium Size: 135 gal. (511 L).
Foods & Feeding: Meaty foods, including fresh or frozen seafoods, frozen preparations, frozen or live brine shrimp, mysid shrimp, live black worms, cleaned earthworms, live grass shrimp, and even small feeder fish. Feed at least 2 times a day.
Aquarium Suitability Index: 4.
Reef Aquarium Compatibility: Ignores corals, but will feed on small fishes and ornamental crustaceans, including shrimps, crabs, brittlestars, and polychaete worms. Will also eat mantis shrimps.
Captive Care: Juveniles, regularly seen in the aquarium trade, are durable, attractively marked, and interesting to watch. Can be kept in small groups, up to 5 individuals, in bigger aquariums (135 gal. [511 L] or larger), but all specimens should be introduced simultaneously. Grows too large for many home systems. It buries at night, so fine coral sand or live sand should be used as substrate (create a layer about 4 in. [10 cm] deep). This species may jump out of the aquarium if frightened; a cover is required.

Labroides dimidiatus (Valenciennes, 1839)
Bluestreak Cleaner Wrasse (Cleaner Wrasse)

Maximum Length: 3.9 in. (10 cm).
Range: Indo-Pacific.
Minimum Aquarium Size: 30 gal. (114 L).
Foods & Feeding: Difficult to feed. May accept meaty foods, including chopped fresh or frozen seafoods, frozen preparations for carnivores, frozen or live brine shrimp, mysid shrimp, and live black worms. Feed at least 3 times a day.
Aquarium Suitability Index: 2.
Reef Aquarium Compatibility: Excellent. (An occasional specimen will nip at and irritate the mantles of tridacnid clams.)
Captive Care: One of a group of small cleaner wrasses that exist by grooming other fishes, this is the most common and durable of the genus. However, even this species will fare poorly unless kept with a large community of fishes from which it can browse mucus and parasites. This species is more likely to accept substitute foods, although not with gusto. In general, most aquarists are well advised to avoid cleaner wrasses, both because they have low survival rates in captivity and because their removal from the reef may deprive wild populations of valuable parasite-cleaning services.

Labroides bicolor
Bicolor Cleaner Wrasse
Max. Length: 4.7 in. (12 cm).
Aquarium Suitability: 2.

Labroides dimidiatus (variant)
Bluestreak Cleaner Wrasse
Max. Length: 3.9 in. (10 cm).
Aquarium Suitability: 2.

Labroides pectoralis
Blackspot Cleaner Wrasse
Max. Length: 3.1 in. (8 cm).
Aquarium Suitability: 2.

Labroides phthirophagus
Hawaiian Cleaner Wrasse
Max. Length: 3.9 in. (10 cm).
Aquarium Suitability: 1.

Labroides rubrolabiatus
Redlipped Cleaner Wrasse
Max. Length: 3.5 in. (9 cm).
Aquarium Suitability: 2.

Labropsis alleni
Allen's Wrasse
Max. Length: 3.9 in. (10 cm).
Aquarium Suitability: 2.

Larabicus quadrilineatus (Rüppell, 1835)
Red Sea Cleaner Wrasse

Maximum Length: 4.5 in. (11.5 cm).
Range: Red Sea.
Minimum Aquarium Size: 55 gal. (208 L).
Foods & Feeding: Adults are difficult to feed, as their natural diet consists only of stony coral polyps. Offer finely chopped seafoods and vitamin-enriched, live brine shrimp. They will also pick at live rock. Feed at least 3 times a day.
Aquarium Suitability Index: 2.
Reef Aquarium Compatibility: Adults will eat small-polyped stony corals; young are not destructive.
Captive Care: A brilliantly colored Red Sea rarity that typically defies the best husbandry efforts of aquarists. Juveniles exhibit the typical feeding behavior of cleaner wrasses, but their diet changes as they grow and adults feed almost exclusively on the polyps of stony corals. Keep just one per aquarium and only with placid tankmates. A juvenile may be tolerated by some of the more-aggressive species because of the cleaning services it provides, however, the author has had this wrasse eaten by groupers.

Macropharyngodon geoffroyi (Quoy & Gaimard, 1824)
Potter's Leopard Wrasse

Maximum Length: 6.2 in. (16 cm).
Range: Hawaiian Islands.
Minimum Aquarium Size: 55 gal. (208 L).
Foods & Feeding: Must be kept in a tank with live rock, which will enable it to forage continually on the associated micro-invertebrate fauna (e.g., foraminiferans). Feed supplemental foods daily, unless the system provides ample supplies of live food. Offer frozen preparations for carnivores, frozen or live brine shrimp, mysid shrimp, and live black worms. Feed several times a day.
Aquarium Suitability Index: 2.
Reef Aquarium Compatibility: Excellent.
Captive Care: Although beautiful, this Hawaiian endemic requires some special care and will starve if not kept in an established reef-type system with productive live rock. Competes poorly for food, and must not be housed with aggressive tankmates. Provide a 2.0-in. (5-cm) layer of fine sand where it can bury at night. Rarely aggressive toward other species or members of its own species (males may squabble). To keep more than one individual, add them simultaneously and include only one male per tank.

Macropharyngodon meleagris (Valenciennes, 1839)
Leopard Wrasse

Maximum Length: 5.9 in. (15 cm).
Range: Eastern Indian Ocean to Western Pacific.
Minimum Aquarium Size: 30 gal. (114 L).
Foods & Feeding: Difficult to feed. House in a well-established tank aquascaped with live rock and sand. Supplement with meaty foods: fresh or frozen seafoods, frozen preparations for carnivores, frozen or live brine shrimp, mysid shrimp, and live black worms. Feed several times a day, depending on the amount of food provided by natural populations of organisms in the rock and sand.
Aquarium Suitability Index: 2. ◣
Reef Aquarium Compatibility: Excellent.
Captive Care: This species' brilliant colors and modest size are typical of a desirable genus made challenging to keep by its feeding habits. Without live rock and its associated populations of microinvertebrate fauna (e.g., foraminiferans and amphipods), a *Macropharyngodon* spp. wrasse will usually starve to death. Sporting large teeth in a tiny mouth, it is rarely aggressive and should be placed with other accommodating species. Two males will fight, but females may be kept in groups. One may transform into a male.

Novaculichthys taeniourus (Lacépède, 1801)
Rockmover Wrasse (Dragon Wrasse)

Maximum Length: 11.8 in. (30 cm).
Range: Indo-Pacific.
Minimum Aquarium Size: 75 gal. (284 L).
Foods & Feeding: Meaty foods, including chopped, fresh or frozen seafoods, krill, frozen or live brine shrimp, mysid shrimp, live black worms, cleaned earthworms, flake food, live grass shrimp, and even small feeder fish. Feed at least 3 times a day.
Aquarium Suitability Index: 4. ◤
Reef Aquarium Compatibility: Will eat small fishes, ornamental crustaceans, and many other motile invertebrates (including snails, serpent stars, bristleworms and mantis shrimps). Notorious for flipping over large pieces of rock and rubble and will also turn over live corals.
Captive Care: A handsome, fascinating-to-watch wrasse for larger aquariums. Juveniles are suitable for the community tank, but as they grow they become very aggressive. Keep with more-belligerent or larger fishes. Limit one specimen per tank. This species buries and will require 2-4 in. (5 to 10 cm) of fine sand substrate on the aquarium bottom. Even large individuals will jump from uncovered tanks.

Oxycheilinus bimaculatus Valenciennes, 1840
Twinspot Maori Wrasse (Red Longjaw Wrasse)

Maximum Length: 5.9 in. (15 cm).
Range: Indo-Pacific.
Minimum Aquarium Size: 30 gal. (114 L).
Foods & Feeding: Meaty foods, including fresh or frozen seafoods, frozen preparations for carnivores, frozen or live brine shrimp, mysid shrimp, live black worms, flake food, live grass shrimp, and even small feeder fish. Feed at least 3 times a day.
Aquarium Suitability Index: 5. ■
Reef Aquarium Compatibility: Will eat small fishes, ornamental crustaceans, and many other motile invertebrates (including snails and serpent stars). Will also eat bristleworms and small mantis shrimps.
Captive Care: Usually sold as the Red Longjaw Wrasse, this species is the smallest member of its genus and is attractively marked. (So-called Maori wrasses are found both in this genus and the closely related *Cheilinus*.) It is a fairly durable fish that will quickly acclimate to captive life. Although it becomes quite aggressive once it has fully adjusted to its new home, if introduced to a tank that already contains pugnacious species, it may have difficulty acclimating. Males display an elongated point on the upper lobe of the tail fin.

Paracheilinus carpenteri Randall & Harmelin-Vivien, 1977
Carpenter's Flasher Wrasse (Redfin Flasher Wrasse)

Maximum Length: 3.1 in. (8 cm).
Range: Indonesia and Philippines.
Minimum Aquarium Size: 20 gal. (76 L).
Foods & Feeding: Varied diet of meaty foods, including finely chopped seafoods, mysid shrimp, and enriched preparations with added vitamins, amino acids, and color-enhancing pigments. Feed at least 3 times a day.
Aquarium Suitability Index: 4.
Reef Aquarium Compatibility: Excellent.
Captive Care: With males that strike dramatic fin-flaring poses, this is a great reef aquarium species that will adapt readily to captivity, especially if housed with other peaceful fishes. Best kept in small groups to encourage "flashing," but add all individuals at the same time or put the females in before the male. Rarely aggressive toward other fishes and easily bullied itself. If persistently harassed when introduced to a tank, it will hide and never come out to feed. To keep it with potentially quarrelsome fishes, the wrasse should be the first fish in the tank. A good diet of enriched foods is required to maintain health and color intensity.

Paracheilinus filamentosus Allen, 1974
Filamented Flasher Wrasse

Maximum Length: 3.9 in. (10 cm).
Range: Western Pacific.
Minimum Aquarium Size: 20 gal. (76 L).
Foods & Feeding: Varied diet required to maintain vibrant coloration. Include finely chopped seafoods, mysid shrimp, and frozen preparations with added amino acids and color-enhancing pigments. Feed at least 3 times a day.
Aquarium Suitability Index: 4.
Reef Aquarium Compatibility: Excellent.
Captive Care: A great reef aquarium fish, especially when kept in groups, which will provoke male flasher wrasses to perform colorful displays, important in courtship and in defending females from neighboring rivals. Solitary males occasionally "flash" at their reflections in the aquarium glass. Adapt readily to captivity, especially if housed with other peaceful fishes. Best kept in small groups, but add all individuals at the same time or put the females in before the male. Except for close relatives (e.g., fairy wrasses) and other small planktivores (e.g., fire gobies), it is rarely aggressive. Groups serve as "dither" fish, encouraging other shy fishes to move into the open.

Paracheilinus angulatus
Lyretail or Angular Flasher Wrasse
Max. Length: 2.8 in. (7 cm).
Aquarium Suitability: 4.

Paracheilinus filamentosus (variant)
Filamented Flasher Wrasse
Max. Length: 3.9 in. (10 cm).
Aquarium Suitability: 4.

Paracheilinus lineopunctatus
Dot-and-Dash Flasher Wrasse
Max. Length: 2.6 in. (6.5 cm).
Aquarium Suitability: 4.

Paracheilinus mccoskeri
McCosker's Flasher Wrasse
Max. Length: 2.8 in. (7 cm).
Aquarium Suitability: 4.

Paracheilinus sp.
Pink Flasher Wrasse
Max. Length: 3.1 in. (8 cm).
Aquarium Suitability: 4.

Paracheilinus flavianalis
Yellowfin Flasher Wrasse
Max. Length: 3.1 in. (8 cm).
Aquarium Suitability: 4.

Paracheilinus octotaenia Fourmanoir, 1955
Eightline Flasher Wrasse (Red Sea Flasher Wrasse)

Maximum Length: 3.5 in. (9 cm).
Range: Red Sea.
Minimum Aquarium Size: 20 gal. (76 L).
Foods & Feeding: Varied diet, including finely chopped seafoods, mysid shrimp, and frozen preparations with added amino acids and pigments to ensure maintenance of vibrant coloration Feed at least 3 times a day.
Aquarium Suitability Index: 4.

Captive Care: A relative newcomer to the aquarium world, this brilliantly colored species is a welcome addition to the reef aquarium or peaceful fish tank. It is the most aggressive member of the genus; males will usually dominate other flasher wrasses if kept in mixed aggregations. Males should be kept singly, unless the tank is very large (135 gal. [511 L] or larger). When creating groups, house one male with several females so that aggression is dispersed. Best kept with less-aggressive fish species. Very likely to jump out of an open aquarium.

Pseudocheilinus evanidus Jordan & Evermann, 1903
Secretive Wrasse (Striated Wrasse)

Maximum Length: 3.1 in. (8 cm).
Range: Indo-Pacific.
Minimum Aquarium Size: 20 gal. (76 L).
Foods & Feeding: Prefers live grass shrimp but will eat frozen brine shrimp and chopped seafoods. Feed at least 2 times a day, depending on availability of live foods.
Aquarium Suitability Index: 3.
Reef Aquarium Compatibility: Not harmful to sessile invertebrates; adult specimens will eat ornamental shrimps. Will eat small fireworms.
Captive Care: This is a cryptic species that requires suitable caves and crevices where it can hide and seem to vanish for considerable periods of time. It often ships poorly and can be a challenge to acclimate successfully. Does best in aquariums with live rock aquascaping. It has a territorial, scrappy disposition, and will battle fiercely with its own kind, as well as other members of the genus. It should be kept with larger, moderately boisterous fishes, and even in an aggressive community tank, it should be one of the first fishes introduced. Will jump from open aquariums.

Pseudocheilinus hexataenia (Bleeker, 1857)
Sixline Wrasse

Maximum Length: 3.0 in. (7.5 cm).
Range: Indo-Pacific.
Minimum Aquarium Size: 20 gal. (76 L).
Foods & Feeding: Meaty foods, including finely chopped seafoods, mysid shrimp, and enriched frozen preparations. Feed at least 2 times a day; less if kept in a tank with productive live rock.
Aquarium Suitability Index: 5.
Reef Aquarium Compatibility: Excellent. Will aid in controlling pyramidellid snails and commensal flatworms. Larger specimens may eat ornamental shrimps.
Captive Care: An active, attractive species that will constantly forage on live rock for small crustaceans, this wrasse often ships poorly, but once acclimated, it is a good aquarium fish. It is a smaller, less-aggressive species than *P. octotaenia*, page 312, and better suited for the community tank. However, it will often behave aggressively toward peaceful wrasses and shy, inoffensive species. Several specimens can be housed in the same tank, but fighting may occur if population densities are too high. Because this is a secretive species, it needs numerous hiding places.

Pseudocheilinus octotaenia Jenkins, 1900
Eightline Wrasse

Maximum Length: 5.3 in. (13.5 cm).
Range: Indo-Pacific.
Minimum Aquarium Size: 20 gal. (76 L).
Foods & Feeding: Meaty foods, including finely chopped seafoods, mysid shrimp, and enriched frozen preparations. Feed at least 2 times a day; less if kept in a tank with productive live rock.
Aquarium Suitability Index: 4. ◣
Reef Aquarium Compatibility: Harmless with corals and clams, but a predator on small crabs and other crustaceans (including ornamental shrimps), and small snails. Also preys on bristleworms, small urchins, pyramidellid snails, and commensal flatworms.
Captive Care: Larger than the similar-looking *P. hexataenia*, page 311, this species is also much more aggressively inclined; it frequently assaults smaller tankmates, shredding fins and removing scales quite effectively with its large canine teeth. Will grasp small sea urchins in its mouth and bash them against hard substrate until they are broken into smaller, edible pieces. Best kept singly and with larger or more-belligerent fishes. If kept in an aggressive community tank, this species should be added first.

Pseudocheilinus tetrataenia Schultz, 1960
Fourline Wrasse

Maximum Length: 2.9 in. (7.3 cm).
Range: Western and Central Pacific.
Minimum Aquarium Size: 20 gal. (76 L).
Foods & Feeding: Meaty foods, including finely chopped seafoods, mysid shrimp, and enriched frozen preparations. Feed at least 2 times a day; less if kept in a tank with productive live rock.
Aquarium Suitability Index: 5. ▆
Reef Aquarium Compatibility: Excellent. Will aid in controlling pyramidellid snails and commensal flatworms; may attack ornamental shrimps.
Captive Care: A small species usually imported from the Hawaiian Islands, this fish often ships poorly but will prove to be a good aquarium fish once it settles in. It is suited to less-belligerent community tanks and smaller reef aquariums, but may behave aggressively toward peaceful wrasses (e.g., flasher, fairy, and leopard wrasses) and shy, inoffensive species (e.g., gobies, dart gobies). Somewhat secretive, it does best in an aquarium with live rock where it can hide and forage.

MALE

Pseudojuloides cerasinus (Snyder, 1904)
Smalltail Wrasse (Pencil Wrasse)

Maximum Length: 4.7 in. (12 cm).
Range: Indo-Pacific.
Minimum Aquarium Size: 30 gal. (114 L).
Foods & Feeding: Difficult to feed; even when it does eat it tends to pine away. Keep in a tank with live rock and feed vitamin-enriched live brine shrimp and frozen mysid shrimp at least 3 times a day.
Aquarium Suitability Index: 2.
Reef Aquarium Compatibility: Not harmful to sessile invertebrates, but adult specimens may attack more-delicate ornamental shrimps. Will eat small fireworms.
Captive Care: Should be avoided by the vast majority of aquarists. Some reef aquarists have had success keeping it in tanks full of healthy live rock with a productive refugium attached. Provide it with plenty of hiding places, including a layer of sand in which it can bury when threatened or at night. Do not house with aggressive tank-mates. Keep only one male per tank. Two or more females can be kept together or with a male. Females are light red or orange.

MALE

Pseudojuloides sp.
Pink Pencil Wrasse

Maximum Length: 3.9 in. (10 cm).

Range: Philippines.

Minimum Aquarium Size: 30 gal. (114 L).

Foods & Feeding: Difficult to feed; even when it does eat it tends to pine away. Does best if kept in a tank with live rock and fed vitamin-enriched live brine shrimp and frozen mysid shrimp at least 3 times a day.

Aquarium Suitability Index: 2.

Reef Aquarium Compatibility: Not harmful to sessile invertebrates; adult specimens may attack more-delicate ornamental shrimps. Will eat small fireworms.

Captive Care: The long, slender pencil wrasses have showy coloration but tend to be a challenge to keep successfully in the aquarium. Chances of success are increased in a tank full of healthy live rock with a productive refugium attached to provide a regular supply of live foods. These fishes must have plenty of hiding places, a layer of fine sand in which they can bury when threatened or at night, and nonaggressive tankmates. Keep only one male per tank; two or more females can be placed together or with a male.

MAIN PHOTO, ADULT; INSET, JUVENILE

Pseudodax moluccanus (Valenciennes, 1839)
Chiseltooth Wrasse

Maximum Length: 9.8 in. (25 cm).
Range: Indo-Pacific.
Minimum Aquarium Size: 75 gal. (284 L).
Foods & Feeding: Meaty foods, including finely chopped shrimp, squid, or marine fish flesh, and frozen mysid shrimp. Finicky specimens may require vitamin-enriched live brine shrimp or small grass shrimp. Feed at least 3 times a day.
Aquarium Suitability Index: 3.
Reef Aquarium Compatibility: Not harmful to sessile invertebrates; adult specimens may eat more-delicate ornamental shrimps and small clams. Will consume small fireworms and fanworms.
Captive Care: Not as flashy as some of the other wrasses, this is a handsome species nonetheless. Juveniles are black with blue lines and act as part-time cleaners. This species tends to ship poorly, but juveniles will acclimate better than larger specimens. Provide good hiding places, including a layer of fine sand in which they can bury when threatened and at night. Adults can hold their own with more-aggressive fishes once they have acclimated. Keep only one male per tank; two or more females can be housed together or with a male.

Stethojulis balteata (Quoy & Gaimard, 1824)
Belted Wrasse

Maximum Length: 5.9 in. (15 cm).
Range: Hawaiian Islands and Johnston Atoll.
Minimum Aquarium Size: 55 gal. (208 L).
Foods & Feeding: Difficult to feed. Even when eating, it tends to pine away. Does best if kept in a tank with live rock and fed meaty foods, including vitamin-enriched live brine shrimp and frozen mysid shrimp. Feed at least 3 times a day.
Aquarium Suitability Index: 2.
Reef Aquarium Compatibility: Not harmful to sessile invertebrates, but adult specimens may eat more-delicate, small ornamental shrimps.
Captive Care: This beautiful wrasse usually does not fare well in captivity. In the wild, it feeds by taking mouthfuls of sand and spitting out the inedibles and lives on relatively small prey items. Chances of success increase slightly in a tank full of healthy live rock, live sand, and a productive refugium attached. Provide with plenty of hiding places, including a layer of sand in which it can bury when threatened and at night. Avoid placing it with aggressive tankmates. Males should be kept singly, but a male and one or more females can share the same tank.

Thalassoma lunare (Linnaeus, 1758)
Moon Wrasse (Lunare Wrasse)

Maximum Length: 9.8 in. (25 cm).
Range: Indo-Pacific.
Minimum Aquarium Size: 75 gal. (284 L).
Foods & Feeding: Meaty foods, including chopped, fresh or frozen seafoods, frozen preparations for carnivores, frozen or live brine shrimp, mysid shrimp, flake foods. Feed at least 3 times a day.
Aquarium Suitability Index: 5. ▔▔
Reef Aquarium Compatibility: Harmless with corals, but will eat small fishes, ornamental crustaceans, and many other motile invertebrates, including snails, serpent stars, bristleworms, and mantis shrimps.
Captive Care: This and other members of the genus *Thalassoma* start as drab juveniles but grow into exceptionally beautiful and hardy adults that make great display specimens. They need plenty of swimming room and will harass new introductions to the aquarium if they are smaller or similar in shape. This species is highly predatory and will make short work of smaller fishes; keep with more-belligerent or larger fishes. A male and female can occupy the same tank if it is at least 125 gal. (473 L). *Thalassoma* spp. wrasses do not bury in the sand, but hide among rockwork at night or when frightened.

Thalassoma bifasciatum (male)
Bluehead Wrasse
Max. Length: 7.1 in. (18 cm).
Aquarium Suitability: 4.

Thalassoma duperrey (male)
Saddle Wrasse
Max. Length: 9.8 in. (25 cm).
Aquarium Suitability: 4.

Thalassoma hardwicke (male)
Hardwick's or Sixbar Wrasse
Max. Length: 7.9 in. (20 cm).
Aquarium Suitability: 4.

Thalassoma lucasanum (female)
Rainbow Wrasse
Max. Length: 3.9 in. (10 cm).
Aquarium Suitability: 4.

Thalassoma lucasanum (male)
Rainbow Wrasse
Max. Length: 3.9 in. (10 cm).
Aquarium Suitability: 4.

Thalassoma lutescens (female)
Sunset or Banana Wrasse
Max. Length: 11.8 in. (30 cm).
Aquarium Suitability: 4.

Xyrichtys pavo Valenciennes, 1840
Blue Razorfish (Indian Fish, Pavo Razorfish)

Maximum Length: 16.1 in. (41 cm).
Range: Indo-Pacific.
Minimum Aquarium Size: 180 gal. (681 L).
Foods & Feeding: Meaty foods, including chopped fresh or frozen seafoods, frozen preparations for carnivores, frozen or live brine shrimp, mysid shrimp, live black worms, cleaned earthworms, flake food, live grass shrimp, and even small feeder fish. Feed at least 2 times a day.
Aquarium Suitability Index: 3.
Reef Aquarium Compatibility: Will eat small fishes, ornamental crustaceans, and many other motile invertebrates (including snails and serpent stars). Will also eat bristleworms and mantis shrimps.
Captive Care: The razorfishes have the astonishing ability to dive headfirst into the substrate when threatened and actually swim under the sand. Require a large tank, with plenty of open sand bottom at least 3-4 in. (8-10 cm) deep for adults. Large specimens often ship poorly; smaller individuals tend to acclimate more readily. Do not keep with members of its own kind, or with other razorfishes.

Cetoscarus bicolor (Rüppell, 1829)
Bicolor Parrotfish

Maximum Length: 31.5 in. (80 cm).
Range: Indo-Pacific.
Minimum Aquarium Size: 300 gal. (1,136 L).
Foods & Feeding: Varied diet, including chopped fresh or frozen seafoods, frozen preparations for herbivores, frozen or live brine shrimp, mysid shrimp, and flake food. Also provide pieces of live rock and/or other calcareous coral skeletons for it to graze on. Feed at least 3 times a day.
Aquarium Suitability Index: 2.
Reef Aquarium Compatibility: Will bite chunks from live stony corals. Can be kept with soft corals, and is safe with motile invertebrates.
Captive Care: This and other parrotfishes make very poor aquarium subjects. They naturally feed on algae that encrusts the reef, crunching up substantial amounts of coral with their beaklike dental plates. They are difficult to feed and get too large for the vast majority of home tanks. In the wild, they sweep freely across the reef and often act painfully confined in an aquarium. This species is not aggressive toward other species, with the possible exception of other parrotfishes. It may fight with members of its own species.

Scarus taeniopterus Desmarest, 1831
Princess Parrotfish

Maximum Length: 13.8 in. (35 cm).
Range: Tropical Western Atlantic.
Minimum Aquarium Size: 135 gal. (511 L).
Foods & Feeding: Difficult to feed. Offer a varied diet including chopped fresh or frozen seafoods, frozen preparations for herbivores, frozen or live brine shrimp, mysid shrimp, and flake food. Provide pieces of live rock and/or calcareous coral skeletons for it to graze on. Plaster of Paris feeding blocks, impregnated with food, can also be used. Feed at least 5 times a day.
Aquarium Suitability Index: 3.
Reef Aquarium Compatibility: Should not be kept with stony corals, as it will rasp on them. Can be kept with soft corals.
Captive Care: A favorite of Caribbean divers and snorkelers, this is one of a number of parrotfishes that is best appreciated in the wild. It ranges widely, grazing on algae throughout the day and does poorly in a confined space. Will typically starve to death if kept in an aquarium without microalgae. Peaceful with other species, but may fight with members of its own kind. Although smaller than others in the genus, it requires a large aquarium and efficient filtration.

Pholidichthys leucotaenia Bleeker, 1856
Convict Blenny (Convict Worm Blenny)

Maximum Length: 5.5 in. (14 cm).
Range: Indo-Pacific.
Minimum Aquarium Size: 20 gal. (76 L).
Foods & Feeding: Meaty foods, such as frozen mysid shrimp, vitamin-enriched brine shrimp, finely chopped table shrimp, and frozen preparations for carnivores. Feed at least 2 times a day (probably less often in a reef aquarium).
Aquarium Suitability Index: 5.
Reef Aquarium Compatibility: Will not harm sessile invertebrates, although adults will eat ornamental shrimps and possibly small crabs. May bury corals placed on or near the bottom.
Captive Care: Easily one of the hardest-working fishes that can be placed in a marine aquarium. It will dig extensive tunnels in the sand, often leading to aquascape avalanches. Be sure all rock is placed on the bottom of the tank before adding substrate. A group of juveniles may mimic schools of the venomous *Plotosus lineatus*, page 45. Adults are often very cryptic, hiding out in their subterranean homes. Fairly disease-resistant, it can withstand suboptimal water conditions and has spawned in captivity.

Parapercis schauinslandi (Steindachner, 1900)
Schauinsland's Sand Perch (Redspotted Sand Perch, Red Grubfish)

Maximum Length: 5.1 in. (13 cm).
Range: Indo-Pacific.
Minimum Aquarium Size: 30 gal. (114 L).
Foods & Feeding: Meaty foods, including frozen prepared foods, chopped fresh or frozen seafoods, and live foods. Feed 1-2 times a day, less often if kept in a tank with live rock or live sand.
Aquarium Suitability Index: 5. ▉
Reef Aquarium Compatibility: A great choice for the deep-water reef aquarium, although larger specimens may attack smaller ornamental shrimps. Will often acclimate to the higher light levels present in a shallow-water reef tank.
Captive Care: This appealing bottom dweller is a durable aquarium fish and the least aggressive species in this family. Even so, small specimens may harass other fishes, especially in a smaller aquarium, and they will become more pugnacious with increasing size and age. A small aggregation of these fish can be kept in a larger tank if introduced simultaneously. Will not hesitate to jump out of an open tank if frightened in any way—the aquarium must be covered.

Atrosalarias fuscus (Rüppell, 1835)
Highfin Blenny

Maximum Length: 5.7 in. (14.5 cm).
Range: Indo-Pacific.
Minimum Aquarium Size: 55 gal. (208 L).
Foods & Feeding: Vegetable matter, including frozen and dried foods containing marine algae and the blue-green alga *Spirulina*. Usually will not thrive unless a crop of microalgae (its natural source of food) is present in the aquarium.
Aquarium Suitability Index: 3.
Reef Aquarium Compatibility: May nip at and eat some small-polyped stony corals.
Captive Care: This comical looking fish spends its time hopping from one spot to another on the substrate, rasping at algae growth or perching in repose, ever-alert to its surroundings. If deprived of its natural herbivorous diet, it is likely to starve. Should only be kept in well-established systems with live rock and some constant microalgae growth. Usually not bothered by its tankmates, with the possible exception of predatory species. Keep only one per tank, unless a male-female pair is obtained.

Ecsenius bicolor (Day, 1888)
Bicolor Blenny

Maximum Length: 3.9 in. (10 cm).
Range: Indo-Pacific.
Minimum Aquarium Size: 20 gal. (76 L).
Foods & Feeding: Vegetable matter, including frozen and dried foods containing marine algae and the blue-green alga *Spirulina*. Usually will not thrive unless a crop of microalgae (its natural source of food) is present in the aquarium.
Aquarium Suitability Index: 4.
Reef Aquarium Compatibility: An occasional specimen may nip at and eat some small-polyped stony corals. Some may bite large-polyped stony corals and clam mantles.
Captive Care: An attractive blenny, interesting to observe and easy to keep in aquariums with natural microalgae growth. Spends most of its time perching on or picking at the substrate and is usually ignored by its tankmates. May behave aggressively toward members of its own species, closely related forms, or smaller bottom-dwelling species. May pick on gobies and firefishes. Keep only one per tank, except in the case of a male-female pair. May jump out of an uncovered aquarium.

Ecsenius gravieri (Pellegrin, 1906)
Red Sea Mimic Blenny

Maximum Length: 3.1 in. (8 cm).
Range: Red Sea.
Minimum Aquarium Size: 20 gal. (76 L).
Foods & Feeding: Vegetable matter, including frozen foods that contain marine algae or the blue-green alga *Spirulina*. Will do best when microalgae (its natural source of food) is available for grazing.
Aquarium Suitability Index: 4.
Reef Aquarium Compatibility: Occasionally will eat some small-polyped stony corals. May bite large-polyped stony corals and clam mantles.
Captive Care: This curious and harmless species mimics *Meiacanthus nigrolineatus*, page 332, which has venomous fangs and is avoided by experienced predators. It is easy to keep in established aquariums that contain some microalgae. Will spend most of its time perched on or picking at the substrate, usually ignored by its tankmates. May behave aggressively toward conspecifics, closely related forms, or smaller bottom-dwellers. Keep only one per tank, except in a male-female pair.

Ecsenius midas Starck, 1969
Midas Blenny

Maximum Length: 3.9 in. (10 cm).
Range: Indo-Pacific.
Minimum Aquarium Size: 20 gal. (76 L).
Foods & Feeding: Varied diet, including finely chopped crustacean flesh, mysid shrimp, vitamin-enriched brine shrimp, as well as frozen preparations for herbivores. Feed 3 times a day.
Aquarium Suitability Index: 5. ▆
Reef Aquarium Compatibility: Excellent.
Captive Care: This slinky, colorful fish makes a great display species and is one of the best blennies for the reef aquarium. Unlike most of its close relatives, this species feeds mostly on zooplankton, rather than algae. Spends its time tucked in small holes or swimming in the water column, usually ignored by its tankmates. Will sometimes pick on small planktivores. The author has observed this species biting and tearing the fins of a firefish and a goby. It is most likely to become a behavioral problem in smaller aquariums.

Exallias brevis (Kner, 1868)
Leopard Blenny (Honeycomb Blenny)

Maximum Length: 5.7 in. (14.5 cm).
Range: Indo-Pacific.
Minimum Aquarium Size: 55 gal. (208 L).
Foods & Feeding: Try frozen preparations for herbivores, mysid shrimp, and vitamin enriched-brine shrimp. Usually will not eat in captivity. If it does, feed 3 times a day.
Aquarium Suitability Index: 2. ◤
Reef Aquarium Compatibility: Will feed on small-polyped stony corals.
Captive Care: Although very attractive, this blenny should not be acquired unless the aquarist is aware of and prepared to supply its specialized diet. This blenny feeds almost exclusively on small-polyped stony coral polyps and spends its time tucked into crevices or among stony coral branches, especially those of *Pocillopora* spp. It is territorial, defending its food source from members of its own species and any other possible food competitors.

Istiblennius chrysospilos (Bleeker, 1857)
Redspotted Blenny (Redspotted Rockskipper)

Maximum Length: 5.1 in. (13 cm).
Range: Western and South Pacific.
Minimum Aquarium Size: 30 gal. (114 L).
Foods & Feeding: Vegetable matter, including frozen and dried foods containing marine algae and the blue-green alga *Spirulina*. Usually will not thrive unless a growth of microalgae (its natural source of food) is present in the aquarium.
Aquarium Suitability Index: 3.
Reef Aquarium Compatibility: An occasional specimen may nip at stony coral polyps or clam mantles.
Captive Care: This is an appealing fish that requires conditions similar to the shallow reefs and tidepools where it naturally occurs. It should only be kept in well-established tanks with sufficient lights and nutrients to sustain an ongoing supply of microalgae growth. It spends its time in repose on the substrate, hopping from one spot to another or rasping at the substrate. Usually not bothered by its tankmates, with the possible exception of predatory species. Keep only one specimen per tank, unless a male-female pair is acquired.

Meiacanthus atrodorsalis (Günther, 1877)
Yellowtail Fang Blenny (Lyretail Fang Blenny)

Maximum Length: 4.3 in. (11 cm).
Range: Indo-Pacific.
Minimum Aquarium Size: 20 gal. (76 L).
Foods & Feeding: Varied diet, including finely chopped crustacean flesh, mysid shrimp, vitamin-enriched brine shrimp, as well as frozen preparations for herbivores. Will usually do poorly unless kept in a tank with live rock, where it can continually hunt and feed on its natural prey, small crustaceans. Feed 3 times a day.
Aquarium Suitability Index: 3. ▨ **V**
Reef Aquarium Compatibility: Excellent.
Captive Care: One of the reputed black sheep of the blenny clan, this species has venomous fangs that it will employ if attacked. For this reason, it is rarely harassed by other fishes, and it spends most of its time swimming or hovering in the water column. In reality, it rarely bothers other fishes, with the possible exception of congeners. Only one should be housed per tank, except in large systems or unless a pair is acquired. May be harassed by damsels and other aggressive species, but will bite the inside of a predator's mouth if ingested, and will usually be promptly spit out, no worse for wear.

Meiacanthus bundoon
Bundoon Fang Blenny
Max. Length: 3.1 in. (8 cm).
Aquarium Suitability: 3. **V**

Meiacanthus grammistes
Striped Fang Blenny
Max. Length: 4.3 in. (11 cm).
Aquarium Suitability: 3. **V**

Meiacanthus mossambicus
Mozambique Fang Blenny
Max. Length: 3.9 in. (10 cm).
Aquarium Suitability: 3. **V**

Meiacanthus nigrolineatus
Blackline Fang Blenny
Max. Length: 3.7 in. (9.5 cm).
Aquarium Suitability: 3. **V**

Meiacanthus ovalaunensis
Canary Fang Blenny
Max. Length: 4.3 in. (11 cm).
Aquarium Suitability: 3. **V**

Meiacanthus smithi
Smith's Fang Blenny
Max. Length: 3.1 in. (8 cm).
Aquarium Suitability: 3. **V**

Ophioblennius atlanticus (Cuvier, 1836)
Redlip Blenny

Maximum Length: 4.7 in. (12 cm).
Range: Tropical Western Atlantic.
Minimum Aquarium Size: 20 gal. (76 L).
Foods & Feeding: Vegetable matter, including frozen and dried foods containing marine algae and the blue-green alga *Spirulina*. Does best if a crop of microalgae (its natural source of food) is growing in the aquarium.
Aquarium Suitability Index: 4.
Reef Aquarium Compatibility: May nip at stony corals and clam mantles.
Captive Care: Familiar to Caribbean snorkelers, this is a likable fish that is interesting to watch and easy to keep, provided it is placed in a well-established aquarium with a constant crop of microalgae. Will spend much of its time perching on the aquascaping, hopping from rock to rock and picking at the substrate. Usually ignored by its tankmates, but may behave aggressively toward members of its own species, closely related forms, or any fish that enters its territory. Large specimens can be very territorial, especially in smaller aquariums. Keep singly or in a male-female pair.

Parablennius marmoreus (Poey, 1875)
Seaweed Blenny

Maximum Length: 4.7 in. (12 cm).
Range: Tropical Western Atlantic.
Minimum Aquarium Size: 20 gal. (76 L).
Foods & Feeding: Vegetable matter, including frozen and dried foods containing marine algae and the blue-green alga *Spirulina*. Does best if a crop of microalgae (its natural source of food) is growing in the aquarium.
Aquarium Suitability Index: 4.
Reef Aquarium Compatibility: May nip at stony corals and clam mantles.
Captive Care: One of a number of well-camouflaged blennies that depend on good grazing for their survival. This species should be housed in a well-established tank that contains a growth of microalgae. It will help control nuisance algae, but may find insufficient grazing in smaller tanks. Spends most of its time sitting on the substrate. Usually ignored by its tankmates, although it may behave aggressively toward members of its own species, closely related forms, or any smaller fishes that enter its territory. Keep only one per tank, except in a larger aquarium or if a male-female pair is obtained.

Plagiotremus rhinorhynchos (Bleeker, 1852)
Bluestriped Fang Blenny ("Pacific Neon Goby")

Maximum Length: 4.7 in. (12 cm).
Range: Indo-Pacific.
Minimum Aquarium Size: 20 gal. (76 L).
Foods & Feeding: Feeds on the scales and body slime of other fishes. Will eat live brine shrimp. Some will also consume finely chopped seafoods. Feed 3 times a day.
Aquarium Suitability Index: 3.
Reef Aquarium Compatibility: Harmless to ornamental invertebrates but difficult to house with other fishes.
Captive Care: One of the so-called sabretoothed blennies, this fish will bite its tankmates unless they have toxic body slime. Should be kept on its own in a specimen tank, or with protected fishes, such as puffers. Juveniles mimic the Bluestreak Cleaner Wrasse (*Labroides dimidiatus*), page 299, while adults with an orange color form often swim among schools of Lyretail Anthias (*Pseudanthias squamipinnis*), page 91. Keep only one per tank.

Salarias fasciatus (Bloch, 1786)
Jeweled Rockskipper (Jeweled Blenny, Lawnmower Blenny)

Maximum Length: 5.1 in. (13 cm).
Range: Indo-Pacific.
Minimum Aquarium Size: 55 gal. (208 L).
Foods & Feeding: Vegetable matter, including frozen and dried foods containing marine algae and the blue-green alga *Spirulina*. Does best if a crop of microalgae (its natural source of food) is present in the aquarium.
Aquarium Suitability Index: 4.
Reef Aquarium Compatibility: May nip at stony corals and clam mantles. Its feeding activity stirs up sediment, putting detritus into suspension where it can be removed by mechanical filters.
Captive Care: This is a utility fish acquired by many aquarists to help control filamentous and film algae. (It will leave curious, full-lipped "kiss marks" on the walls of the aquarium where it rasps away algal growth.) May starve in tanks that are not well established or that have insufficient algae. Large individuals will attack fish tankmates, including other blenny species, especially in smaller aquariums. Keep singly, unless in a large system or if a male-female pair is obtained. Never keep with seahorses or pipefishes, which it will harass.

Dactylopus dactylopus (Bennett, 1837)
Finger Dragonet

Maximum Length: 7.1 in. (18 cm).
Range: Western Pacific.
Minimum Aquarium Size: 55 gal. (208 L).
Foods & Feeding: Challenging to feed. House in a tank furnished with a bed of well-established live sand, which provides live natural foods. Offer meaty foods, including shaved shrimp or vitamin-enriched live brine shrimp, using a long pipette, rigid air-line tubing, or a poultry baster to deposit items near the fish on the substrate. In a tank without live sand, feed 3 times a day.
Aquarium Suitability Index: 2.
Reef Aquarium Compatibility: Excellent.
Captive Care: This odd fish is a definite conversation piece, with exotic finnage, including a fingerlike pelvic ray. Peaceful except with conspecifics (males will fight) and possibly other dragonets. It is an easy target for nipping and will have difficulty competing with aggressive feeders. Needs plenty of open sand bottom and will bury itself when threatened or at night. May need special feeding, especially in an aquarium with aggressive feeders, where most food will be consumed before the bottom-feeding dragonet has a chance.

Synchiropus ocellatus (Pallas, 1770)
Ocellated Dragonet (Scooter Dragonet)

Maximum Length: 2.4 in. (6 cm).
Range: Western Pacific.
Minimum Aquarium Size: 20 gal. (76 L).
Foods & Feeding: Challenging to feed. House in a tank furnished with a bed of well-established live sand, which provides live natural foods. Offer meaty foods, including shaved shrimp or vitamin-enriched live brine shrimp, using a long pipette, rigid air-line tubing, or a poultry baster to deposit items near the fish on the substrate. In a tank without live sand, feed 3 times a day.
Aquarium Suitability Index: 2.
Reef Aquarium Compatibility: Excellent.
Captive Care: Males sport brighter colors and a larger first dorsal fin, which is erected and spread wide when displaying to less-ornate females or rivals. To keep more than one, choose two or three females with a single male. Unlike the mandarinfishes, more than one male can be kept in a medium-sized aquarium if all are introduced simultaneously. More-pugnacious tankmates may pester the dragonet and prevent it from getting enough to eat; best kept with docile species.

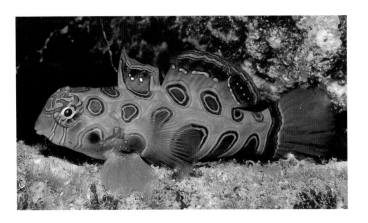

Synchiropus picturatus (Peters, 1876)
Spotted Mandarinfish (Psychedelic Mandarinfish, Picture Dragonet)

Maximum Length: 2.8 in. (7 cm).
Range: Western Pacific.
Minimum Aquarium Size: 20 gal. (76 L).
Foods & Feeding: Challenging to feed. Must be provided with plenty of natural prey, which can be introduced on live rock and live sand. Will eat vitamin-enriched live brine shrimp and live black worms, but is a methodical feeder that does not fare well with competitors.
Aquarium Suitability Index: 2.
Reef Aquarium Compatibility: Excellent. Will eat brown flatworms, which can reach plague proportions in certain reef aquariums.
Captive Care: This exquisite fish should only be kept in an established aquarium with live substrate and plenty of hiding places; it will starve in a new or barren tank. Should not be kept with anemones, which will eat this fish. This is a great choice for reef aquariums. It will ignore other species, but males will attack male conspecifics, as well as male *S. splendidus.* May bury itself in the sand at night or if threatened. Males have a more-elongate first dorsal spine than females.

Synchiropus splendidus (Herre, 1927)
Green Mandarinfish (Striped Mandarinfish)

Maximum Length: 3.1 in. (8 cm).
Range: Western Pacific.
Minimum Aquarium Size: 20 gal. (76 L).
Foods & Feeding: Challenging to feed. Must be provided with plenty of natural prey, which can be introduced on live rock and live sand. Will eat vitamin-enriched live brine shrimp and live black worms, but is a methodical feeder that does not fare well with competitors.
Aquarium Suitability Index: 2.
Reef Aquarium Compatibility: Excellent.
Captive Care: This ornate species with its mazelike patterns of green, orange and blue is a longstanding favorite species that has an unfortunate survival record among aquarists. This fish too often starves in newly set up or sterile tanks. It must be kept in a well-established aquarium with live substrate and plenty of hiding places. Will ignore other fish species, but males will attack male conspecifics. Although the mandarins apparently exude a noxious slime that deters potential fish predators, they will be eaten by sea anemones. It may bury in the sand at night or if threatened. Males have a more-elongate first dorsal spine than females. Has spawned in captivity.

Synchiropus stellatus Smith, 1963
Stellate Dragonet (Starry Dragonet)

Maximum Length: 2.4 in. (6 cm).
Range: Western Pacific.
Minimum Aquarium Size: 20 gal. (76 L).
Foods & Feeding: Challenging to feed. House in a tank furnished with a bed of well-established live sand, which provides live natural foods. Offer meaty foods, including shaved shrimp or vitamin-enriched live brine shrimp, using a long pipette, rigid air-line tubing, or a poultry baster to deposit items near the fish on the substrate. In a tank without live sand, feed 3 times a day.
Aquarium Suitability Index: 2.
Reef Aquarium Compatibility: Excellent.
Captive Care: An ideal reef aquarium species, with brightly colored males erecting a flamboyant first dorsal fin to attract females or warn rivals. To keep more than one, choose two or three females with a single male. This species is mostly indifferent to other fishes, but may be pestered by more-pugnacious tankmates. As with other dragonets, the large cheek spines can become entangled in the mesh of a fishnet. Use a specimen container if capture is necessary.

Amblyeleotris guttata (Fowler, 1938)
Orangespotted Shrimp Goby

Maximum Length: 3.5 in. (9 cm).
Range: Western Pacific.
Minimum Aquarium Size: 20 gal. (76 L).
Foods & Feeding: Meaty foods, including fresh or frozen mysid shrimp, vitamin-enriched brine shrimp, finely chopped table shrimp, and frozen preparations for carnivores. Feed at least 2 times a day.
Aquarium Suitability Index: 4.
Reef Aquarium Compatibility: Excellent, although it is a possible threat to small, delicate ornamental shrimps.
Captive Care: Members of this genus form symbiotic partnerships with nearly blind alpheid shrimps—the fish providing watchful eyes and the shrimp digging a burrow, which they share. Also known as prawn gobies, they are well suited to aquarium life and not aggressive, except possibly toward conspecifics (this applies particularly to male specimens). The goby will survive without the shrimp, but they make a fascinating display when acquired together. (This species usually lives in the burrows of *Alpheus ochrostriatus*.) Provide them with a bed of fine sand and loose coral rubble. May jump out of an open aquarium when startled.

Amblyeleotris randalli Hoese & Steene, 1978
Randall's Shrimp Goby

Maximum Length: 3.5 in. (9 cm).
Range: Western Pacific.
Minimum Aquarium Size: 20 gal. (76 L).
Foods & Feeding: Meaty foods, including fresh or frozen mysid shrimp, vitamin-enriched brine shrimp, finely chopped table shrimp, and frozen preparations for carnivores. Feed at least 2 times a day.
Aquarium Suitability Index: 4.
Reef Aquarium Compatibility: Excellent, although it is a possible threat to small, delicate ornamental shrimps.
Captive Care: This is probably the most spectacular member of the genus, with males that display a fanlike dorsal fin that bears a dramatic "eyespot." This species may not eat for several days after it is introduced, but will usually acclimate and begin eating.Can be kept with other shrimp gobies and may even share a burrow with another species. Conspecifics will occasionally quarrel if kept together, usually without serious consequences unless the aquarium is small. Occasionally its large dorsal fin is a target for species that like to nip fins or remove parasites (such as the Longfin Bannerfish, *Heniochus acuminatus*).

Amblyeleotris diagonalis
Diagonally-banded Shrimp Goby
Max. Length: 3.4 in. (8.5 cm).
Aquarium Suitability: 4.

Amblyeleotris latifasciata
Spottail or Metallic Shrimp Goby
Max. Length: 5.1 in. (13 cm).
Aquarium Suitability: 4.

Amblyeleotris periophthalma
Broadbanded Shrimp Goby
Max. Length: 3.1 in. (8 cm).
Aquarium Suitability: 4.

Amblyeleotris steinitzi
Steinitz's Shrimp Goby
Max. Length: 3.5 in. (9 cm).
Aquarium Suitability: 4.

Amblyeleotris wheeleri
Wheeler's Shrimp Goby
Max. Length: 3.5 in. (9 cm).
Aquarium Suitability: 4.

Cryptocentrus cyanotaenia
Bluebanded Shrimp Goby
Max. Length: 5.5 in. (14 cm).
Aquarium Suitability: 4.

Amblygobius rainfordi (Whitley, 1940)
Rainford's Goby (Old Glory)

Maximum Length: 2.6 in. (6.5 cm).
Range: Western and Central Pacific.
Minimum Aquarium Size: 20 gal. (76 L).
Foods & Feeding: Varied diet, including small crustaceans, such as vitamin-enriched live and frozen brine shrimp, mysid shrimp, and prepared foods for herbivores. Will typically do best with some filamentous algae and live rock. Feed 2 times a day, depending on availability of live food sources within the aquarium.
Aquarium Suitability Index: 4.
Reef Aquarium Compatibility: Excellent.
Captive Care: This is a wonderful little fish that is rarely aggressive toward other species. May starve if placed in a new aquarium or one without live rock and sand to provide grazing opportunities. Juveniles can be kept together in medium-sized tanks if introduced together, but adults often quarrel. It is best to keep one per tank, unless the system is large and affords many hiding places. Can be kept with other members of the genus, but do not house with fishes like dottybacks, hawkfishes, and sand perches, which are prone to picking on small, substrate-bound fishes.

Amblygobius phalaena (Valenciennes, 1837)
Brownbarred Goby

Maximum Length: 5.9 in. (15 cm).
Range: Indo-Pacific.
Minimum Aquarium Size: 20 gal. (76 L).
Foods & Feeding: Varied diet, including small crustaceans, such as vitamin-enriched live and frozen brine shrimp and mysid shrimp, as well as prepared foods for herbivores. Eats large quantities of algae in the wild and will do better if provided with similar fare in the aquarium. Feed 3 times a day, depending on the availability of natural live foods in the system.
Aquarium Suitability Index: 4.
Reef Aquarium Compatibility: Usually not considered a threat to sessile invertebrates, but may attack zoanthids.
Captive Care: One of the larger gobies, this species can be employed in a utility role to help keep the upper layers of aquarium sand stirred by taking in mouthfuls and then expelling them through its gills. It will also eat some filamentous algae. Best kept singly, unless a male-female pair is acquired. Pugnacious fishes, such as dottybacks, hawkfishes, and sand perches, may harass these gobies. May jump out of an open aquarium.

Cryptocentrus cinctus (Herre, 1936)
Yellow Shrimp Goby (Yellow Watchman Goby)

Maximum Length: 2.8 in. (7 cm).
Range: Indo-Pacific.
Minimum Aquarium Size: 20 gal. (76 L).
Foods & Feeding: Meaty foods, such as fresh or frozen mysid shrimp, vitamin-enriched brine shrimp, finely chopped table shrimp, and frozen preparations for carnivores. Feed at least 2 times a day.
Aquarium Suitability Index: 4.
Reef Aquarium Compatibility: Will not harm sessile invertebrates, but larger specimens will eat smaller ornamental shrimps.
Captive Care: This is a fine aquarium species and the most common shrimp goby in the aquarium trade. Can be yellow, light brown, or white overall with blue spots on the head, dorsal fin, and flanks, often with 4-5 dusky bars on the body. It readily adapts to captive living and has even spawned in reef aquariums. Provide a sand bottom with live rock or coral rubble to form hiding places. Placing two individuals together in the same tank can be risky unless they are a male-female pair. Will attack other shrimp gobies, especially in smaller aquariums. May jump out of an open aquarium.

Cryptocentrus leptocephalus Bleeker, 1876
Pinkspotted Shrimp Goby (Singapore Shrimp Goby)

Maximum Length: 5.9 in. (15 cm).
Range: Eastern Indian Ocean and Western Pacific.
Minimum Aquarium Size: 30 gal. (114 L).
Foods & Feeding: Meaty foods, such as fresh or frozen mysid shrimp, vitamin-enriched brine shrimp, finely chopped table shrimp, and frozen preparations for carnivores. Feed at least 2 times a day.
Aquarium Suitability Index: 4.
Reef Aquarium Compatibility: Will not harm sessile invertebrates, but will eat ornamental shrimps.
Captive Care: This is one of the most handsome members of this group, but also one of the more aggressive. Larger specimens will often attack other gobies and even smaller, unrelated fishes like assessors and wrasses. It is more likely to pose a behavioral problem if space is limited and it is one of the first introductions to the tank. Aggression usually takes the form of jaw gaping and lateral displays, but if it escalates, the goby may bite and do physical harm to the intruding fish. Conspecifics will usually fight as well, if they are not a male-female pair. (When mated pairs of shrimp gobies are offered for sale, they should never be split up.)

Cryptocentrus pavoninoides Bleeker, 1849
Blackfinned Shrimp Goby

Maximum Length: 5.1 in. (13 cm).
Range: Western Pacific.
Minimum Aquarium Size: 30 gal. (114 L).
Foods & Feeding: Meaty foods, such as fresh or frozen mysid shrimp, vitamin-enriched brine shrimp, finely chopped table shrimp, and frozen preparations for carnivores. Feed at least 2 times a day.
Aquarium Suitability Index: 4.
Reef Aquarium Compatibility: Will not harm sessile invertebrates, but will eat ornamental shrimps.
Captive Care: This is a wonderful aquarium fish with two color phases that may represent sexual dichromatism. One form is yellowish orange overall with distinct bars on the body, numerous spots on the face, and bold orange markings on the median fins. The other color form is brown to olive drab overall with blue spots on the head and body. Displays bars only when it is threatened, and the orange markings on the fins are not as striking. This is a peaceful species that may be kept in groups and with other gobies. It may chase more-diminutive shrimp gobies and smaller, bottom-dwelling fishes.

Gobiodon okinawae Sawada, Arai & Abe, 1972
Yellow Clown Goby

Maximum Length: 1.4 in. (3.5 cm).
Range: Indonesia and the Philippines.
Minimum Aquarium Size: 20 gal. (76 L).
Foods & Feeding: Meaty foods, including vitamin-enriched live and brine shrimp, frozen mysid shrimp, finely shaved table shrimp, and frozen food for carnivores. In a reef tank, it can be fed once a day; in a tank without live substrate, feed several times a day.
Aquarium Suitability Index: 4.
Reef Aquarium Compatibility: Excellent. Will nip small coral polyps but will not do irreparable damage.
Captive Care: Although diminutive, this is a fascinating fish to keep in the aquarium, especially in smaller tanks. It does best if housed with live or faux corals of the branching type. Rarely aggressive toward other fishes, but it will fight with members of its own kind in smaller tanks. If there are several fish and enough coral heads to go around, they will disperse or form male-female pairs. Will spawn in captivity, laying demersal eggs among coral branches. Best kept with other docile species. Members of this genus are thought to have a noxious body slime that deters most predatory fishes from eating them.

Gobiosoma evelynae Böhlke & Robbins, 1968
Sharknose Goby (Cleaner Goby)

Maximum Length: 1.6 in. (4 cm).
Range: Tropical Eastern Atlantic.
Minimum Aquarium Size: 10 gal. (38 L).
Foods & Feeding: Meaty foods, including vitamin-enriched live and frozen brine shrimp, frozen mysid shrimp, finely shaved table shrimp, and frozen food for carnivores. In a reef tank, it can be fed once a day; in a tank without live substrate, feed several times a day.
Aquarium Suitability Index: 4.
Reef Aquarium Compatibility: Very good.
Captive Care: This beautiful cleaning species will actually nip ich cysts off other fishes and may even remove the viral infection *Lymphocystis*. Unlike the cleaner wrasses, these gobies are not totally dependent on fish parasites and slime, but will also eat other foods. Be sure it gets enough to eat if kept with more-aggressive tankmates. This species is a great addition to a reef tank for parasite control. It is not uncommon for male-female pairs to spawn in the aquarium. In most cases, the eggs are laid in a crevice or empty shell, and both parents defend the eggs.

Gobiosoma oceanops (Jordan, 1904)
Neon Goby

Maximum Length: 2.0 in. (5 cm).
Range: Tropical Eastern Atlantic.
Minimum Aquarium Size: 10 gal. (38 L).
Foods & Feeding: Meaty foods, including vitamin-enriched live and frozen brine shrimp, frozen mysid shrimp, finely shaved table shrimp, and frozen food for carnivores. In a reef tank, it can be fed once a day; in a tank without live substrate, feed several times a day.
Aquarium Suitability Index: 4. ◥
Reef Aquarium Compatibility: A great addition to the reef aquarium, especially the small-polyped stony coral tank.
Captive Care: A bright, endearing cleaner species that will service tankmates and help control some diseases. Will actually nip ich cysts off other fishes and may even remove the viral infection *Lymphocystis*. Although rarely aggressive toward other fishes, it will fight with members of its own kind, especially in smaller tanks. It is not uncommon for pairs to spawn in the aquarium. In most cases, eggs are laid in a crevice or empty shell, and both parents defend the eggs aggressively. Fry are easily raised on rotifers and *Artemia* nauplii.

Istigobius decoratus (Herre, 1927)
Decorated Goby

Maximum Length: 4.7 in. (12 cm).
Range: Indo-Pacific.
Minimum Aquarium Size: 20 gal. (76 L).
Foods & Feeding: Meaty foods, including vitamin-enriched live and frozen brine shrimp, frozen mysid shrimp, finely shaved table shrimp, and frozen food for carnivores. In a reef tank, it can be fed once a day; in a tank without live substrate, feed several times a day.
Aquarium Suitability Index: 4.
Reef Aquarium Compatibility: Excellent.
Captive Care: A typical bottom-hugging goby that can be employed in a utility role to help keep the upper layers of live sand stirred. It will take up mouthfuls of substrate and then expel them through its gills. Will behave aggressively toward members of its own and closely related species. Keep only one per tank unless a male-female pair is acquired. May be harassed by more-aggressive bottom-dwelling species, including hawkfishes and sand perches.

Signigobius biocellatus Hoese & Allen, 1977
Signal Goby (Twinspot Goby, Crabeye Goby)

Maximum Length: 2.6 in. (6.5 cm).
Range: Western Pacific.
Minimum Aquarium Size: 20 gal. (76 L).
Foods & Feeding: Difficult to feed. Meaty foods, including vitamin-enriched live and frozen brine shrimp and mysid shrimp, live black worms, as well as prepared foods for carnivores. Typically feeds on the bottom only, taking mouthfuls of substrate, along with the food that lands on or lives within the sand.
Aquarium Suitability Index: 2.
Reef Aquarium Compatibility: Harmless with corals and clams, but may eat ornamental crustaceans.
Captive Care: Thought to mimic a crab as it hops along on the bottom with its two eyespot-clad dorsal fins erect. Unfortunately, it is difficult to keep and most individuals slowly starve to death. To succeed, use live sand as a substrate, attach a richly populated refugium to the tank, and feed the fish frequently. Deworming may also help. Usually sold in pairs (often found in pairs in the wild) and are thought to do poorly if kept singly. Do not keep with aggressive fishes, including bottom-feeding food competitors.

Stonogobiops nematodes Hoese & Randall, 1982
Blackray Shrimp Goby (Highfin Shrimp Goby)

Maximum Length: 2.0 in. (5 cm).
Range: Indonesia and the Philippines.
Minimum Aquarium Size: 20 gal. (76 L).
Foods & Feeding: Meaty foods, including fresh or frozen mysid shrimp, vitamin-enriched brine shrimp, finely chopped table shrimp, and frozen preparations for carnivores. Feed at least 2 times a day.
Aquarium Suitability Index: 4.
Reef Aquarium Compatibility: Excellent.
Captive Care: This delightful little fish makes a wonderful addition to the passive community tank. Adults live in pairs and hover several inches from the entrance of the burrow. Ideally, the aquarist should try to acquire a mated pair, along with its symbiont shrimp, *Alpheus randalli.* Not aggressive toward other bottom-oriented fishes, except at feeding time, and often dominated by more-pugnacious species. They might not get enough to eat if kept with overly aggressive or larger tankmates. Individuals of the same sex will fight, especially two males in a smaller aquarium (under 55 gal. [208 L]). Sometimes they will bite other fish species and hold on tenaciously. If startled, they will occasionally bury under the sand.

Stonogobiops sp.
Whiteray Shrimp Goby (Clown Shrimp Goby)

Maximum Length: 2.0 in. (5 cm).
Range: Eastern Indian Ocean and Western Pacific.
Minimum Aquarium Size: 20 gal. (76 L).
Foods & Feeding: Meaty foods, including fresh or frozen mysid shrimp, vitamin-enriched brine shrimp, finely chopped table shrimp, and frozen preparations for carnivores. Feed at least 2 times a day.
Aquarium Suitability Index: 4.
Reef Aquarium Compatibility: Excellent.
Captive Care: This recent, unnamed arrival to the aquarium trade is a marvelous addition to the passive community tank. Adults live in pairs and hover several inches from the entrance to the burrow. Not aggressive toward other bottom-oriented fishes, except at feeding time, and often dominated by more-pugnacious species. Should be housed with other peaceful species. Can be kept in pairs, but individuals of the same sex will fight, especially two males in a smaller aquarium (under 55 gal. [208 L]). Provide a bed of sand and coral rubble where they can burrow and hide. Have been known to jump out of an open tank when frightened.

Valenciennea puellaris (Tomiyama, 1956)
Orangespotted Sleeper Goby (Maiden Goby)

Maximum Length: 5.5 in. (14 cm).
Range: Indo-west-Pacific.
Minimum Aquarium Size: 55 gal. (208 L).
Foods & Feeding: Difficult to feed. Meaty foods, including small crustaceans like vitamin-enriched live and frozen brine shrimp and mysid shrimp, live black worms, as well as prepared foods for carnivores. Feed several times a day.
Aquarium Suitability Index: 2-3. ◣ ▧
Reef Aquarium Compatibility: Excellent. Will eat smaller bristleworms and also desirable infaunal invertebrates in live sand.
Captive Care: The sleeper gobies are sometimes employed as working fishes in reef tanks with substrate because their feeding activities take them deeper into the sand bed than many other gobies. Unfortunately, they are difficult to keep—many slowly starve to death. To improve the chances of success, keep them in a tank with live sand and a well-established refugium; be sure they are well fed. Deworming may help. Can be kept in male-female pairs (especially in a smaller tank); otherwise they may quarrel with each other and with other sleeper gobies. This species' color varies over its range.

Valenciennea helsdingeni
Twostripe Sleeper Goby
Max. Length: 6.3 in. (16 cm).
Aquarium Suitability: 2.

Valenciennea limicola
Muddy Sleeper Goby
Max. Length: 2.8 in. (7 cm).
Aquarium Suitability: 3.

Valenciennea longipinnis
Longfinned Sleeper Goby
Max. Length: 5.9 in. (15 cm).
Aquarium Suitability: 3.

Valenciennea sexguttata
Sixspot Sleeper Goby
Max. Length: 5.5 in. (14 cm).
Aquarium Suitability: 3.

Valenciennea strigata
Yellowheaded Sleeper Goby
Max. Length: 7.1 in. (18 cm).
Aquarium Suitability: 2.

Valenciennea wardii
Ward's or Tiger Sleeper Goby
Max. Length: 5.1 in. (13 cm).
Aquarium Suitability: 2-3.

Gunnelichthys curiosus Dawson, 1968
Curious Wormfish

Maximum Length: 4.5 in. (11.5 cm).
Range: Indo-Pacific.
Minimum Aquarium Size: 30 gal. (114 L).
Foods & Feeding: Meaty foods, such as frozen mysid shrimp, vitamin-enriched brine shrimp, finely chopped table shrimp, and frozen preparations for carnivores. Feed at least 2-3 times a day, depending on the availability of live foods in the aquarium.
Aquarium Suitability Index: 3.
Reef Aquarium Compatibility: Excellent.
Captive Care: This unusual fish is best kept with peaceful species in a tank with a fine sand substrate. Will bury in soft substrate when threatened and at night and does best with a bed of live sand and coral rubble. It is harmless and can be kept in pairs or groups, although it is prudent to add all of them to the tank at once. Do not keep with aggressive fishes or predatory species (it is easily caught and eaten by even small piscivores).

Nemateleotris decora Randall & Allen, 1973
Purple Firefish (Purple Dartfish, Decorated Dartfish, Flame Firefish)

Maximum Length: 3.5 in. (9 cm).
Range: Indo-west-Pacific.
Minimum Aquarium Size: 20 gal. (76 L).
Foods & Feeding: Meaty foods, including finely chopped or shaved fresh or frozen seafood, frozen preparations for carnivores, frozen and live brine shrimp, and mysid shrimp. A planktivore, it feeds mostly on prey suspended in the water column, but will pick food off the substrate on occasion. Feed at least once a day.
Aquarium Suitability Index: 5.
Reef Aquarium Compatibility: Excellent.
Captive Care: A gorgeous, hovering fish that is disease-resistant and readily acclimates to the home aquarium. Provide plenty of hiding places; an aquarium bottom covered with loose coral rubble is ideal. The most aggressive of the firefishes, it should be housed singly or in male-female pairs. More-pugnacious fishes will cause it to hide constantly and starve to death. Colors may fade if not provided with an enriched, varied diet. Will jump through small openings.

Nemateleotris magnifica Fowler, 1938
Fire Goby (Firefish, Fire Dartfish, Magnificent Dartfish)

Maximum Length: 3.1 in. (8 cm).
Range: Indo-Pacific.
Minimum Aquarium Size: 20 gal. (76 L).
Foods & Feeding: Meaty foods, including finely chopped or shaved fresh or frozen seafood, frozen preparations for carnivores, frozen and live brine shrimp and mysid shrimp. A planktivore, it feeds most on prey suspended in the water column, but will pick food off the substrate on occasion. Feed at least once a day.
Aquarium Suitability Index: 5.
Reef Aquarium Compatibility: Excellent.
Captive Care: A lovely but timid species that should be housed with other passive fishes. If housed with aggressive tankmates, it will hide and not feed. Keep singly, unless the tank is very large or a male-female pair is obtained. If kept in groups, one individual will usually start chasing the others, often until it kills them all. Provide coral rubble as suitable hiding places. Prone to leaping from shipping bags and open aquariums. Colors may fade if it is not provided with a varied diet.

Oxymetopon cyanoctenosum Klausewitz & Condé, 1981
Bluebarred Ribbon Goby (Razor Goby)

Maximum Length: 7.9 in. (20 cm).
Range: Western Pacific.
Minimum Aquarium Size: 55 gal. (208 L).
Foods & Feeding: Live brine shrimp may be needed to initiate feeding. Try to switch to finely chopped or shaved fresh or frozen seafood, frozen preparations for carnivores, and mysid shrimp. A planktivore, it feeds mostly on prey suspended in the water column, but will pick food off the substrate on occasion. Feed at least 2 times a day.
Aquarium Suitability Index: 2.
Reef Aquarium Compatibility: Excellent, but prefers dim lighting.
Captive Care: This unusual goby is attractive but somewhat of a recluse that is best kept in a tank on its own or with other docile species. When housed with aggressive tankmates, it will hide constantly and starve to death. Requires ample swimming room and good hiding places, such as a flat rock on live sand with a hollow underneath. This species is easily "spooked" by human movements. Place tank in a low traffic area, move slowly when the fish is out, and do not turn off all lights suddenly. Will spend more time in the open if the tank is dimly lit. Will leap from uncovered aquariums.

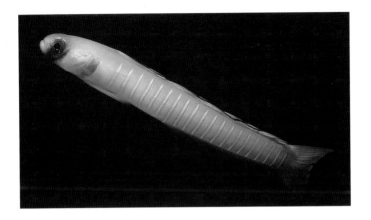

Ptereleotris zebra Fowler, 1938
Zebra Dart Goby (Zebra Dartfish, Barred Dartfish, Bar Goby)

Maximum Length: 4.3 in. (11 cm).
Range: Indo-west-Pacific.
Minimum Aquarium Size: 20 gal. (76 L).
Foods & Feeding: Meaty foods, including finely chopped or shaved fresh or frozen seafood, frozen preparations for carnivores, frozen and live brine shrimp, and mysid shrimp. A planktivore, it feeds mostly on prey suspended in the water column, but will pick food off the substrate on occasion. Feed 1-2 times a day.
Aquarium Suitability Index: 4.
Reef Aquarium Compatibility: Excellent.
Captive Care: One of the most peaceful of aquarium fishes, delicately attractive and highly disease-resistant. Must have less-aggressive tank-mates, such as other dart gobies, and numerous places to hide, including a sand-covered bottom. It will bury in finer sand substrates at night or when threatened. Best kept in pairs or small groups. It will often hide for a week or two, but once acclimated, will swim freely about the tank. Prone to jumping from small openings. Has spawned in captivity, laying grey eggs in its burrow or cave that are tended by the female.

Nemateleotris helfrichi
Helfrich's Firefish, Helfrich's Dartfish
Max: Length: 2.4 in. (6 cm).
Aquarium Suitability: 5. ◼

Ptereleotris evides
Scissortail Dartfish, Scissortail Goby
Max. Length: 5.5 in. (14 cm).
Aquarium Suitability: 4. ◢

Ptereleotris hanae
Filamented Dartfish
Max. Length: 4.7 in. (12 cm).
Aquarium Suitability: 4. ◢

Ptereleotris heteroptera
Spottail Dartfish, Blue Gudgeon Goby
Max. Length: 4.7 in. (12 cm).
Aquarium Suitability: 4. ◢

Ptereleotris microlepis
Green Dartfish, Green Gudgeon Goby
Max. Length: 5.1 in. (13 cm).
Aquarium Suitability: 4. ◢

Ptereleotris monoptera
Monofin Dartfish
Max. Length: 4.7 in. (12 cm).
Aquarium Suitability: 4. ◢

Chaetodipterus faber (Broussonet, 1782)
Atlantic Spadefish

Maximum Length: 35.8 in. (91 cm).
Range: Tropical Western Atlantic.
Minimum Aquarium Size: 500 gal. (1,893 L).
Foods & Feeding: Varied diet, including meaty foods, such as pieces of fresh shrimp, scallop, and vitamin-enriched brine shrimp, as well as frozen preparations for herbivores. Feed 2-3 times a day.
Aquarium Suitability Index: 4.
Reef Aquarium Compatibility: Will eat many types of sessile invertebrates, including some corals and anemones.
Captive Care: Forming impressive schools in the wild, this elegantly shaped fish has an appearance suggestive of the large angelfishes. For the aquarist with an immense tank, it will readily adapt to captivity, and it can be kept in pairs or groups. Small specimens are shy and often picked on by more-aggressive tankmates, and they should only be housed with more-peaceful species. Adults become more self-assured and succumb less often to tankmate aggression. As this fish matures, it becomes more active and needs plenty of swimming space. Unfortunately, it gets too large for most home aquariums.

Platax orbicularis (Forsskål, 1775)
Orbiculate Batfish (Orbic Platax, Orbic Batfish)

Maximum Length: 22.4 in. (57 cm).
Range: Indo-Pacific.
Minimum Aquarium Size: 200 gal. (757 L).
Foods & Feeding: Varied diet, including meaty foods, such as pieces of fresh shrimp, scallop, vitamin-enriched brine shrimp, and frozen preparations for herbivores. Feed 3 times a day.
Aquarium Suitability Index: 3.
Reef Aquarium Compatibility: Will eat many types of sessile invertebrates, including some corals and anemones.
Captive Care: Unusual and interesting, juveniles of this species are often purchased by well-intentioned hobbyists who do not recognize their growth potential. This is a hardy species, although it often comes down with ich (easily treated with copper-based medications). It should be kept in a deep tank and provided with plenty of unobstructed swimming room. Juveniles should be housed with nonaggressive species. They are generally peaceful, and more than one can be kept per tank. Adults can be housed with moderately aggressive forms, but do not keep with potential fin nippers, such as puffers. They will learn to take food from the aquarist's fingers.

Platax pinnatus (Linnaeus, 1758)
Pinnate Batfish (Pinnate Platax, Redfin Batfish)

Maximum Length: 17.7 in. (45 cm).
Range: Western Pacific.
Minimum Aquarium Size: 200 gal. (757 L).
Foods & Feeding: Often difficult to feed and thus best left in the wild. Some individuals will take vitamin-enriched brine shrimp, live black worms, small pieces of fresh shrimp, squid, frozen mysid shrimp, and frozen preparations for herbivores. Feed 3 times a day.
Aquarium Suitability Index: 2. ◣
Reef Aquarium Compatibility: Will eat many types of sessile invertebrates, including some corals and anemones.
Captive Care: The exquisite juveniles of this species appear with some regularity in the aquarium trade, but they should be avoided by all but the most experienced aquarists. Most will refuse to feed and are destined to starve. House in a deep tank and provide with plenty of unobstructed swimming room. Unlike its relatives, it is shy and will need suitable hiding places and nonaggressive tankmates. A peaceful species—more than one can be kept per tank. Again, specimens that feed and thrive are the exception, not the rule.

Platax teira Forsskål, 1775
Longfin Batfish (Longfin Platax, Teira Batfish)

Maximum Length: 23.6 in. (60 cm).
Range: Indo-west-Pacific.
Minimum Aquarium Size: 200 gal. (757 L).
Foods & Feeding: Varied diet, including meaty foods, such as pieces of fresh shrimp, scallop, vitamin-enriched brine shrimp, as well as frozen preparations for herbivores. Feed 3 times a day.
Aquarium Suitability Index: 3.
Reef Aquarium Compatibility: Adults will eat many types of sessile invertebrates, including some corals and anemones.
Captive Care: This fish has beautiful, long, flowing fins and can become a true pet—feeding from its owners fingers—but unfortunately it will outgrow the majority of home aquariums. Like its cousins, it is susceptible to ich (easily treated with copper-based medications). Should be kept in a deep tank and provided with plenty of unobstructed swimming room and only moderate currents. Juveniles should be housed with peaceful species. They are not aggressive; more than one can be kept per tank. Adults can be housed with moderately aggressive forms, but not with potential fin nippers.

Siganus vulpinus (Schlegel & Müller, 1844)
Foxface Rabbitfish

Maximum Length: 9.4 in. (24 cm).
Range: Western Pacific
Minimum Aquarium Size: 75 gal. (284 L).
Foods & Feeding: Varied diet, mostly vegetable matter. Feed dried and frozen herbivore foods that contain marine algae and the blue-green alga *Spirulina*. Supplement with pieces of zucchini, broccoli, leaf lettuce, and sushi nori (dried seaweed). Feed 2-3 times a day.
Aquarium Suitability Index: 4. ◣ **V**
Reef Aquarium Compatibility: Will browse on desirable and undesirable algae. If well fed, will typically ignore corals, although some will nip and even eat large-polyped species and certain soft coral polyps.
Captive Care: The rabbitfishes are attractive and hardy fishes that fare well even in newly established aquariums. Some have been known to survive "wipe outs" that killed every other fish in the tank. This species is among the more aggressive in the genus. Juveniles will often put up with conspecifics, but adults will fight unless they are of the opposite sex and pair up. Will ignore unrelated fish species. Venomous spines; handle with care.

Siganus corallinus
Coral Rabbitfish
Max. Length: 11.0 in. (28 cm).
Aquarium Suitability: 4. **V**

Siganus guttatus
Goldspotted Rabbitfish
Max. Length: 15.7 in. (40 cm).
Aquarium Suitability: 4. **V**

Siganus magnifica
Magnificent Rabbitfish
Max. Length: 9.1 in. (23 cm).
Aquarium Suitability: 4. **V**

Siganus puellis
Masked Rabbitfish
Max. Length: 15.0 in. (38 cm).
Aquarium Suitability: 4. **V**

Siganus unimaculatus
Onespot Foxface Rabbitfish
Max. Length: 7.9 in. (20 cm).
Aquarium Suitability: 4. **V**

Siganus virgatus
Virgate Rabbitfish
Max. Length: 11.8 in. (30 cm).
Aquarium Suitability: 4. **V**

Zanclus cornutus (Linnaeus, 1758)
Moorish Idol

Maximum Length: 6.3 in. (16 cm).
Range: Indo-Pacific.
Minimum Aquarium Size: 100 gal. (379 L).
Foods & Feeding: Very difficult to feed. Varied diet, including finely chopped table shrimp, squid, clams, mysid shrimp, vitamin-enriched live brine shrimp, live black worms, as well as vegetable matter. Also offer foods with *Spirulina* and various marine algae. Feed several times a day. Reluctant feeders may require live rock with rich coralline algae and sponge growth (their natural fare) to survive acclimation.
Aquarium Suitability Index: 2.
Reef Aquarium Compatibility: An occasional individual will nip large-polyped stony corals as well as certain soft coral polyps.
Captive Care: This glorious fish has been on the want list of most marine aquarists at one time or another. Unfortunately, it is difficult to keep. In most cases it will refuse to eat or will never take food with gusto and will slowly starve or decline in health. Several can be kept together. Needs plenty of unobstructed swimming space as well as holes or crevices into which it can dive when threatened.

Acanthurus achilles Shaw, 1803
Achilles Surgeonfish

Maximum Length: 9.4 in. (24 cm).
Range: Indo-Pacific.
Minimum Aquarium Size: 100 gal. (379 L).
Foods & Feeding: Varied diet, mostly vegetable matter. Feed dried and frozen herbivore foods that contain marine algae and the blue-green alga *Spirulina*. Supplement with pieces of zucchini, broccoli, leaf lettuce, and sushi nori (dried seaweed). Feed 3 times a day.
Aquarium Suitability Index: 3.
Reef Aquarium Compatibility: Generally safe. Browses on filamentous microalgae and small fleshy macroalgae. If underfed, an occasional individual may nip at large-polyped stony corals.
Captive Care: A handsome fish, but one of the more-demanding members of the *Acanthurus* clan. Needs a large aquarium, plenty of unobstructed swimming room, and prefers turbulent water flow. In a small tank, it will nervously pace back and forth along the front of the tank and gradually pine away. Can be aggressive and will often harry other acanthurids. Keep singly unless the system is very large. Spends a major part of its day grazing and must be provided a daily feeding of vegetable matter, preferably including marine algae.

Acanthurus coeruleus Bloch & Schneider, 1801
Atlantic Blue Tang (Blue Tang)

Maximum Length: 9.1 in. (23 cm).
Range: Tropical Atlantic.
Minimum Aquarium Size: 75 gal. (284 L).
Foods & Feeding: Varied diet, mostly vegetable matter. Feed dried and frozen herbivore foods that contain marine algae and the blue-green alga *Spirulina*. Supplement with pieces of zucchini, broccoli, leaf lettuce, and sushi nori (dried seaweed). Feed 3 times a day.
Aquarium Suitability Index: 4.
Reef Aquarium Compatibility: Generally safe. Browses on filamentous microalgae and small fleshy macroalgae. If underfed, an occasional individual may nip at large-polyped stony corals.
Captive Care: A lovely addition to the Caribbean biotope aquarium. Although usually well-behaved in larger aquariums, it can be quite belligerent in smaller tanks. Best kept singly, but small groups can be housed in extra-large aquariums (180 gal. [681 L] or larger). Juveniles are yellow overall with a blue ring around the eye and blue trim on the median fins. Adults are blue overall, although the intensity of the blue can vary depending on the individual's "mood." Some small adults may also have a yellow tail.

Acanthurus japonicus (Fowler, 1946)
Powder Brown Surgeonfish

Maximum Length: 8.3 in. (21 cm).
Range: Western Pacific.
Minimum Aquarium Size: 75 gal. (284 L).
Foods & Feeding: Varied diet, mostly vegetable matter. Feed dried and frozen herbivore foods that contain marine algae and the blue-green alga *Spirulina.* Supplement with pieces of zucchini, broccoli, leaf lettuce, and sushi nori (dried seaweed). Feed 3 times a day.
Aquarium Suitability Index: 3.
Reef Aquarium Compatibility: Generally safe. Browses on filamentous microalgae and small fleshy macroalgae. If underfed, an occasional individual may nip at large-polyped stony corals.
Captive Care: Faring poorly during collection and shipping, this species has a reputation for being delicate and hard to acclimate. The similar *A. nigricans,* page 377, is a much more durable fish. Both are relatively quiet and shy when first introduced and require suitable hiding places to refuge in if threatened. The Powder Brown can be a finicky eater; a tank with flourishing algae will ensure it gets enough to eat during acclimation. Keep only one per tank, and do not mix with more-aggressive acanthurids.

Acanthurus leucosternon Bennett, 1832
Powder Blue Surgeonfish

Maximum Length: 9.1 in. (23 cm).
Range: Indian Ocean.
Minimum Aquarium Size: 100 gal. (379 L).
Foods & Feeding: Varied diet, mostly vegetable matter. Feed dried and frozen herbivore foods that contain marine algae and the blue-green alga *Spirulina*. Supplement with pieces of zucchini, broccoli, leaf lettuce, and sushi nori (dried seaweed). Feed 3 times a day.
Aquarium Suitability Index: 3.
Reef Aquarium Compatibility: Generally safe. Browses on filamentous microalgae and small fleshy macroalgae. If underfed, an occasional individual may nip at large-polyped stony corals.
Captive Care: This is one of the most beautiful fishes available to the marine aquarist, but it requires special care. It is very susceptible to ich, a weakness common in this family but exaggerated in this species. It is extremely hostile toward other surgeonfishes, especially those similar in form and color. Except in very large systems, it should be the only surgeonfish or tang present. This species is sexually dimorphic: males are considerably smaller than females.

Acanthurus lineatus (Linnaeus, 1758)
Lined Surgeonfish (Clown Surgeonfish)

Maximum Length: 15.0 in. (38 cm).
Range: Indo-Pacific.
Minimum Aquarium Size: 180 gal. (681 L).
Foods & Feeding: Varied diet, mostly vegetable matter. Feed dried and frozen herbivore foods that contain marine algae and the blue-green alga *Spirulina*. Supplement with pieces of zucchini, broccoli, leaf lettuce, and sushi nori (dried seaweed). Feed 3 times a day.
Aquarium Suitability Index: 3.
Reef Aquarium Compatibility: Generally safe. Browses on larger filamentous algae and small fleshy macroalgae. If underfed, an occasional individual may nip at large-polyped stony corals.
Captive Care: A bellicose beauty, this species is at the top of the aggressive acanthurid hierarchy. It has a larger caudal peduncle spine than almost all other surgeonfishes—and a hair-trigger willingness to use it. Avoid keeping with other members of the family, except in a huge aquarium. Will attack other species with similar food habits or shape. Very active; needs lots of unobstructed swimming room and clean, highly oxygenated seawater. Young, emaciated specimens are most commonly available but are difficult to revive.

Acanthurus nigricans (Linnaeus, 1758)
Whitecheek Surgeonfish

Maximum Length: 8.3 in. (21 cm).
Range: Tropical-pan-Pacific.
Minimum Aquarium Size: 75 gal. (284 L).
Foods & Feeding: Varied diet, mostly vegetable matter. Feed dried and frozen herbivore foods that contain marine algae and the blue-green alga *Spirulina*. Supplement with pieces of zucchini, broccoli, leaf lettuce, and sushi nori (dried seaweed). Feed 3 times a day.
Aquarium Suitability Index: 4.
Reef Aquarium Compatibility: Generally safe. Browses on filamentous microalgae and small fleshy macroalgae. If underfed, an occasional individual may nip at large-polyped stony corals.
Captive Care: This is a lovely species—similar to but more durable than its close relative, *A. japonicus*, page 374. It can be relatively shy when first acquired and should be provided with suitable hiding places to refuge in if threatened. Keep only one per tank, except in very large systems. Once acclimated, some individuals will behave aggressively toward other acanthurids or food competitors introduced later. Do not keep with more-aggressive acanthurids.

MAIN PHOTO, JUVENILE; INSET, ADULT

Acanthurus olivaceus Foster, 1801
Orangeshoulder Surgeonfish (Orangeband Surgeonfish)

Maximum Length: 13.8 in. (35 cm).
Range: Western Pacific.
Minimum Aquarium Size: 135 gal. (511 L).
Foods & Feeding: Varied diet, mostly vegetable matter. Feed dried and frozen herbivore foods that contain marine algae and the blue-green alga *Spirulina*. Supplement with pieces of zucchini, broccoli, leaf lettuce, and sushi nori (dried seaweed). Feed 3 times a day.
Aquarium Suitability Index: 4.
Reef Aquarium Compatibility: Rarely bothers corals. Feeds by sucking filamentous algae, diatoms, and detritus off the sand surface.
Captive Care: This is a large, eyecatching fish with a more-peaceful disposition than some others in the genus. Best housed in a large tank with plenty of swimming room and an open sand bottom for grazing. Will usually ignore tankmates, including other acanthurids, but house only one per tank, unless keeping an adult and a juvenile in a large system. If placing with other surgeonfishes (except *A. nigricans* and *A. triostegus,* which are less aggressive) add this species first. Juveniles are yellow overall and lack the characteristic orange shoulder patch, which develops as it grows.

MAIN PHOTO, JUVENILE; INSET, ADULT

Acanthurus pyroferus Kittlitz, 1834
Chocolate Surgeonfish (Mimic Surgeonfish)

Maximum Length: 9.8 in. (25 cm).
Range: Indo-Pacific.
Minimum Aquarium Size: 75 gal. (284 L).
Foods & Feeding: Varied diet, mostly vegetable matter. Feed dried and frozen herbivore foods that contain marine algae and the blue-green alga *Spirulina*. Supplement with pieces of zucchini, broccoli, leaf lettuce, and sushi nori (dried seaweed). Feed 3 times a day.
Aquarium Suitability Index: 4.
Reef Aquarium Compatibility: Generally safe. Browses on filamentous microalgae and small fleshy macroalgae. If underfed, an occasional individual may nip at large-polyped stony corals.
Captive Care: In a classic example of Batesian mimicry, juveniles of this species mimic either the Lemonpeel (*Centropyge flavissima*) or the Halfblack (*C. vroliki*) Angelfish, pages 215 and 220. The more-palat-able surgeonfish thus resembles the spiny and less-appetizing an-gelfish model. As it grows larger than the angelfish model, it begins to develop adult coloration. Juveniles tend to be durable and do well in a medium- to large-sized aquarium. Only moderately aggressive, but keep just one specimen (of the same color) per tank.

Acanthurus sohal (Forsskål, 1775)
Sohal Surgeonfish

Maximum Length: 15.7 in. (40 cm).
Range: Red Sea and the Arabian Gulf.
Minimum Aquarium Size: 180 gal. (681 L).
Foods & Feeding: Varied diet, mostly vegetable matter. Feed dried and frozen herbivore foods that contain marine algae and the blue-green alga *Spirulina*. Supplement with pieces of zucchini, broccoli, leaf lettuce, and sushi nori (dried seaweed). Feed 3 times a day.
Aquarium Suitability Index: 4.
Reef Aquarium Compatibility: Generally safe. Browses on filamentous microalgae and small fleshy macroalgae. If underfed, an occasional individual may nip at large-polyped stony corals.
Captive Care: A poster fish for the Red Sea, but one of the most notorious acanthurids in captivity. Highly territorial—it will dash from one side of the tank to the other and chastise other fishes, especially other surgeonfishes and food competitors. (In the wild it will attack parrotfishes and triggerfishes.) The caudal spines are very large, possibly venomous, and highly effective weapons. It is not uncommon for this terror to kill its rivals in captivity. Adults must be kept in larger aquariums that afford plenty of open swimming space.

Acanthurus triostegus (Linnaeus, 1758)
Convict Surgeonfish

Maximum Length: 10.2 in. (26 cm).
Range: Indo-Pacific.
Minimum Aquarium Size: 75 gal. (284 L).
Foods & Feeding: Varied diet, mostly vegetable matter. Feed dried and frozen herbivore foods that contain marine algae and the blue-green alga *Spirulina*. Supplement with pieces of zucchini, broccoli, leaf lettuce, and sushi nori (dried seaweed). Feed 3 times a day.
Aquarium Suitability Index: 4.
Reef Aquarium Compatibility: Generally safe. Browses on filamentous microalgae and small fleshy macroalgae. If underfed, an occasional individual may nip at large-polyped stony corals.
Captive Care: This is the pacifist of the surgeonfish clan. Endowed with a small caudal spine, it is one of the least aggressive *Acanthurus* spp. Rarely bothers heterospecifics. Juveniles, especially, may squabble with each other. To keep more than one subadult or adult, add them simultaneously. Groups make very pleasing displays in public aquariums and very large home systems. They are more likely to be bullied by other acanthurids, and it is best to keep them with acanthurids from other genera, such as *Naso* and *Zebrasoma*.

Acanthurus tristis Tickell, 1888
Indian Ocean Mimic Surgeonfish

Maximum Length: 9.8 in. (25 cm).
Range: Indian Ocean.
Minimum Aquarium Size: 75 gal. (284 L).
Foods & Feeding: Varied diet, mostly vegetable matter. Feed dried and frozen herbivore foods that contain marine algae and the blue-green alga *Spirulina.* Supplement with pieces of zucchini, broccoli, leaf lettuce, and sushi nori (dried seaweed). Feed 3 times a day.
Aquarium Suitability Index: 4.
Reef Aquarium Compatibility: Generally safe. Browses on filamentous microalgae and small fleshy macroalgae. If underfed, an occasional individual may nip at large-polyped stony corals.
Captive Care: Juveniles of this species mimic Eibl's Angelfish (*Centropyge eibli*), page 213. The relationship, like those of the Chocolate Surgeonfish (*A. pyroferus*) and its *Centropyge* models, is Batesian. (The juvenile surgeonfish avoids predation because it resembles the less-palatable angelfish.) This is a desirable species that can be housed in an aquarium as small as 75 gal. (284 L). Not overly aggressive, except toward members of its own kind, it will feed on a wide array of aquarium fare.

Ctenochaetus hawaiiensis Randall, 1955
Black Surgeonfish (Chevron Tang)

Maximum Length: 11.0 in. (28 cm).
Range: Central Pacific.
Minimum Aquarium Size: 100 gal. (379 L).
Foods & Feeding: Varied diet, mostly vegetable matter such as dried marine algae, frozen herbivore rations, the blue-green alga *Spirulina*, slices of zucchini, and broccoli. Feed at least 3 times a day.
Aquarium Suitability Index: 4.
Reef Aquarium Compatibility: Rarely bothers sessile invertebrates. Like other surgeonfishes and tangs, is prone to ich, which is difficult to treat in a tank with invertebrates.
Captive Care: From a radiant juvenile with a blue herringbone pattern on an orange background, this surgeonfish grows into a dark olive-brown adult with thin lines on the body. It is not an overly aggressive fish and will usually coexist easily with most tankmates. Exceptions include members of its own species and close relatives. Keep only one specimen per tank. It is likely to be picked on by other surgeonfishes. Spends a major part of its day grazing, so vegetable matter must be introduced daily in an aquarium without microalgae.

MAIN PHOTO, PACIFIC FORM; INSET, INDIAN OCEAN FORM

Ctenochaetus strigosus (Bennett, 1828)
Goldring Bristletooth (Yelloweye Bristletooth, Yelloweye Surgeonfish, Kole's Tang)

Maximum Length: 7.1 in. (18 cm).
Range: Indo-Pacific.
Minimum Aquarium Size: 75 gal. (284 L).
Foods & Feeding: Varied diet, mostly vegetable matter such as dried marine algae, frozen herbivore rations, the blue-green alga *Spirulina*, slices of zucchini, and broccoli. Feed at least 3 times a day.
Aquarium Suitability Index: 4.
Reef Aquarium Compatibility: Excellent.
Captive Care: Subtly handsome with a gold ring around the eye, adults of this species collected in the Indian Ocean bear spots, while Pacific specimens show distinct stripes. Juveniles of both forms are a bright yellow that gradually fades to a less-flamboyant brown. This is not an overly aggressive fish and will usually not bother fish tankmates, with the possible exception of close relatives. Conspecifics will battle each other, and it is best to keep only one specimen per tank. It is likely to be picked on by more-aggressive surgeonfishes. Does best in a tank with a healthy growth of microalgae to satisfy its constant grazing habits.

Naso brevirostris (Valenciennes, 1835)
Spotted Unicornfish (Paletail Unicornfish)

Maximum Length: 23.6 in. (60 cm).
Range: Indo-Pacific.
Minimum Aquarium Size: 180 gal. (681 L).
Foods & Feeding: Varied diet, mostly of vegetable matter, including the blue-green alga *Spirulina*, dried seaweed available from pet shops or Asian food stores, and frozen herbivore rations. Juveniles and small adults spend their days grazing and require portions of vegetable matter daily in an aquarium without microalgae. Adults feed on zooplankton and should be fed mysid shrimp, vitamin-enriched brine shrimp, and other meaty marine foods. Feed at least 3 times a day.
Aquarium Suitability Index: 4.
Reef Aquarium Compatibility: Harmless to sessile invertebrates.
Captive Care: This unusual "horned" species attains an appreciable size and is also quite active, making it an interesting choice for a large tank with plenty of unobstructed swimming space. It is rarely aggressive toward tankmates, although it may squabble with members of its own kind. The horn, or forehead spike, elongates with maturity. This species may jump out of an open aquarium.

Naso lituratus (Foster & Schneider, 1801)
Orangespine Unicornfish (Naso Tang)

Maximum Length: 18.1 in. (46 cm).
Range: Indo-Pacific.
Minimum Aquarium Size: 135 gal. (511 L).
Foods & Feeding: Varied diet, mostly vegetable matter such as dried marine algae, especially brown varieties, available from pet shops or Asian food stores, *Spirulina*, herbivore rations, and frozen meaty foods for planktivores. Feed at least 3 times a day.
Aquarium Suitability Index: 4.
Reef Aquarium Compatibility: Will graze on macroalgae, but is safe with most invertebrates. Rare individuals may nip at large-polyped corals.
Captive Care: This is a handsome, very active fish that can make a wonderful display specimen if provided with plenty of swimming space and suitable hiding places. Some specimens are reluctant to feed on anything but brown macroalgae, although most will take a variety of foods. Usually not aggressive toward tankmates, except for members of its own species and possibly related forms. The characteristic orange patches on the caudal peduncle surround large, permanently erect spines that can cause deep cuts and are easily entangled in a fish net. May jump out of an open aquarium.

Naso unicornis (Forsskål, 1775)
Bluespine Unicornfish

Maximum Length: 27.1 in. (69 cm).
Range: Indo-Pacific.
Minimum Aquarium Size: 200 gal. (757 L).
Foods & Feeding: Varied diet, mostly vegetable matter such as the blue-green alga *Spirulina*, slices of zucchini, broccoli, and the dried seaweed available from pet shops or Asian food stores. Spends a major part of its day grazing, so vegetable matter should be introduced daily in an aquarium without microalgae. Frozen foods should be offered at least 3 times a day.
Aquarium Suitability Index: 4.
Reef Aquarium Compatibility: Feeds mostly on brown macroalgae and will eliminate any such plants present in a reef tank. A rare individual may nip at large-polyped corals.
Captive Care: This is a fairly durable fish that will require a very large tank with plenty of unobstructed swimming space. It is usually not aggressive toward its tankmates, except for members of its own species and possibly related forms. It has large, permanently erect caudal peduncle spines that are marked by blue spots and are easily entangled in a fish net—as well as a threat to the aquarist.

Paracanthurus hepatus (Linnaeus, 1766)
Palette Surgeonfish (Pacific Blue Tang)

Maximum Length: 12.2 in. (31 cm).
Range: Indo-Pacific.
Minimum Aquarium Size: 100 gal. (379 L).
Foods & Feeding: Meaty foods to satisfy its zooplankton diet, including finely chopped fresh or frozen shrimp, mysid shrimp, and vitamin-enriched brine shrimp. It will also eat frozen preparations for herbivores. Feed at least 3 times a day.
Aquarium Suitability Index: 3.
Reef Aquarium Compatibility: Rarely bothers sessile invertebrates.
Captive Care: Beloved by aquarists for its shocking blue coloration and beautiful appearance, this fish can be a challenge to keep. It is prone to contracting ich and other skin parasites and is very susceptible to lateral line and fin erosion (like many surgeonfishes). It is shy at first and should be provided with branching corals or other suitable shelter sites. It is not an overly aggressive fish and will usually not bother fish tankmates, with the possible exception of close relatives. Juveniles can be kept in groups, but adults will quarrel unless given sufficient space. It may be picked on by more-aggressive acanthurids and other pugnacious species.

Zebrasoma desjardinii (Bloch, 1797)
Indian Ocean Sailfin Tang (Red Sea Sailfin Tang)

Maximum Length: 15.7 in. (40 cm).
Range: Central and South Pacific.
Minimum Aquarium Size: 135 gal. (511 L).
Foods & Feeding: Varied diet, mostly vegetable matter. Feed dried and frozen herbivore foods that contain marine algae and the blue-green alga *Spirulina*. Supplement with pieces of zucchini, broccoli, leaf lettuce, and sushi nori (dried seaweed). Feed 3 times a day.
Aquarium Suitability Index: 4.
Reef Aquarium Compatibility: Generally safe and desirable. Browses on filamentous microalgae and small fleshy macroalgae. If under-fed, an occasional individual may nip at large-polyped stony corals.
Captive Care: A wonderful aquarium fish, although it is one of the largest members of the genus and will grow to need a large tank. (The author reserves the common name "tang" for members of *Zebrasoma*.) It is the least feisty member of the family, although it may behave aggressively toward conspecifics. Keep only one; except in an extra-large tank. One of the best choices for controlling undesirable filamentous algae in the reef aquarium; an occasional individual will even eat nuisance bubble algae.

Zebrasoma flavescens (Bennett, 1828)
Yellow Tang

Maximum Length: 7.9 in. (20 cm).
Range: Central and South Pacific.
Minimum Aquarium Size: 75 gal. (284 L).
Foods & Feeding: Varied diet, mostly vegetable matter. Feed dried and frozen herbivore foods that contain marine algae and the blue-green alga *Spirulina.* Supplement with pieces of zucchini, broccoli, leaf lettuce, and sushi nori (dried seaweed). Feed 3 times a day.
Aquarium Suitability Index: 4.
Reef Aquarium Compatibility: Generally safe and desirable. Browses on filamentous microalgae and small fleshy macroalgae. If under-fed, an individual may nip at stony corals and even soft corals.
Captive Care: One of the mainstay species in the marine hobby, this species brings a splash of bright color to any aquarium. However, it must be fed a diet appropriate for active herbivores, or its beautiful yellow color will fade and it may develop head and lateral line ero-sion. Can be very aggressive once established, especially in a smaller tank. It may refuse to tolerate the presence of other tangs or sur-geonfishes. Keep only one, except in large tanks (135 gal. [511 L]), where groups should be introduced simultaneously.

Zebrasoma scopas (Cuvier, 1829)
Brown Tang (Scopas Tang)

Maximum Length: 7.9 in. (20 cm).
Range: Central and South Pacific.
Minimum Aquarium Size: 75 gal. (284 L).
Foods & Feeding: Varied diet, mostly vegetable matter. Feed dried and frozen herbivore foods that contain marine algae and the blue-green alga *Spirulina*. Supplement with pieces of zucchini, broccoli, leaf lettuce, and sushi nori (dried seaweed). Feed 3 times a day.
Aquarium Suitability Index: 4.
Reef Aquarium Compatibility: Generally safe and desirable. Browses on filamentous microalgae and small fleshy macroalgae. If under-fed, an individual may nip at stony corals and even soft corals.
Captive Care: Less gaudy than the related *Z. flavescens*, page 390, its more-subdued coloration and constant grazing activities make it appealing to some aquarists. One of the most aggressive zebraso-mids and very territorial, especially toward other members of this genus. (Tangs often maintain territories from which they exclude conspecifics and similar-looking fishes.) Keep only one, unless in a very large system. A proper herbivorous diet will help retain healthy colors and prevent head and lateral line erosion.

Zebrasoma veliferum (Bloch, 1797)
Sailfin Tang

Maximum Length: 15.7 in. (40 cm).
Range: Central and South Pacific.
Minimum Aquarium Size: 135 gal. (511 L).
Foods & Feeding: Varied diet, mostly vegetable matter. Feed dried and frozen herbivore foods that contain marine algae and the blue-green alga *Spirulina*. Supplement with pieces of zucchini, broccoli, leaf lettuce, and sushi nori (dried seaweed). Feed 3 times a day.
Aquarium Suitability Index: 4.
Reef Aquarium Compatibility: Generally safe and desirable. Browses on filamentous microalgae and small fleshy macroalgae. If underfed, an individual may nip at stony corals and even soft corals.
Captive Care: One of largest members of the genus but a hardy and commendable species for aquarists with spacious tanks. This is the least aggressive member of the genus and family, although it may behave aggressively toward members of its own kind. To keep more than one, especially a male and female, an extra-large tank is essential. Must receive a diet rich in vegetable matter, or it will tend to fade and develop head and lateral line erosion. Very similar to the *Z. desjardinii*, page 389.

Zebrasoma xanthurum (Blyth, 1852)
Purple Tang

Maximum Length: 9.8 in. (25 cm).
Range: Red Sea.
Minimum Aquarium Size: 100 gal. (379 L).
Foods & Feeding: Varied diet, mostly vegetable matter. Feed dried and frozen herbivore foods that contain marine algae and the blue-green alga *Spirulina*. Supplement with slices of zucchini, broccoli, leaf lettuce, and sushi nori (dried seaweed). Feed 3 times a day.
Aquarium Suitability Index: 4.
Reef Aquarium Compatibility: Generally safe and desirable. Browses on filamentous microalgae and small fleshy macroalgae. If underfed, an individual may nip at stony corals and even soft corals.
Captive Care: This beautiful Red Sea fish was once rare and extravagantly priced in the aquarium world but is now readily available. The most belligerent member of the genus, it will fight fiercely with members of its own species and other tangs. Should be the last fish introduced into the community tank, unless housed with large, equally belligerent species. Best kept as the sole surgeonfish in a home aquarium, unless in an extra-large tank. Must be fed a proper herbivorous diet to retain color and prevent head and lateral line erosion.

Balistapus undulatus (Park, 1797)
Undulate Triggerfish (Orangelined Triggerfish, Orangetailed Triggerfish)

Maximum Length: 11.8 in. (30 cm).
Range: Indo-Pacific.
Minimum Aquarium Size: 55 gal. (208 L).
Foods & Feeding: Mixed diet of meaty foods, including chopped shrimp, squid, clams, and fish. Also frozen rations with marine algae and vitamin-enriched foods. Feed no fewer than 3 times a day.
Aquarium Suitability Index: 5. ▪
Reef Aquarium Compatibility: Not suitable. Feeds on a wide range of invertebrates.
Captive Care: An exceptionally beautiful species often called the most belligerent marine aquarium fish available. Because it is so attractive, hardy, and has a great repertoire of behaviors, it is a favorite with some aquarists. Best kept singly in an aquarium of its own; even if housed with other aggressive species, it is likely to attack tankmates sooner or later. Often shy at first, but in time many specimens learn to associate their caretaker with food and swim near the surface waiting for a tasty morsel. Use care when working in a tank housing this fish: it will bite the hand that feeds it.

Balistes vetula Linnaeus, 1758
Queen Triggerfish

Maximum Length: 23.6 in. (60 cm).
Range: Tropical Atlantic.
Minimum Aquarium Size: 200 gal. (757 L).
Foods & Feeding: Mixed diet of meaty foods, including chopped shrimp, squid, clams, and fish. Also frozen rations with marine algae and vitamin-enriched foods. Feed no fewer than 3 times a day.
Aquarium Suitability Index: 5.
Reef Aquarium Compatibility: Not suitable. Eats many invertebrates.
Captive Care: Truly the most regal triggerfish of the Tropical Atlantic and Caribbean. Unfortunately, it gets larger and more aggressive than most aquarists can handle. Juveniles and adolescents can be kept with larger fish species, but they will begin to wreak havoc on their tankmates as they mature. An adult will have to be housed on its own, except in a very large aquarium—even then there is always a chance that it will attack its tankmates. Such large, menacing individuals can decimate the population of an aquarium and are not easily passed along to other aquarists. As with other aggressive triggerfishes, it is notorious for rearranging aquarium decor and may even bite and break heater tubes, air-line tubing, and plastic siphons.

Balistoides conspicillum (Bloch & Schneider, 1801)
Clown Triggerfish

Maximum Length: 19.9 in. (50 cm).
Range: Indo-Pacific.
Minimum Aquarium Size: 135 gal. (511 L).
Foods & Feeding: Mixed diet of meaty foods, including chopped shrimp, squid, clams, and fish. Also frozen rations with marine algae and vitamin-enriched foods. Feed no fewer than 3 times a day.
Aquarium Suitability Index: 3-5 (age dependent).
Reef Aquarium Compatibility: Not suitable.
Captive Care: Dramatic, almost bizarre, coloration makes this species a prize among aquarists, despite a number of drawbacks. The mortality rates of very small juveniles (often available in large numbers and sold as "tiny" Clown Triggerfish) are often high. Larger juveniles, adolescents, and adults, are typically very hardy. Sadly, some manifest a Jekyll and Hyde personality: amiable for many months, then suddenly turning nasty—nipping and even killing their tankmates. To keep this trigger with other fishes, place it in a very large tank with plenty of suitable hiding places. Keep only one and house with large fishes or fishes of equal belligerence. Grows quickly if well fed. Has been known to attack its owners.

Melichthys vidua (Solander, 1844)
Pinktail Triggerfish

Maximum Length: 13.8 in. (35 cm).
Range: Indo-Pacific.
Minimum Aquarium Size: 75 gal. (284 L).
Foods & Feeding: Mixed diet of meaty foods, including chopped shrimp, squid, clams, and fish. Also frozen rations with marine algae and vitamin-enriched foods. Feed no fewer than 3 times a day.
Aquarium Suitability Index: 4.
Reef Aquarium Compatibility: One of the few triggers that can be kept in the reef aquarium. Will usually ignore sessile invertebrates, but larger specimens may eat ornamental shrimps.
Captive Care: This is an attractive species with subtle beauty that does not fit the usual aggressive profile of the triggerfishes. Can be retiring when initially introduced, but will become quite tame over time, and is even more sociable than the *O. niger* triggerfish. Because of its hardiness and more-passive disposition, it is a great choice for the beginning aquarist. Can be kept with peaceful fishes of equal size or larger, or with more-aggressive fishes that are smaller. Unlike some of its cousins, this fish is less likely to rearrange the aquarium decor or dig holes in the substrate.

Odonus niger (Rüppell, 1837)
Niger Triggerfish (Redtooth Triggerfish)

Maximum Length: 19.7 in. (50 cm)—including the long tail lobes.
Range: Indo-Pacific.
Minimum Aquarium Size: 75 gal. (284 L).
Foods & Feeding: Mixed diet of meaty foods, including chopped shrimp, squid, clams, and fish. Also frozen rations with marine algae and vitamin-enriched foods. Feed no fewer than 3 times a day.
Aquarium Suitability Index: 5. ▮
Reef Aquarium Compatibility: Can be housed in a reef aquarium, but may nip at sponges, tunicates, ornamental crustaceans, and snails. Harmless to corals. To keep with a cleaner shrimp, add the crustacean first.
Captive Care: An excellent aquarium fish, relatively peaceful and quite handsome when well-fed and properly illuminated. Usually not hostile to tankmates, it tends to be shy at first, becoming bolder with time. More than one can be kept per tank if they are added simultaneously as juveniles to a large tank. Should be provided with a piece of live rock with a hole where it can retreat if threatened. It may bite: before handling aquarium decorations to clean or relocate them, make sure you know where your triggerfish is.

Pseudobalistes fuscus (Bloch & Schneider, 1801)
Bluelined Triggerfish (Blue Triggerfish, Rippled Triggerfish, Yellowspotted Triggerfish)

Maximum Length: 21.7 in. (55 cm).
Range: Indo-Pacific.
Minimum Aquarium Size: 200 gal. (757 L).
Foods & Feeding: Mixed diet of meaty foods, including chopped shrimp, squid, clams, and fish. Also frozen rations with marine algae and vitamin-enriched foods. Feed no fewer than 3 times a day.
Aquarium Suitability Index: 5. ▆
Reef Aquarium Compatibility: Not suitable. Eats many invertebrates.
Captive Care: A flamboyant menace of a fish that can attain large proportions. Juveniles are brightly colored and may fit into a community tank, but subadult and adult specimens are belligerent and tend to become more subdued in color. Best kept with large and aggressive fish species in a very large aquarium. This is one of the worst of the triggerfishes when it comes to rearranging its aquarium aquascapes, including pieces of rock. It will blow jets of water at the substrate in search of infaunal invertebrates, and will sometimes chase, and attempt to nip, any fish that comes too close during this behavior. Larger specimens can inflict a painful bite.

Rhinecanthus aculeatus (Linnaeus, 1758)
Picasso Triggerfish (Humuhumu Triggerfish)

Maximum Length: 9.8 in. (25 cm).
Range: Indo-Pacific.
Minimum Aquarium Size: 55 gal. (208 L).
Foods & Feeding: Mixed diet of meaty foods, including chopped shrimp, squid, clams, and fish. Also frozen rations with marine algae and vitamin-enriched foods. Feed no fewer than 3 times a day.
Aquarium Suitability Index: 5.
Reef Aquarium Compatibility: Will attack many invertebrates, with the exception of large, stinging cnidarians, such as the carpet anemones (*Stichodactyla* spp.).
Captive Care: A species for modern art lovers or anyone who desires a fish that thinks it's a dog. Juveniles are relatively mild-mannered and will learn to eat from their owners' fingers. Belligerence will increase with age, and they should be kept with fish equal in size or larger. If introduced simultaneously into a larger tank, they can be housed with members of the same genus. Juveniles are compatible with members of their own species, but fights are likely to become more frequent as they mature. Will occasionally bite heater tubes and air-line tubing and may rearrange aquarium decor.

Rhinecanthus assasi
Assasi or Arabian Picasso Triggerfish
Max. Length: 11.8 in. (30 cm).
Aquarium Suitability: 5. ■■■

Rhinecanthus rectangulus
Rectangular Triggerfish
Max. Length: 11.8 in. (30 cm).
Aquarium Suitability: 5. ■■■

Rhinecanthus verrucosus
Blackbelly or "Bursa" Triggerfish
Max. Length: 9.1 in. (23 cm).
Aquarium Suitability: 5. ■■■

Sufflamen chrysopterus
Halfmoon Triggerfish
Max. Length: 11.8 in. (30 cm).
Aquarium Suitability: 5. ■■■

Sufflamen bursa (Bloch & Schneider, 1801)
Scimitar Triggerfish (Scythe Triggerfish, Bursa Triggerfish)

Maximum length: 9.4 in. (24 cm).
Range: Indo-Pacific.
Minimum Aquarium Size: 55 gal. (208 L).
Foods & Feeding: Mixed diet of meaty foods, including chopped shrimp, squid, clams, and fish. Also frozen rations with marine algae and vitamin-enriched foods. Feed no fewer than 3 times a day.
Aquarium Suitability Index: 5. ▆
Reef Aquarium Compatibility: Will attack many invertebrates, with the exception of large, stinging cnidarians, such as the carpet anemones (*Stichodactyla* spp.).
Captive Care: Although known as the "Pallid Triggerfish" in Australia, this species is handsome in a nongarish way and is much less aggressive than many of its relatives. Juveniles are mild mannered, while adults can be more antagonistic, especially to newly introduced tankmates. To keep a larger specimen with other fishes, be sure it is the last fish introduced. It may be shy at first, but in time it will recognize the aquarist as a source of food and will become more brazen.

Xanthichthys auromarginatus (Bennett, 1831)
Bluechin Triggerfish (Gilded Triggerfish)

Maximum Length: 8.7 in. (22 cm).
Range: Indo-Pacific.
Minimum Aquarium Size: 75 gal. (284 L).
Foods & Feeding: Mixed diet of meaty foods, including chopped shrimp, squid, clams, and fish. Also frozen rations with marine algae and vitamin-enriched foods. Feed no fewer than 3 times a day.
Aquarium Suitability Index: 5.
Reef Aquarium Compatibility: One of the few triggers that can be kept in the reef aquarium. Less destructive and will usually ignore sessile invertebrates, but larger specimens may eat ornamental shrimps.
Captive Care: One of the more-congenial triggerfishes and well suited to the moderately aggressive community tank. Can even be kept in small groups (one male and two or more females) in a large aquarium. It is sexually dichromatic: males sport a blue patch on the throat and yellow fin margins. Will typically spend much of its time hiding when first introduced, but will become bolder with time. Provide with plenty of open swimming space. Some specimens will spit water out of openings in the tank top; be sure there are no electrical outlets nearby.

Xanthichthys mento (Jordan & Gilbert, 1882)
Crosshatch Triggerfish

Maximum Length: 11.4 in. (29 cm).
Range: Indo-Pacific.
Minimum Aquarium Size: 75 gal. (284 L).
Foods & Feeding: Mixed diet of meaty foods, including chopped shrimp, squid, clams, and fish. Also frozen rations with marine algae and vitamin-enriched foods. Feed no fewer than 3 times a day.
Aquarium Suitability Index: 5. ▇
Reef Aquarium Compatibility: One of the few triggers that can be kept in the reef aquarium. Less destructive and will usually ignore sessile invertebrates, but larger specimens may eat ornamental shrimps.
Captive Care: A hardy, desirable species that will fit into a number of different aquarium settings. It is rarely aggressive toward its tank-mates unless they are much smaller and/or introduced to the aquarium after it is. To keep more than one per tank, the tank should be at least 100 gal. [379 L]; add one male and several females simultaneously. Males and females are sexually dichromatic: males have a red tail and females do not. Can be shy when first introduced, but will become quite tame in time. Appreciates swift water movement and plenty of swimming space.

Xanthichthys ringens (Linnaeus, 1758)
Sargassum Triggerfish

Maximum Length: 13.8 in. (35 cm).
Range: Indo-Pacific.
Minimum Aquarium Size: 75 gal. (284 L).
Foods & Feeding: Mixed diet of meaty foods, including chopped shrimp, squid, clams, and fish. Also frozen rations with marine algae and vitamin-enriched foods. Feed no fewer than 3 times a day.
Aquarium Suitability Index: 4.
Reef Aquarium Compatibility: One of the few triggers that can be kept in the reef aquarium. Will usually ignore sessile invertebrates, but larger specimens may eat ornamental shrimps.
Captive Care: A very gregarious fish and the best of the triggers for the community aquarium. Can be kept in small groups in medium-sized aquariums. Some individuals may pick on smaller fishes, especially those introduced after they have acclimated. Aggression is more likely in a smaller aquarium, where space and shelter sites are limited. Appreciates strong water movement and plenty of swimming space. Rarely rearranges aquarium decor and is not a great threat to equipment in its tank.

Chaetodermis penicilligera (Cuvier, 1817)
Tasseled Filefish (Leafy Filefish)

Maximum Length: 12.2 in. (31 cm).
Range: Indo-Pacific.
Minimum Aquarium Size: 100 gal. (379 L).
Foods & Feeding: Mixed diet of meaty foods, including chopped shrimp, squid, clams, and fish. Also frozen rations with marine algae and vitamin-enriched foods. Feed no fewer than 3 times a day.
Aquarium Suitability Index: 3.
Reef Aquarium Compatibility: Should not be housed with invertebrates with the exception of large, stinging cnidarians, like the carpet anemones (_Stichodactyla_ spp.). Feeds on a wide range of invertebrates.
Captive Care: This curiosity usually lives in weedy areas on rocky reefs, hence the unusual camouflage. It tends to be shy when first added to the tank and will have a difficult time adjusting if kept with more-belligerent tankmates. Must have at least one suitable shelter site. Will usually not bother fish tankmates, with the possible exception of members of its own or related kinds. Do not keep with fishes that may nip off its skin flaps (e.g., pufferfishes, certain triggerfishes).

Oxymonacanthus longirostris (Bloch & Schneider, 1801)
Longnose Filefish (Orangespotted Filefish)

Maximum Length: 4.7 in. (12 cm).
Range: Indo-Pacific.
Minimum Aquarium Size: 20 gal. (76 L).
Foods & Feeding: Difficult to feed. An obligatory coral feeder, it specializes on the polyps of *Acropora*. Will occasionally be coaxed into eating live brine shrimp, but this rarely meets its nutritional needs. Feed several times a day.
Aquarium Suitability Index: 1. ▀▀▀
Reef Aquarium Compatibility: Can be kept in the reef aquarium, although it may nip the polyps of small-polyped stony corals.
Captive Care: This little beauty should be avoided by the vast majority of aquarists because it rarely accepts aquarium fare. It should only be kept with more-docile species and rarely behaves aggressively toward its tankmates. Certain specimens (possibly males) may quarrel with each other, but can be kept in small groups in medium-sized aquariums. Contrary to some reports, keeping a group will not necessarily increase the chances of survival. Provide branching corals (either live, dead skeletons, or faux) for it to refuge in when threatened or at night.

Paraluteres prionurus (Bleeker, 1851)
Saddled Filefish (Mimic Filefish)

Maximum Length: 3.9 in. (10 cm).
Range: Indo-Pacific.
Minimum Aquarium Size: 20 gal. (76 L).
Foods & Feeding: Mixed diet of meaty foods, including chopped shrimp, squid, clams, and fish. Also frozen rations with marine algae and vitamin-enriched foods. Feed no fewer than 3 times a day.
Aquarium Suitability Index: 4.
Reef Aquarium Compatibility: Although less destructive than some of the larger filefishes, it is risky to add this fish to a tank with sessile invertebrates, with the exception of potent sea anemones, like the members of the genus *Stichodactyla*.
Captive Care: This is a boldly colored species and one of the hardiest of the filefish clan in captive conditions. It mimics the poisonous Saddled Toby (*Canthigaster valentini*), page 421. Because of their close resemblance, predators learn to avoid this filefish, as well as the noxious toby. Does best when kept with more-docile fishes. May be kept in pairs (male-female), but males may fight. This mimic filefish may be picked on by its model toby if they are housed together.

Pervagor janthinosoma (Bleeker, 1853)
Blackbar Filefish

Maximum Length: 5.5 in. (14 cm).
Range: Indo-Pacific.
Minimum Aquarium Size: 30 gal. (114 L).
Foods & Feeding: Difficult to feed. Can usually be coaxed into eating live brine shrimp, which should be soaked in a marine vitamin supplement. To entice it to feed, try smashing shrimp or squid flesh into the interstices of a coral skeleton or a piece of live rock. Once it is feeding, try switching it to a mixed diet, including a wide range of marine animal flesh, as well as frozen preparations for herbivores, mysid shrimp, and freeze-dried krill soaked in a vitamin supplement. Will also eat algae, and vegetable matter should be offered. Feed no fewer than 3 times a day.
Aquarium Suitability Index: 3.
Reef Aquarium Compatibility: Not recommended.
Captive Care: A fish best avoided by the beginning aquarist. It can be a challenge to feed initially and can be quite shy when first added to the aquarium. Usually fares worse when kept with belligerent species or more-aggressive food competitors. Keep only one or in male-female pairs. Provide with suitable shelter sites.

Pervagor melanocephalus (Bleeker, 1853)
Blackheaded Filefish

Maximum Length: 3.9 in. (10 cm).
Range: Indo-Pacific.
Minimum Aquarium Size: 20 gal. (76 L).
Foods & Feeding: Difficult to feed. Can usually be coaxed into eating live brine shrimp, which should be soaked in a marine vitamin supplement. To entice it to feed, try smashing shrimp or squid flesh into the interstices of a coral skeleton or a piece of live rock. Once it is feeding, try switching it to a mixed diet, including a wide range of marine animal flesh, as well as frozen preparations for herbivores, mysid shrimp, and freeze-dried krill soaked in a vitamin supplement. Will also eat algae, and vegetable matter should be offered. Feed no fewer than 3 times a day.
Aquarium Suitability Index: 3.
Reef Aquarium Compatibility: Not recommended.
Captive Care: This can be a demanding species—a challenge to feed initially and quite shy when first added to the aquarium. Usually fares much better with peaceful, noncompetitive tankmates. Keep singly or in male-female pairs. May quarrel with closely related species. Provide with suitable shelter sites.

Pervagor spilosoma (Lay & Bennett, 1839)
Fantail Filefish (Hawaiian Filefish)

Maximum Length: 7.1 in. (18 cm).
Range: Indo-Pacific.
Minimum Aquarium Size: 55 gal. (208 L).
Foods & Feeding: Varied diet, including shaved shrimp, squid, and scallop, mysid shrimp, and freeze-dried krill soaked in a vitamin supplement. Also frozen preparations containing marine algae. Feed no fewer than 3 times a day.
Aquarium Suitability Index: 4.
Reef Aquarium Compatibility: Should not be housed with invertebrates with the exception of large, stinging cnidarians, like the carpet anemones (*Stichodactyla* spp.).
Captive Care: One of the most desirable filefishes for the home aquarium: hardy, brightly colorful, and relatively small. This species is best kept singly, unless a male-female pair is acquired. May fight with other members its genus. Rarely bothers other fish species, except possibly those with elaborate finnage (long fin filaments are an irresistible target).

Acanthostracion quadricornis (Linnaeus, 1758)
Scrawled Cowfish

Maximum Length: 18.9 in. (48 cm).
Range: Indo-Pacific.
Minimum Aquarium Size: 180 gal. (681 L).
Foods & Feeding: Varied diet of meaty foods, including chopped shrimp, squid, clams, fish, mysid shrimp, and enriched freeze-dried krill. Also herbivore preparations containing marine algae. Do not offer floating food: this species may ingest air at the water's surface, causing buoyancy problems. Feed no fewer than 3 times a day.
Aquarium Suitability Index: 3.
Reef Aquarium Compatibility: Not recommended.
Captive Care: This odd creature is an interesting addition to the larger community tank. It does best when housed with other placid species and is usually indifferent toward its tankmates. Provide plenty of swimming room and avoid sudden movements—adults are easily startled and may collide with the glass (resulting in broken "horns") or even leap out of an open tank. Can be kept in groups or pairs, although adult specimens (possibly males) may chase and nip at each other. Reportedly can release toxins when stressed (like other boxfishes); remove a dying specimen or prevent it from being harassed.

Lactoria cornuta (Linnaeus, 1758)
Longhorn Cowfish (Longhorn Boxfish)

Maximum Length: 18.1 in. (46 cm).
Range: Indo-Pacific.
Minimum Aquarium Size: 180 gal. (681 L).
Foods & Feeding: Varied diet of meaty foods, including chopped shrimp, squid, clams, fish, mysid shrimp, and enriched freeze-dried krill. Also herbivore preparations containing marine algae. Do not offer floating food: this species may ingest air at the water's surface, causing buoyancy problems. Feed no fewer than 3 times a day.
Aquarium Suitability Index: 3.
Reef Aquarium Compatibility: Not recommended.
Captive Care: An interesting fish, although cute yellow juveniles grow large, become less colorful, and the long horns get progressively shorter. Fares best if not kept with aggressive food competitors. It will sometimes swim at the surface and spit water at feeding time. Adults are easily startled by sudden movement or by turning on the room lights when the tank is dark—they may collide with the glass or become wedged in the decor. When stressed, it can exude a toxin that may wipe out an entire tank; remove the source of the stress or the boxfish immediately if it is observed being harried or dying.

Lactoria fornasini (Bianconi, 1846)
Thornback Cowfish (Bluelined Cowfish, Thornback Boxfish)

Maximum Length: 5.9 in. (15 cm).
Range: Indo-Pacific.
Minimum Aquarium Size: 55 gal. (208 L).
Foods & Feeding: Varied diet of meaty foods, including chopped shrimp, squid, clams, fish, mysid shrimp, and enriched freeze-dried krill. Also herbivore preparations containing marine algae. Do not offer floating food: this species may ingest air at the water's surface, causing buoyancy problems. Feed no fewer than 3 times a day.
Aquarium Suitability Index: 3.
Reef Aquarium Compatibility: Not recommended. Its eclectic diet includes many invertebrates, and it may itself fall prey to large stinging anemones.
Captive Care: This smaller cowfish will readily adapt to aquarium life if kept with other passive fish species. More than one can be kept, although two adult males may quarrel. Typically indifferent toward other fish tankmates. Will fare better if not kept with aggressive food competitors. Although reported to exude the same toxic slime as other boxfishes, it is apparently less apt to do so or the toxin is not as lethal, as poisonings are very rarely reported.

Ostracion cubicus Linnaeus, 1758
Cube Boxfish (Yellow Boxfish)

Maximum Length: 17.7 in. (45 cm).
Range: Indo-Pacific.
Minimum Aquarium Size: 180 gal. (681 L).
Foods & Feeding: Varied diet of meaty foods, including chopped shrimp, squid, clams, fish, mysid shrimp, and enriched freeze-dried krill. Also herbivore preparations containing marine algae. Do not offer floating food: this species may ingest air at the water's surface, causing buoyancy problems. Feed no fewer than 3 times a day.
Aquarium Suitability Index: 3.
Reef Aquarium Compatibility: Not recommended.
Captive Care: This is a personable fish that requires a certain amount of special care. It tends to be very shy at first and may refuse to accept food for several days or even weeks. Provide caves or crevices in which it can hide, plenty of swimming room, and docile tankmates. Can jump out of an open aquarium. When stressed, it can exude a toxin that may wipe out an entire tank (including the boxfish itself); if the fish is being irritated by its tankmates or near death, remove the source of the stress or the boxfish immediately. The effects of this toxin are nonreversible.

MAIN PHOTO, MALE; INSET, FEMALE

Ostracion meleagris Shaw, 1796
Spotted Boxfish (Blue Boxfish)

Maximum Length: 6.3 in. (16 cm).
Range: Indo-Pacific.
Minimum Aquarium Size: 55 gal. (208 L).
Foods & Feeding: Difficult to feed. Live, vitamin-enriched brine shrimp may be needed to initiate a feeding response. Once eating, offer a varied diet, including a wide range of meaty marine foods, as well as frozen preparations for herbivores. Do not offer floating food: it may ingest air at the water's surface, causing buoyancy problems. Feed no fewer than 3 times a day. Starving specimens exhibit concave body sides; a healthy fish's sides will appear straight.
Aquarium Suitability Index: 3.
Reef Aquarium Compatibility: Not recommended.
Captive Care: Keeping this beautiful fish is akin to playing Russian roulette with its tankmates: it is the most notorious boxfish for exuding ostracitoxin when stressed, which can fatally poison an entire tank. If the fish is being harried by its tankmates or dying, remove the source of the stress or the boxfish immediately. Keep singly or in pairs—but not two males. The male is dark with blue mottling; the female is brown with white spots.

Arothron mappa (Lesson, 1930)
Map Puffer

Maximum Length: 25.6 in. (65 cm).
Range: Indo-west-Pacific.
Minimum Aquarium Size: 240 gal. (908 L).
Foods & Feeding: Varied diet of meaty foods, including chopped shrimp, squid, clams, enriched krill, and fish—as well as preparations designed for herbivores. Feed no fewer than 3 times a day.
Aquarium Suitability Index: 3.
Reef Aquarium Compatibility: Not recommended. Eats sessile invertebrates and coralline algae.
Captive Care: This is a prized fish among advanced aquarists, with highly variable and sometimes magnificent color patterns. It is also a species that demands an enormous aquarium and some dedicated husbandry. It will probably need to be dewormed and the teeth may have to be filed down to prevent overgrowth, which can impede feeding. Best kept singly, although it is not aggressive toward other fishes, even other puffer species. Tends to be shy at first, and the tank should have a large cave or overhang where the puffer can take shelter. Will chew up hard coral skeletons, faux corals, and aquarium equipment.

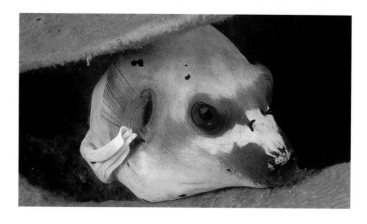

Arothron nigropunctatus (Bloch & Schneider, 1801)
Blackspotted Puffer

Maximum Length: 13.0 in. (33 cm).
Range: Indo-Pacific.
Minimum Aquarium Size: 75 gal. (284 L).
Foods & Feeding: Varied diet of meaty foods, including chopped shrimp, squid, clams, enriched krill, and fish—as well as preparations designed for herbivores. Feed no fewer than 3 times a day.
Aquarium Suitability Index: 4.
Reef Aquarium Compatibility: Not recommended.
Captive Care: This is the most commonly seen member of its genus, which offers large, showpiece specimens that are too destructive for reef aquariums but that tend to become family pets in larger community "fish-only" tanks. Their color is highly variable: individuals range from brown to blue-gray, with varying amounts of yellow and black spots. Rare individuals may be completely black, all gold, or even orange overall. (Compare to *A. meleagris*, page 419.) May be shy and refuse food at first, after which it will become bold if not kept with overly competitive tankmates. Rarely aggressive; more than one can be kept in the same tank. Can also be kept with other *Arothron* spp., except more-aggressive forms.

Arothron diadematus
Masked or Panda Puffer
Max Length: 11.8 in. (30 cm).
Aquarium Suitability: 3.

Arothron hispidus
Whitespotted or Hispid Puffer
Max. Length: 18.9 in. (48 cm).
Aquarium Suitability: 3.

Arothron immaculatus
Immaculate Puffer
Max. Length: 11.0 in. (28 cm).
Aquarium Suitability: 3.

Arothron manilensis
Manila or Striped Puffer
Max. Length: 12.2 in. (31 cm).
Aquarium Suitability: 3.

Arothron meleagris
Guinea Fowl or Golden Puffer
Max. Length: 19.7 in. (50 cm).
Aquarium Suitability: 3.

Arothron stellatus
Starry or Stellate Puffer
Max. Length: 47.0 in. (120 cm).
Aquarium Suitability: 2.

Canthigaster jactator (Jenkins, 1901)
Whitespotted Toby (Hawaiian Whitespotted Toby)

Maximum Length: 3.5 in. (9 cm).
Range: Hawaiian Islands.
Minimum Aquarium Size: 20 gal. (76 L).
Foods & Feeding: Varied diet of meaty foods, including chopped shrimp, squid, clams, enriched krill, and fish—as well as preparations designed for herbivores. Feed no fewer than 3 times a day.
Aquarium Suitability Index: 3.
Reef Aquarium Compatibility: Not recommended. Feeds on a wide range of invertebrates.
Captive Care: Members of this genus are known as tobies or sharpnose puffers and offer the aquarist some of the same behaviors as the larger puffers without the need for a very large aquarium. This species, unfortunately, is a notorious nipper, often biting the fins of its tank-mates and leaving telltale signs: perfect circular holes. It is particularly prone to this destructive behavior when kept in smaller tanks. Best kept singly, unless in a male-female pair or in a spacious tank. Deworming may be necessary and the ever-growing teeth may have to be clipped to enable the toby to feed. Offering hard-shelled inverte-brates can help wear the teeth down.

Canthigaster valentini (Bleeker, 1853)
Saddled Toby (Blacksaddled Toby, Valentini Toby)

Maximum Length: 3.9 in. (10 cm).
Range: Indo-Pacific.
Minimum Aquarium Size: 20 gal. (76 L).
Foods & Feeding: Varied diet of meaty foods, including chopped shrimp, squid, clams, enriched krill, and fish—as well as preparations designed for herbivores. Feed no fewer than 3 times a day.
Aquarium Suitability Index: 3.
Reef Aquarium Compatibility: Not recommended.
Captive Care: This is a hardy, commendable species that is mimicked by the Saddled Filefish (*Paraluteres prionurus*), page 408. An occasional specimen will nip fins, especially long and elaborate ones. Like other tobies, it may behave aggressively toward conspecifics unless a member of the opposite sex can be acquired. Even then, males may chase and nip females, but it is also possible that spawning may occur. Females have been observed to lay their eggs on a clump of filamentous algae. Males grow larger than females and have blue-green iridescent lines radiating from the back of the eyes, blue-gray lines on a light orange background under the lower jaw, and a blue-gray patch anterior to the anus.

Canthigaster amboinensis
Ambon Toby
Max. Length: 5.5 in. (14 cm).
Aquarium Suitability: 3.

Canthigaster bennetti
Bennett's Toby
Max. Length: 3.9 in. (10 cm).
Aquarium Suitability: 3.

Canthigaster compressa
Fingerprint Toby
Max. Length: 4.3 in. (11 cm).
Aquarium Suitability: 3.

Canthigaster coronata
Crowned or Threebarred Toby
Max. Length: 5.3 in. (13.5 cm).
Aquarium Suitability: 3.

Canthigaster rostrata
Sharpnose Puffer or Atlantic Toby
Max. Length: 4.3 in. (11 cm).
Aquarium Suitability: 3.

Canthigaster solandri
Ocellated, Solander's, or Spotted Toby
Max. Length: 4.1 in. (10.5 cm).
Aquarium Suitability: 3.

Chilomycterus antillarum Jordan & Rutter, 1897
Web Burrfish

Maximum Length: 9.8 in. (25 cm).
Range: Tropical Western Atlantic.
Minimum Aquarium Size: 75 gal. (284 L).
Foods & Feeding: Varied diet of meaty foods, including chopped shrimp, squid, clams, enriched krill, and fish—as well as preparations designed for herbivores. Feed no fewer than 3 times a day.
Aquarium Suitability Index: 2. ◣
Reef Aquarium Compatibility: Not recommended.
Captive Care: This unusual Western Atlantic species, with its short, fixed spines, is not as easy to keep as its relative the Spiny Puffer (*Diodon holocanthus*). It is often reluctant to feed and many specimens simply waste away. Smaller individuals are usually easier to acclimate and feed, especially if tankmates that compete actively for food are not present. Deworming is a good practice to ensure that internal parasites do not lead to its demise. Will nip at bottom-dwelling fishes, slow-moving fishes, and long-finned fishes, but rarely behaves aggressively toward conspecifics or other members of the family. Usually lives in seagrass meadows and should be provided with plenty of swimming space.

Diodon holocanthus Linnaeus, 1758
Spiny Puffer (Porcupinefish, Balloon Porcupinefish)

Maximum Length: 11.8 in. (30 cm).
Range: Circumtropical,
Minimum Aquarium Size: 75 gal. (284 L).
Foods & Feeding: Varied diet of meaty foods, including chopped shrimp, squid, clams, enriched krill, and fish—as well as preparations designed for herbivores. Feed no fewer than 3 times a day.
Aquarium Suitability Index: 4.
Reef Aquarium Compatibility: Not recommended.
Captive Care: This popular species makes a comical and personable pet. It quickly learns to associate its keeper with food and will come out and "beg" whenever the aquarist is near. Can be hand-fed, but beware: its jaws can deliver a painful bite. May nip fishes in its tank and may attempt to consume smaller, active fishes. May be kept in pairs or groups. This species is nocturnal and may spend most of the day hiding under a ledge or in a crevice. Like other puffers in general, it is prone to ich; be prepared to treat these outbreaks. May need deworming. Refrain from provoking its well-known ability to inflate, as air can become trapped in the alimentary tract. Do not try to catch it with a net: the puffer may inflate and be difficult to extract.

Photography Credits

All photographs by Scott W. Michael,
except as follows:

Gerald R. Allen
244, 297

Foster Bam
365

Fred Bavendam
8, 59

Janine Cairns-Michael
57, 174, 240, 395, 421, 424

Stephen Frink/WaterHouse
160, 228

John P. Hoover
188, 246 (top left), 378 (inset), 385, 423

Paul Humann
57 (top right)

Aaron Norman
386, 409

Allen, G.R. 1991. *Damselfishes of the World.* Mergus, Melle, Germany.

Allen, G.R., R. Steene and M. Allen. 1998. *A Guide to Angelfishes and Butterflyfishes.* Odyssey Publ. (USA) / Tropical Reef Research (Australia).

De Graff, F. 1973. *Marine Aquarium Guide.* The Pet Library Ltd., Harrison, N.J.

Debelius, H. and H. A. Baensch. 1994. *Marine Atlas, Vol. 1.* Mergus (Germany) / Microcosm Ltd. (USA).

Fautin, D.C. and G.R. Allen. 1992. *Field Guide to Anemonefishes and Their Host Anemones.* Western Australian Museum, Perth, Australia.

Haywood, M. 1982. *Popular Fishes for Your Marine Aquarium.* W. Foulsham & Co. Ltd. New York.

Hoover, J.P. 1993. *Hawaii's Fishes; a Guide for Snorkelers, Divers, and Aquarists.* Mutual Publishing, Honolulu, HI.

Humann, P. 1994. *Reef Fish Identification: Florida, Caribbean, Bahamas.* 2nd edition. New World Publ. Jacksonville, FL.

Klocek, R. and J. Kolman. 1976. *Marines (The Fishes).* Marine Hobbyist News, Normal, IL.

Kuiter, R.H. and H. Debelius. 1994. *Southeast Asia Tropical Fish Guide.* IKAN-Underwasserarchiv, Frankfurt, Germany.

Lieske, E. and R. Myers. 1994. *Collins Pocket Guide: Coral Reef Fishes: Indo-Pacific and Caribbean.* HarperCollins Publ., London.

Michael, Scott W. 1998. *Reef Fishes, Vol. 1.* Microcosm Ltd., Shelburne, VT.

Michael, Scott W. *Reef Fishes, Vol. 2.* Manuscript in progress.

Michael, Scott W. *Reef Fishes, Vol. 3.* Manuscript in progress.

Moe, M.A. 1982. *The Marine Aquarium Handbook, Beginner to Breeder.* Norns Pub. Co. Marathon, FL.

Moe, M.A. 1989. *The Marine Aquarium Reference: Systems and Invertebrates.* Green Turtle Publ., Plantation, FL.

Myers, R.F. 1989. *Micronesian Reef Fishes: A Practical Guide to the Identification of the Coral Reef Fishes of the Tropical Western Pacific.* Coral Graphics, Guam.

Thresher, R.E. 1980. *Reef Fish: Behavior and Ecology on the Reef and in the Aquarium.* Palmetto Publ. Co., St. Petersburg, FL.

SPECIES INDEX

The name in parentheses is the preferred common name.

COMMON NAME INDEX

Both preferred and secondary common names are included.

REEF FISHES
A Guide to Their Identification, Behavior, and Captive Care
Scott W. Michael
Foreword by Dr. John E. Randall

THE DEFINITIVE WORK ON THE DAZZLING FISHES OF the world's coral reefs, especially those of interest to marine aquarists. This first volume of a long-anticipated three-volume set covers reef environments, fish behavior, anatomy, taxonomy, and evolution, with hundreds of species accounts and world-class photographs. Reviewers are hailing it as a "must-have reference" for marine fish enthusiasts, as well as for divers, snorkelers, and coral reef naturalists.

624 pages • 8½ x 9¼

ISBN 1-890087-21-1 • Hardcover • MC 103
ISBN 1-890087-45-9 • Softcover • MC 103S

Information: www.microcosm-books.com
Available from T.F.H. Publications, Inc.